FRONTLINE SOUTHERN AFRICA

FRONTLINE SOUTHERN AFRICA

Keith Bernstein
and Toni Strasburg

Foreword by
Kenneth Kaunda

CHRISTOPHER HELM
London

Christopher Helm (Publishers) Ltd, Imperial House,
21-25 North Street, Bromley, Kent BR1 1SD

ISBN 0-7470-3012-X

A CIP catalogue record for this book
is available from the British Library

Typeset by Leaper and Gard, Bristol
Printed and bound in Great Britain by Jolly and Barber Ltd, Rugby

**Dedicated to the people of the Frontline States
and to Hilda and Rusty Bernstein**

FOREWORD

South Africa, at war with its own people, is fighting an undeclared war against its neighbours — the independent frontline states which share its borders. This war is part of South Africa's policy of 'Total Strategy' known as Destabilisation, which involves all forces — political, economic, diplomatic and military. The regional objective is to create and maintain a dependence that will be economically lucrative and politically submissive — and act as a bulwark against the imposition of international sanctions against apartheid.

The main strategy of the South African regime is to carve herself a position of absolute control and domination, so that the Frontline States lose their independence in terms of political and economic decisions. The South African regime knows that it is fighting a losing battle. What it is now trying to achieve by destabilising the Frontline States is to delay the end of apartheid.

Destabilisation is, of course, taking many forms but the conclusion is one: destabilisation leads to death of innocent human beings, either through deprivation or through bullets. Whatever form this takes, it is still a sad development and we condemn it in the strongest possible terms.

The regime is desperate and in desperation it is hitting out at everything and everybody. The racist South African Forces are involved in Namibia, Angola and Mozambique. The Frontline States do not want to go to war with South Africa. They have no capacity to do that. They are merely saying what the rest of the world is saying — they are opposed to apartheid. There is nothing for South Africa to defend itself against in terms of the Frontline States. Its only odious objective is to dominate the Frontline States and reduce them into its satellite states — to turn then into Bantustans. Its aim is domination over the whole region.

This book gives a striking visual account of what is happening inside some of the Frontline States as a result of destabilisation moves by the South African regime. I hope it brings the reality home to many more people. There is nothing new as far as apartheid is concerned, but there would be something new about the situation in South Africa if apartheid ended and we're prepared to make that sacrifice to bring about an end to it.

Kenneth D. Kaunda
PRESIDENT OF THE REPUBLIC OF ZAMBIA
18 November 1987

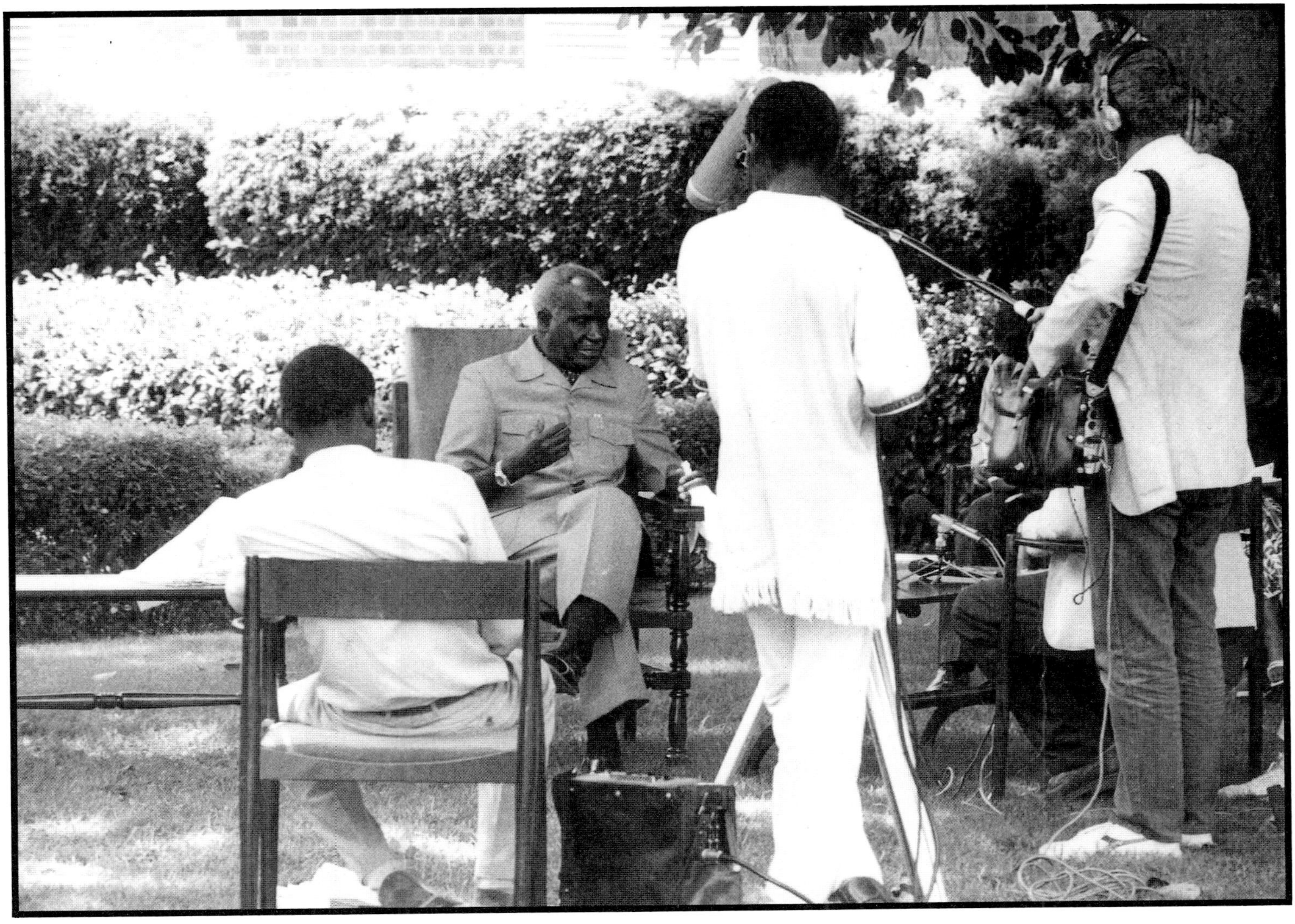

ACKNOWLEDGEMENTS

This book and the film *Destructive Engagement* would not have been possible without the help and support of the many people who gave us introductions, advice, information and hospitality. Not everybody can be acknowledged here but we would like to thank the governments of Mozambique, Zimbabwe, Zambia and Angola, in particular Arlindo Lopes of the Ministry of Information, Mozambique. All our friends at the Institut de Cinema, Maputo; and our many friends in Zambia and Zimbabwe, especially David Martin and Phyllis Johnson who believed in the film all along. Carlos Henriques of TVP Angola who gave us both time and some of his amazing film footage. Geoff Sayers and Brian Beardwood at Oxfam whose help was invaluable, and especially Bill Yates who made part of the journey with us. To Roger James at Central TV and Rod Stoneman at Channel 4 who were generous with their support when the film was in production. To the many organisations who backed the film. To June Peacock and Janice Hartree at Central for their help and kindness, and especially Maggie Coates who was always there even when the money wasn't. To Nigel Skelsey from Keith for confidence. To Steve Hurrell for the introductions and Uma Ram Nath and Peter O'Neill for being go-betweens.

Finally to the rest of the film crew who put up with much to get the film made; Christian Wangler, Adrian Pennink, but particularly Ivan Strasburg who apart from being a wonderful cinematographer is also Toni's husband and always supported the film.

Keith Bernstein
Toni Strasburg

INTRODUCTION

This book does not try to offer a definitive analysis of the total experience of the Frontline States. It came about because of a journey we took in order to make a documentary film about South Africa's war against the Frontline States. We travelled across the width of Africa from Mozambique, on the east coast, to Angola on the west, filming and observing in cities and outlying provinces the effect of South Africa's policy of 'Total Strategy' on the people of these countries.

Our particular attention was drawn to the amazing suffering of the people of Mozambique and Angola, who survive under fearful conditions; and the bulk of the photographs are of these two countries. The picture of life in Zimbabwe and Zambia is less harrowing, but no less important.

Inevitably, because of restrictions of time and money, we were unable to include all of the Frontline States, so that Botswana, Lesotho, Swaziland and Namibia, who have all suffered from their geographical proximity to South Africa, are not represented in this collection of photographs. Nor have we covered the struggle of the African National Congress (ANC) inside South Africa itself.

This does not mean that we do not recognise that these countries too are affected by South Africa's policies. Swaziland and Lesotho have both suffered direct South African attack. Botswana has been unstinting in the help which they give to the thousands of refugees fleeing the conflict. Namibia and the South West Africa People's Organisation (SWAPO) are conducting their own struggle against the illegal occupation of their country by South Africa, and of course the ANC is on the frontline inside South Africa itself.

We hope that readers will want to know more about the subject and go on to further reading. For us it was a journey we felt privileged to have made.

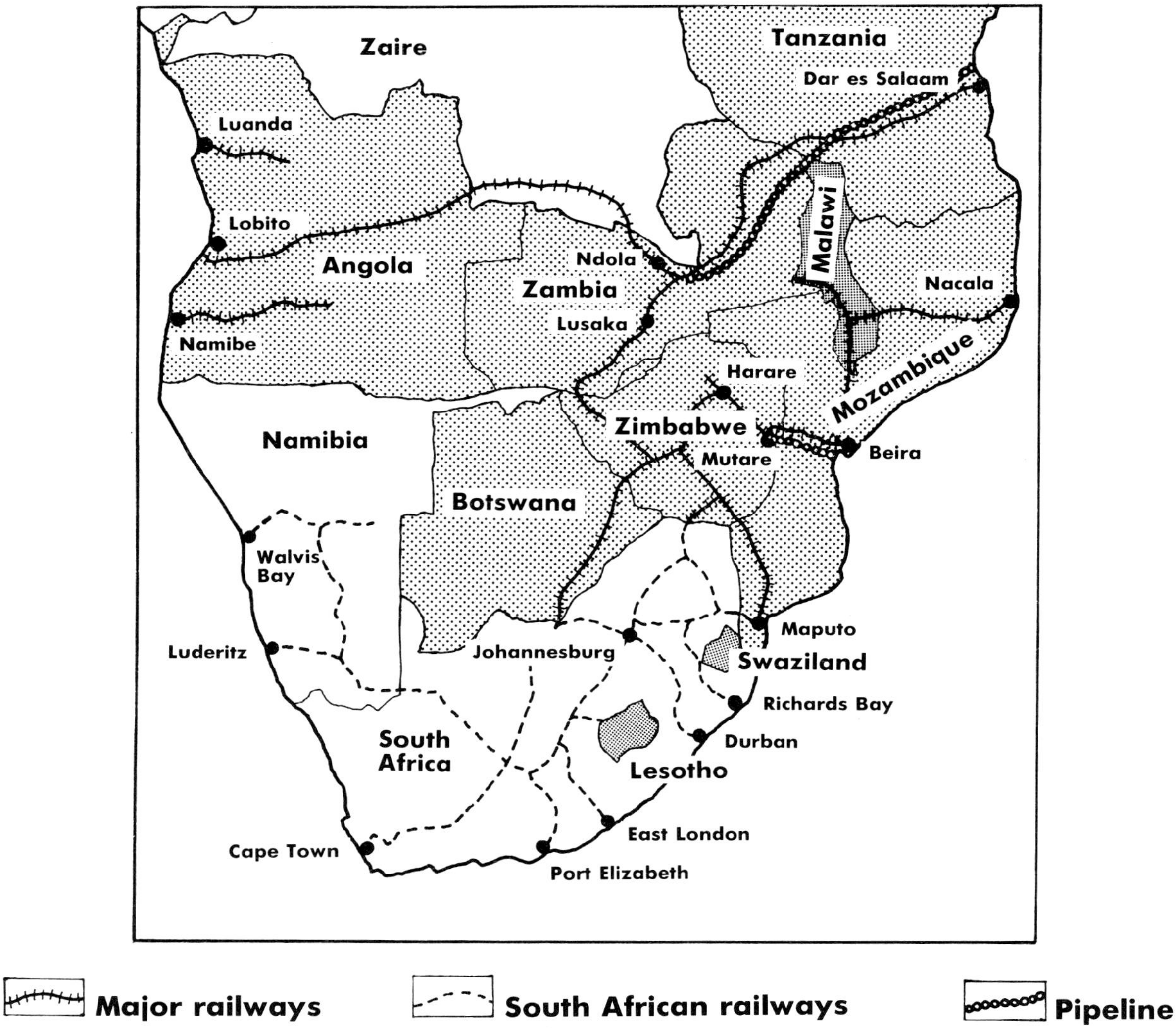

COUNTRY	POPULATION (million)	HEAD OF GOVERNMENT	CAPITAL
Angola	8.7	Jose Eduardo dos Santos (President)	Luanda
Mozambique	13.8	Joaquim Chissano (President)	Maputo
Zambia	6.5	Kenneth Kaunda (President)	Lusaka
Zimbabwe	7.0	Robert Mugabe (President)	Harare
Botswana	1.1	Quett Masire (President)	Gaborone
Malawi	2.0	Kamuzu Banda (Life President)	Lilongwe
Namibia	1.5	South-African controlled	Windhoek

THE FRONTLINE STATES

The term 'Frontline States' refers to the independent states which border South Africa — Angola, Mozambique, Botswana, Zambia and Zimbabwe — and Tanzania which has no common frontier with South Africa but became allied to the border states during the war of liberation in Zimbabwe. Other states affected in the region are Malawi, Lesotho and Swaziland. Angola's border is not with South Africa but with Namibia which is illegally administered by South Africa.

The Road to Independence

Angola and Mozambique

These were both Portuguese colonies. In the post World War II period, national liberation movements grew up in each country. Resistance in Angola came from the MPLA (Movement for the Liberation of Angola), the FNLA (National Liberation Front) and UNITA (National Union for the Total Independence of Angola). In Mozambique it came from Frelimo (Mozambican Liberation Front).

South Africa remained an ally of the Portuguese administration in both colonies until their independence, with treaty arrangements on security, trade and financial links.

Resistance undermined Portuguese colonialism and destabilised the Portuguese government in Lisbon. In 1974 the revolution against the 40-year-old dictatorship in Portugal, then under President Marcello Caetano, signalled the end of attempts to hold the colonies. Power was surrendered in 1975 to the MPLA (which had emerged as the dominant group) in Angola, and to Frelimo in Mozambique.

Portuguese withdrawal was marked by the removal of almost all mobile installations, plant and machinery from the two countries, and the emigration of almost all the administrative, technical and supervisory personnel, who had been closely identified with the colonial regime. Unlike the British and French colonial administrations in Africa, no preparation had been made for African successors.

Angola experienced the earliest and most backward form of European colonialism in Africa. The first Portuguese settlement began on the coast at Luanda in 1575. For centuries it was used as a base for the slave trade which ended in the nineteenth century. It was replaced by a system of forced labour, through which Angola was developed and exploited.

Mozambique was colonised by the Portuguese for over 400 years starting in the early sixteenth century. Like Angola, Mozambique was deemed a province of Portugal and the economy developed to supplement that of Portugal.

Zambia

Formerly the British colony of Northern Rhodesia. In 1953 it became part of the Central African Federation with Southern Rhodesia and Nyasaland, but retained Whitehall administration. The Federation tried to entrench power in the white minorities, but Zambian liberation movements, most notably UNIP (United National Independence Party) led by Kenneth Kaunda, resisted.

In 1963 the Federation, torn by internal dissension and the pressures for independence in its various constituents, was abandoned by the British government and in 1964 Nyasaland became the independent state of Malawi and Northern Rhodesia became Zambia. Southern Rhodesia remained under white minority rule until 1980.

Zimbabwe

Zimbabwe (formerly Rhodesia), although technically a British colony, was never directly ruled from Whitehall. Until 1923 it was administered by the British South Africa Company (BSA). It then became what was called a 'self-governing colony'.

Around the time it became part of the Central African Federation in 1953, a national liberation movement developed among the black majority. Eventually there were two main organisations — the Zimbabwe African National Union (ZANU) led by Robert Mugabe, and the Zimbabwe African People's Union (ZAPU) led by Joshua Nkomo. In the 1970s each organisation developed its own guerrilla forces, and conducted military operations against the minority white regime of Ian Smith.

The British government attempted to intervene politically, and the Smith government broke away from Britain and unilaterally declared itself independent in 1965. By 1979 the guerrilla struggle had seriously undermined the regime and, under pressure from the British government, direct negotiations with Britain and the warring factions produced a ceasefire and in 1980 a general election.

The independent state of Zimbabwe was established under Mugabe as Prime Minister of a black majority government. The white minority which fell from 270,000 to 100,000 retained 20 seats under the constitutional settlement until 1987.

Country Information

ANGOLA — The MPLA government inherited an economy characterised by a low level of production, an illiteracy rate over 90 per cent and an extremely high infant mortality rate. About 85 per cent of the population existed within a subsistence economy.

The sectors principally developed were mineral extraction (oil, diamonds and iron) and agriculture (coffee, cotton, timber, sisal, maize, tobacco and sugar).

Immediately after independence the MPLA started to make efforts towards improving living conditions, but factions within the country, particularly the FNLA and later UNITA, created a situation of almost continuous guerrilla warfare, which hindered growth already hit by years of war and the sudden exodus of most Europeans.

One of the MPLA's main objectives, still nowhere near achieved, has been to restore production to at least pre-independence levels, under a new pattern of management and labour organisation. Today, oil and gas constitute 90 per cent of Angola's exports, with exploration in joint ventures between Sonangol (the Angolan state company) and European and American companies. The United States is in a paradoxical position. Angola is one of its largest African trading partners, yet the American government has refused it diplomatic recognition.

MOZAMBIQUE — Mozambique's economy is largely agricultural, 90 per cent of the workforce being employed in the rural sector. Crops include cashew nuts, tea, sugar, sisal, cotton, copra and oil seeds. It has considerable undeveloped mineral resources such as iron, coal and graphite.

The withdrawal of the Europeans at independence hit the economy heavily. During the colonial period white farmers made up under 1 per cent of agricultural producers, but controlled over 50 per cent of the cultivated farmland.

ZIMBABWE — Zimbabwe is the key to any regional economic grouping. Sitting astride all the main roads and railways, it is the heart of the region. It is also the most industrially advanced of the Frontline States. After South Africa, Zimbabwe has the most broadly based economy of any African country. It has a diversified industrial infrastructure, including a more than 40-year-old iron and steel industry. Its mining, chemical and construction industries are relatively advanced and, except for petroleum-based products, it is almost self-sufficient. The country has always had a strong agricultural base, with tobacco, wheat, maize, sugar and cotton. Minerals such as asbestos, gold, chrome, coal, copper, iron, tin and nickel are extensively mined.

The strength of the economy was maintained for several years after independence, but began to show signs of strain as the situation worsened in South Africa in the mid-1980s.

ZAMBIA — Zambia's chief exports are copper, zinc and cobalt, as well as tobacco and, in good years, maize. Foreign exchange is earned mainly from copper (80-90 per cent). Agriculture has never been properly developed despite its great potential, and as a result the country imports most of its food. Lately, with the collapse of the copper market, emphasis has at last been put on agricultural development.

In 1965 Ian Smith made his Unilateral Declaration of Independence (UDI) in Rhodesia. International sanctions followed and the economic disruption in the region seriously affected Zambia. The long-term decline in copper prices added to the country's difficulties. Zambia was forced into increasing dependence on Western financial institutions, although in 1987 it threw off an International Monetary Fund (IMF) programme for recovery on the grounds that it was making matters worse.

MALAWI — Formerly Nyasaland and from 1953 part of the Central African Federation, Malawi became independent in 1964. President Banda rules with almost dictatorial powers. Unlike all the other Southern African Development Co-ordination Conference (SADCC) countries, Malawi has diplomatic relations with South Africa, contrary to the wishes of the Organisation of African Unity (OAU).

Malawi's economic development amounts to a refinement and improvement of the colonial system, rather than an attempted transformation. It was considered one of the world's poorest nations, and it has received substantial aid from the West, as well as from South Africa. Lilongwe, the new capital, was built with South African aid.

Malawi has no natural resources apart from the land, and therefore agriculture is the most important activity with 90 per cent of the population dependent on agriculture for their survival. Maize, tobacco, sugar and tea are the major crops. Manufacturing has grown in recent years, notably in the provision of farm products.

NAMIBIA — A German colony until the end of World War I, Namibia has become a mandate of the League of Nations entrusted to South Africa. In 1966 the UN ended South Africa's mandate and ordered it to withdraw. It refused to pull out. In the same year, the South West Africa People's Organisation (SWAPO) started its struggle for independence. In 1971 the

International Court of Justice declared South Africa's presence illegal, but it continues to run the territory and the war goes on. A series of South African-controlled administrations have meantime run the country.

Namibia's economy is built almot entirely on the export of raw materials and animal products. Between them agriculture, mining and fishing account for 99 per cent of all exports. The economy is controlled completely by South Africa which aims to extract as much wealth as possible against the day when it might be forced to give up the territory. Ninety per cent of all goods are exported.

Mining is the largest sector producing diamonds, uranium, tin, lithium, copper, lead, zinc and gem-stones. Most mines are owned by foreign multi-nationals, such as the South African de Beers (which produces about one-sixth of the world's annual supply of gem diamonds), and Rio Tinto Zinc. Agriculture consists almost entirely of ranching. Three-quarters of the national cattle herd is owned by whites. During the 1970s some of the world's richest fishing grounds off the Namibian coast were fished to exhaustion.

BOTSWANA — Botswana, formerly Bechuanaland, became a British Protectorate in 1885 and it was effectively under direct British administration until 1965. On several occasions attempts were made to put the territory under South African rule, most notably in 1910 when the Union of South Africa came into being. But the Africans always resisted abandonment by the British and in 1965 power was transferred to an elected local government headed by Seretse Khama.

Most of the land is semi-arid and 75 per cent is agriculturally non-productive. Meat was for long a key export but mining developed substantially after independence, leading to rapid economic growth. Diamonds provide 70 per cent of total foreign exchange earnings. Copper, nickel, iron ore and soda ash are also present together with Africa's largest known coal reserves. Mining is dominated by foreign companies already involved in South Africa.

Lately the country has been hit by several years of drought, resulting in the need for food aid.

Botswana like Lesotho and Swaziland has a Customs Union with South Africa, integrating the economy largely with that of the Republic. Although a Frontline State, Botswana's support for organisations fighting South Africa is constrained because of its vulnerable position.

Relations

South African relations with all the Frontline States have changed drastically since each won its independence. Relations with the Smith regime in Rhodesia (*Zimbabwe*) had been extremely close. South Africa assisted the UDI process by trade and economic means, and provided favourable conditions of supply and transportation for the Smith government, including the supply of military equipment and oil. South Africa and South African-based companies provided the means for Smith to break the oil embargo which the British government tried half-heartedly to impose. Throughout the war in Zimbabwe, South Africa served as the main ally and support base for the regime, while Mozambique and Zambia were the allies and supply bases of the liberation forces. From the time of the fall of the Smith government, South African hostility has not only been manifested by repeated incursion by undercover agents, but also by the secretive support for marauding disaffected bands of 'dissidents', who have created disturbed conditions in those areas where support for Mugabe's party is weakest. Uneasy relations between the two countries are maintained by the Zimbabwean necessity for its imports and exports to pass through South Africa via South African railways to the main ports — Durban and Port Elizabeth. South Africa has repeatedly used both the threat of closure of these routes, and an 'administrative' demonstration of its preparedness to close them, by periodically delaying and obstructing procedures at the frontiers.

Zambia too maintains uneasy diplomatic relations under the same constraints of trade strangulation. It is also where South Africa's main liberation movement, the African National Congress (ANC) has its headquarters, and has been subject to repeated armed incursions by South African units, allegedly attacking ANC bases.

Mozambique inherited the treaty arrangements and agreements which had long existed between South Africa and the former Portuguese authorities. In particular, treaties concerning rail traffic from South Africa to the port at Maputo and those regarding recruitment of Mozambican labour for South Africa's gold mines. Clauses of the latter treaty dealt with South Africa's obligation to remit part of the miners' pay to Mozambique in gold, for 'deferred pay' to the men, thus giving Mozambique its main foreign currency earnings. South Africa has used its economic muscle to hinder the development of independent Mozambique, both by reducing rail traffic almost to a standstill, and by curtailing the recruitment of Mozambican labour for the mines and the 'deferred pay'. South African forces have made periodic incursions across the frontier to attack targets in Mozambique.

During Zimbabwe's war of independence, Mozambique provided bases for the ZANU guerrillas; Smith's government, aided by rebellious remnants of the Portuguese colonial regime, established the MNR also known as Renamo. This mercenary force has been taken over by South Africa since the collapse of the Smith regime. South Africa supplies and finances the MNR, and directs its operations which are designed to destroy the Mozambican economy and infrastructure, destroying roads and transport, and spreading terror and disaffection amongst the people.

In 1984 South Africa and Mozambique signed the Nkomati accord, which bound Mozambique to cease all aid to the ANC, and South Africa to end all aid for the MNR. Although Mozambique stuck to its side of the bargain, closing ANC offices and removing personnel, South Africa has continually violated the agreement and continues to direct and maintain the MNR.

Angola since independence has provided a friendly frontier, and bases and assistance to liberation forces from Namibia. SWAPO guerrillas from Namibia have used Southern Angola as both a base and a haven in retreat from South African military forces. The South Africans have repeatedly staged large-scale incursions into Angola, and maintain an almost continuous presence there, destroying road and rail links, terrorising the population and generally laying waste to vast areas of the country.

They also provide direct assistance to anti-government forces operating in Angola. The main rebel force, known as UNITA, has been established inside Angola by South Africa and the USA, who supply them logistically, and financially.

UNITA's strategy, closely following that of the MNR in Mozambique, is to cripple the country's economy, terrorise the people and destabilise the government. It has no significant programme other than the overthrow of the government. Angola has acquired the services of 30,000 Cuban technicians, doctors and military to help counter the threat.

War

By each day's end, war claims the lives of more than 360 small children in Angola and Mozambique. If this was Europe and not Africa we would not allow it to continue. A Commonwealth report in 1986 called this 'a major armed conflict spilling well beyond South Africa's borders'. Nearly all the media attention has been focused on the violence and oppression within South Africa. But South Africa has concluded that the best way to preserve minority rule is to fight a major war beyond its borders, in the neighbouring countries — the Frontline States. With apartheid under pressure both inside and outside South Africa, Pretoria lashed out. On 30 January 1981, just 10 days after Reagan took office, South African commandos hit the capital of Mozambique. It was South Africa's first official cross-border raid since the invasion of Angola.

South Africa's war combines military, and political action in a mix called 'Destabilisation' or 'Total Strategy'. It is difficult for people outside the region to believe just how hard South Africa is hitting its neighbours. South Africa's 'total strategy' in terms of human cost is incalculable, the economic costs run into tens of billions of dollars. Military action is largely through surrogate armies: UNITA in Angola, MNR in Mozambique and the so-called super ZAPU in Zimbabwe. UNITA and the MNR had been nearly moribiund, but were revitalised with massive new South African support. At the same time economic sanctions were imposed against Zimbabwe and Mozambique.

Economic and military targets were closely linked. The surrogate armies all focused on economic targets, particularly transport links.

Today, Mozambique barely functions. South Africa on its own admission has continued to support the MNR which has systematically destroyed the country. 400,000 lives have been lost in Mozambique alone, half of them children under the age of five. The UNICEF report, published in February 1987, says that 'one of the deadliest weapons of war is the mass terrorism carried out, which has burned crops and farms, destroyed schools and clinics, villages and stores'. Since 1981, 718 health posts have been destroyed. As a result of this systematic wrecking of the infrastructure of Mozambican society there are hundreds of thousands of displaced people in Mozambique. Driven from their land by the MNR they are unable to plant crops. With nearly four million people on the verge of starvation because of the destruction of food crops and transport capacity, famine has become an effective weapon of war.

But South Africa's punitive power is economic as well as military. The destruction of crucial transport links in Mozambique and Angola has heightened the dependence of the countries in the region on South Africa's transport network. This gives South Africa enormous power to exercise economic pressure in these countries.

The increased dependence of Zimbabwe, Zambia and the other landlocked states on South Africa has forced them to send their freight through South Africa, at the additional cost of at least US$300 million per year.

It is crucial to Zimbabwe that Mozambique does not succumb to the MNR, and Zimbabwe, along with Tanzania and Malawi, is now heavily committed to helping Frelimo forces there.

Zambia, despite the fact that it has no borders with South Africa, has not been left alone. Apart from direct South African attack, Zambia has more than 130,000 refugees who have poured in from all over the region.

Undoubtedly Angola and Mozambique have borne the brunt of Pretoria's military aggression in all its varieties. Roughly half the rural population of both countries has been displaced and they are refugees in their own countries.

Angola is subject to repeated invasion by the South African Defence Forces (SADF), who together with the US back the dissident UNITA forces. The war in Angola has cost US$18 billion since the MPLA gained independence in 1975. Like Mozambique, the Angolans inherited a largely illiterate population in a country systematically wrecked by the departing Portuguese. Angola has not had a single day's peace in 25 years.

None of these countries has ever attempted to cross into South Africa, despite the years of aggression. Struggling to build new nations since independence, they have been forced to militarise.

Southern African Development Co-ordination Conference (SADCC)

South Africa has come to dominate the region by controlling much of its industry, trade and transport. The states on the northern borders provide a market for South African goods and cheap labour for the mines.

In response, the Frontline States met in Tanzania in 1979 to prepare a strategy for regional economic alliance. This was the beginning of SADCC, an organisation of nine countries: Angola, Zambia, Zimbabwe, Mozambique, Tanzania, Botswana, Lesotho, Malawi and Swaziland.

As a block they represent 70 million people and command large, untapped reserves of natural resources, including critical reserves of strategic minerals. By co-ordinating and rationalising development, particularly industrial development, they aim to break out of the cycle of economic depression and famine that affects so many sub-Saharan countries and, most importantly, to break the economic stranglehold of South Africa in their region by making alternative trade arrangements.

The nine states of SADCC know that, having won the battle for political independence, co-operation is the only way to win the struggle for economic liberation.

The main aims of SADCC are:

1. To reduce economic dependence, particularly but not only on South Africa.

2. To forge links among themselves to promote equitable regional development.
3. To mobilise resources to national, bilateral and regional development.
4. To secure international co-operation towards the goal of economic liberation. SADCC's central secretariat based in Gaborone, Botswana, is staffed by only six professional officers, and the responsibility for regional programmes is divided among the nine members. This decentralisation was intended to avoid creation of a large expensive bureaucracy, and to make regional advancement dependent on the input and contribution of the member states.

ANGOLA was assigned responsibility for the energy sector, including all forms of power from hydro-electric to woodfuel for rural people.

ZIMBABWE was to co-ordinate food security, developing early warning systems against drought, and training for agricultural advisers for farms and villages.

BOTSWANA was made responsible for agricultural research, livestock production and animal diseases.

LESOTHO was assigned responsibility for soil and water conservation and tourism.

MALAWI was to co-ordinate forestry, fisheries and wildlife.

MOZAMBIQUE was made responsible for the development of transportation and communication.

SWAZILAND was to co-ordinate manpower development.

TANZANIA was to co-ordinate industry and trade.

ZAMBIA was made responsible for mining.

SADCC is still young, but has had some successes. Mozambique has established the Southern African Transport and Communications Commission to enable the rehabilitation of major transport routes. The vital Beira railway and port have been upgraded and kept open, and work started on other essential facilities. Communications projects have made advances, allowing international telephone contacts without dependence on the South African system. Power grids are being extended.

But SADCC continues to face immense obstacles. Botswana, responsible for cattle, has seen its own herds sharply reduced by six consecutive years of drought. Angola, responsible for energy, has fended off armed attacks on its oil installations and US government efforts to convince private American oil companies to withdraw from valuable operations there.

All SADCC countries face the constant threat of South African destruction of their efforts. SADCC estimates South Africa's activities cost them US$10 billion in the organisation's first five years. SADCC depends largely on international financing and aid to fund its programmes, valued at US$5 billion.

In the words of Samora Machel, the late President of Mozambique: 'For the countries of SADCC there is neither help nor charity and we do not want them. What exists are interests ... It is economic interests that move different countries. The nothern industrial countries are going to Angola because they want oil, diamonds and coffee. In Zimbabwe they want chrome and gold. In Swaziland they want iron and coal. Our natural resources are targets and therefore they are also tools for co-operation and not for aid. Therefore, we should not wait for aid, but rather for co-operation.'

Seven years after the independence of Zimbabwe and the founding of SADCC, the war for the control of Southern Africa has dramatically intensified. Pretoria is asserting its claim to be a regional power. In reply SADCC struggles to reduce its economic dependence on South Africa. Destabilisation now costs the SADCC more than US$5 billion per year. Development efforts are undermined. The political fabric is weakened. Whatever the political faults and economic errors of the region's various governments, their efforts have been swamped by destruction from outside.

In the face of this, two responses are required from the international community. First, the neighbouring states need assistance to repair the damage. But to do that alone would just be to treat the symptoms of the disease. The real need is to address the cause. It is clear that South Africa must be stopped. It is also clear, from experience, that diplomatic protest is not enough. If diplomacy fails, the normal recourse of the international community is economic sanctions. Experience in Southern Africa does indicate that they can be effective. But in order to work they must be organised and applied by South Africa's main trading partners — the US, Britain, Japan and Europe. The impact of their sanctions will be greater, and yet the relative cost smaller, than sanctions applied by the Frontline States.

In the words of Oliver Tambo, the President of the ANC, 'The end of apartheid depends on two things. The struggle of the people inside South Africa, and international pressure, which does not have to come from the neighbouring countries. It is up to the international community and no amount of aggression against the Frontline States is going to save apartheid.'

'All the Frontline States — Mozambique, Zimbabwe, Botswana, Zambia and Angola — are living under fear and threat from South Africa. If the situation was different we would have used that money for capital development, or economic development for the better living of our people, but we are forced by circumstances now to go for militarisation.'

Emerson Munangagwe, Minister of State, Zimbabwe

'Well, you must know that South Africa is a prosperous country. Probably it's the most industrialised country in the continent. It has got its own resources. But, in addition, South Africa enjoys considerable support from the western countries. There is a lot of support from Britain, from America, from Germany and France. These countries have got huge investments within South Africa. So then they have got a material interest in helping that regime. They together with Israel have helped considerably in giving South Africa the technical know-how in terms of arms and other strategic industries. South Africa has never wanted to fight a war, a revolutionary war, within its own borders, because it wanted to hide the reality of a civil war from the white population, wanted to convey the impression or the façade of a peaceful country, of a prosperous country where there was peace and stability. I think South Africa faces a crisis it has never faced before. It faces a serious economic crisis. The army is over-stretched, the army is involved in Namibia, in Angola. It's involved with MNR, but now for the first time the army is actually involved within South Africa. The SADF is occupying so many townships.'

Chris Hani, ANC

Mozambique

'Europe does not know terrorism since the Second World War. What Europeans are discussing about terrorism is a picnic, is peanuts, compared to what South Africa's unleashed against the Frontline States.'

Carlos Cardoza, Head of Information Services, Mozambique

With its military and economic might South Africa has, for the last six years, been waging a full-scale war on its neighbours — the Frontline States. With smashed industry, restricted trade, famine and death, the Frontline States are being devastated.

However much South Africa pursues its policy of destabilisation — in this case, a euphemism for war — the opposition of the Frontline States to the apartheid regime remains implacable.

In Mozambique, the South African government and military finance the Mozambique National Resistance, the MNR, who terrorise the population, burning villages and mutilating their captives.

Frelimo troops are required to protect the families in displacement camps against further MNR attacks. Despite the fertility of their land, peasant farmers can do little to cultivate as they are not safe from attack. With 4 million people under threat of starvation in Mozambique today, famine — man-made famine — has proved an effective and devastating weapon of war.

Problems of food distribution are compounded by the lack of roads and the shortage of trucks. Where there are the trucks with food, aid can get at least part of the way, if they can avoid MNR ambushes and mines. But where there are no roads, the food can't reach those who are starving, and in many cases the security situation prevents the people from reaching the relative safety of refugee camps. Not only do the MNR attack food and fuel convoys, but they also kill and maim civilians, often in horrific ways.

Frelimo's forces now have British military training in their fight against the South African-backed MNR. The bandits they capture are taken to rehabilitation camps. Their stories reveal how they were recruited. Some were hungry and were offered food; some were abducted from their villages and forced to join; others who were working illegally in South Africa were offered the choice — prison, or fight for the MNR.

Despite constant denials by the South African government, their continued support for the MNR was brought home by the quantities of weapons captured in February 1987 by Zimbabwean forces in Mozambique's Zambezia province.

'People don't run away from liberation. People don't run away from the ANC in South Africa. People do not run away from Frelimo in Mozambique. They don't run away from the MPLA in Angola. They run away from MNR. Why? Because they are not a liberation movement.

'Some of their (MNR) acts will not become public until very late in this century. Some of them are too horrible to talk about, and the western media would move into a hysteria about African backwardness, instead of blaming the very people who they supported, apartheid in South Africa. The most known acts of terror include cutting off the ears, cutting off lips, off noses, severing arms, you know cut your arm put it in your mouth and say eat Frelimo's food or Machel's food. Destroying villages, massacring peasants, massacring passengers in buses, destroying the livelihood of people, destroying infrastructure that makes life possible in the countryside. It's generalised, it's not — terror is not used as a — how can I put it? — as the behaviour of this or that bandit commander, or this or that person. It has been generalised.

'Europe does not know terrorism since the Second World War. What Europeans are discussing about terrorism is a picnic, is peanuts, compared to what South Africa's unleashed against the Frontline States.

'The costs have not — the costs of the war are not precise yet, they're not known to the dollar. But the war of destabilisation has cost Mozambique something in the region of five thousand million dollars, more than 400,000 lives, 95 or 96 per cent of them civilian lives were lost in this war. I'm not talking about the

Rhodesian aggression or the liberation war against colonialism, or Mozambique's participation in the liberation of Uganda. Just this war alone. Apartheid is a crime against humanity. If it's against humanity, it's not only against the Frontline, so humanity must get involved, the governments of the world must get involved.'

Carlos Cardoza, Head of Information Services, Mozambique

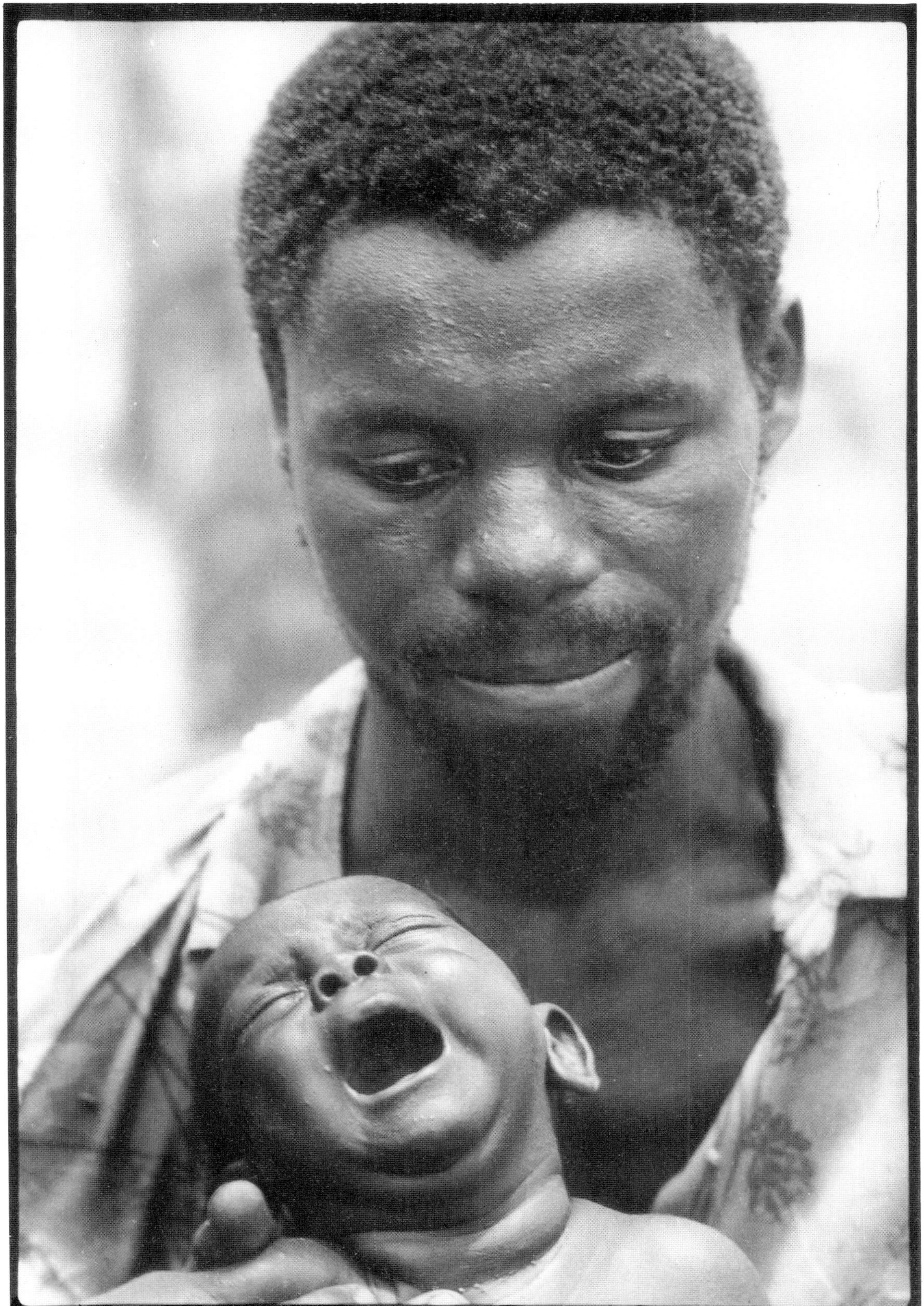

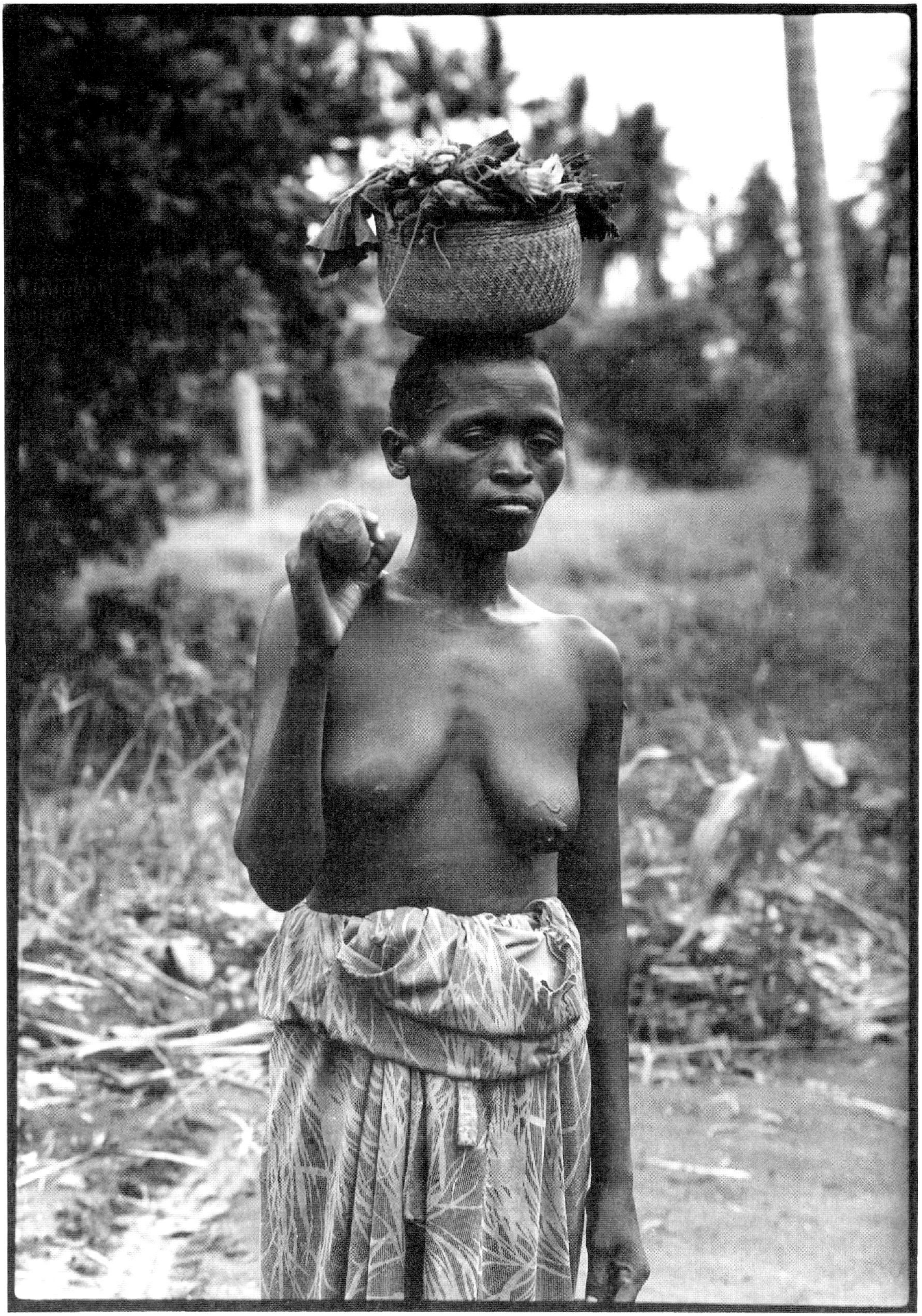

'Well here the first thing is the hunger . . . we have been here for only a short while and have been taking mangoes, at night, for our children. But it seems there are no more now. We think that this is our first pre-occupation. In the first place to have food. Maybe within the next fortnight, our children will be in bad shape — they will have diseases, diarrhoea because of the leaves they are eating.'

Refugee at camp, Mozambique

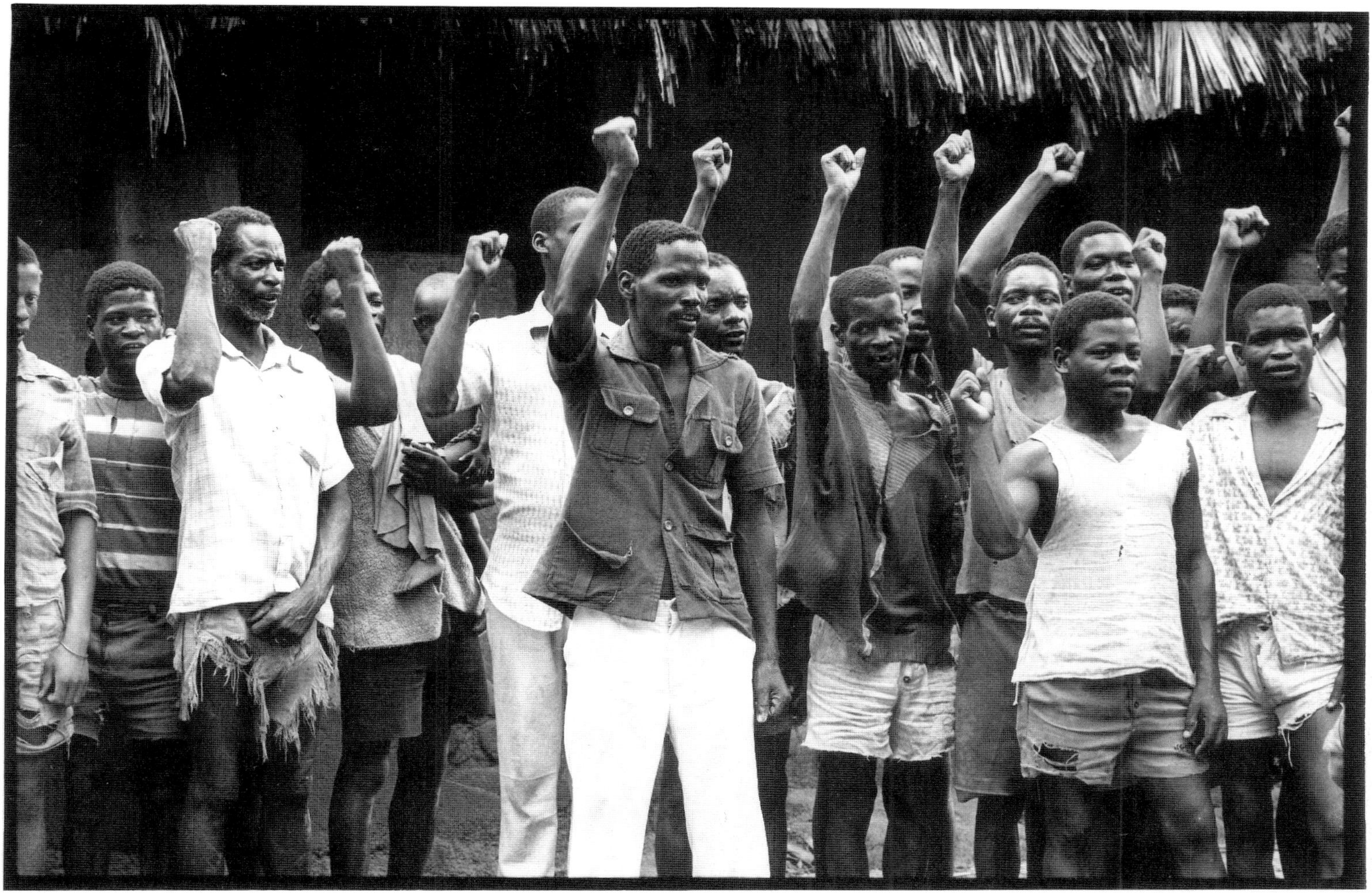

'Well the people who have arrived here fled from the armed bandits, especially in the last couple of months, and they all arrive in very bad condition. That is to say, malnutrition, nude — they don't have any clothes — the armed bandits took everything they had and the people have been using roots and trunks of trees to make clothes. We have received these people and distributed the little we have. They inform us that when the armed bandits arrive they take everything from them and leave the people without anything, completely naked.

We have cases of girls who were violated. They don't spare any girls — 11, 12 years old. And not only the young — also old people, some arrive with their breasts cut off, without their ears and there has also been massive beating to find out who is who and to obtain information on the movement of our troops and if somebody knows, or has been in contact with our troops what happens is a kind of revenge. We have seen that frequently in this district. In respect to these families, and other families arrived in previous years, the biggest problem is first of all food for the families and clothes for them. They arrive in a very difficult condition, they don't have clothes, they don't have food. Beside health problems we have had difficulties with medicines which we receive in reduced quantities. Things are getting worse as more families are constantly arriving.'

Frelimo Major, Mozambique refugee camp

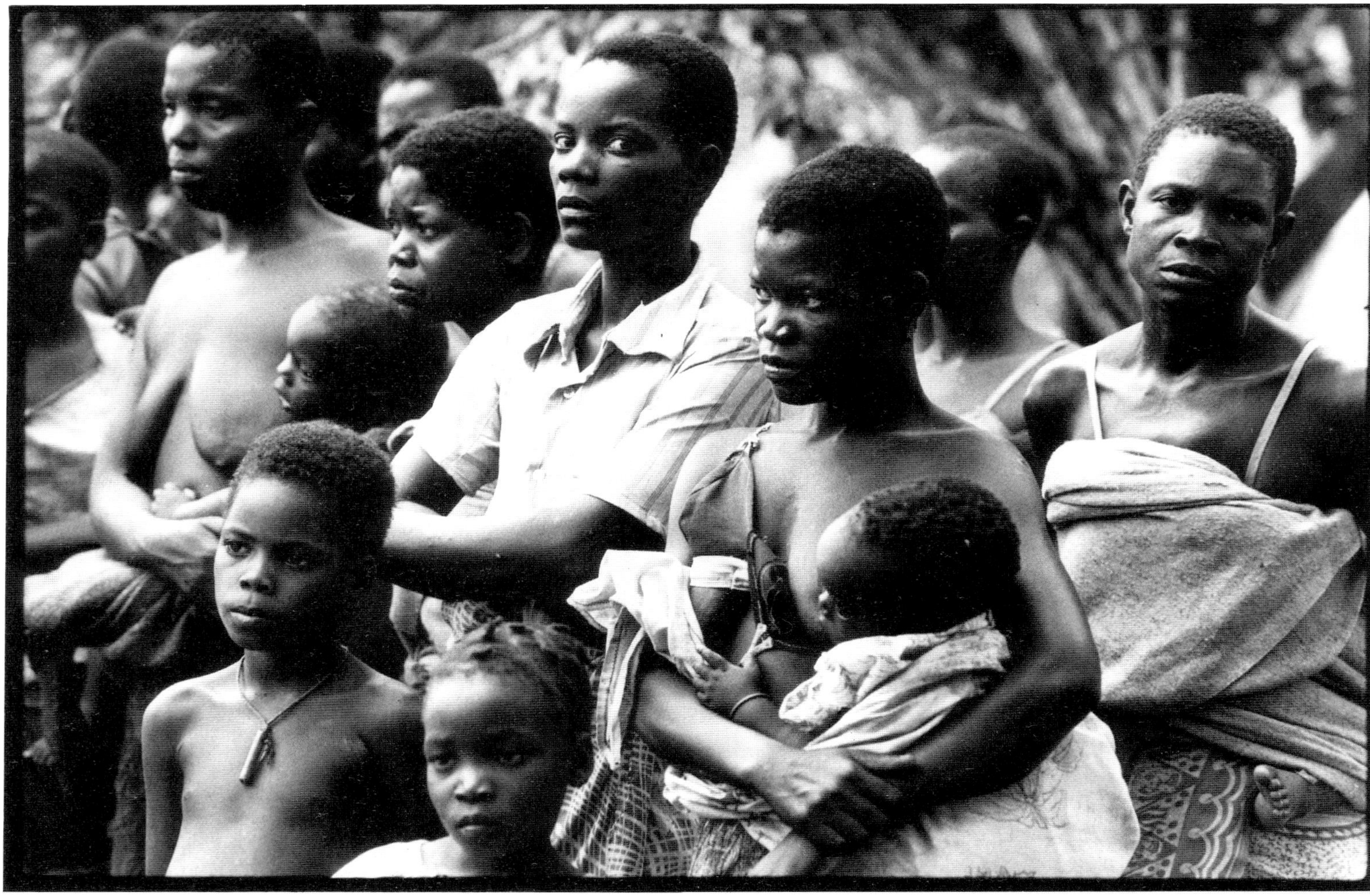

'The biggest needs are, in the first place, regular supplies to the district. Because of transport difficulties this is not possible. We depend on transport via sea or river. It can be by ship from Quelimane to Mabala or by river. There are a few rivers which are linking Macuse to Mabala and from Mahde to Maganja da Costa. Even on this link we have difficulties over a distance of 20-25 km, between Maganwa and Maganja da Costa, where we have to use canoes. It is a big difficulty the flow of the goods. But we are trying hard. If we could get the support of inflatable boats which would enable a quicker movement and take bigger quantities of goods, that could significantly complete the big effort that is being made from Quelimane.'

Commander, Mozambique refugee camp

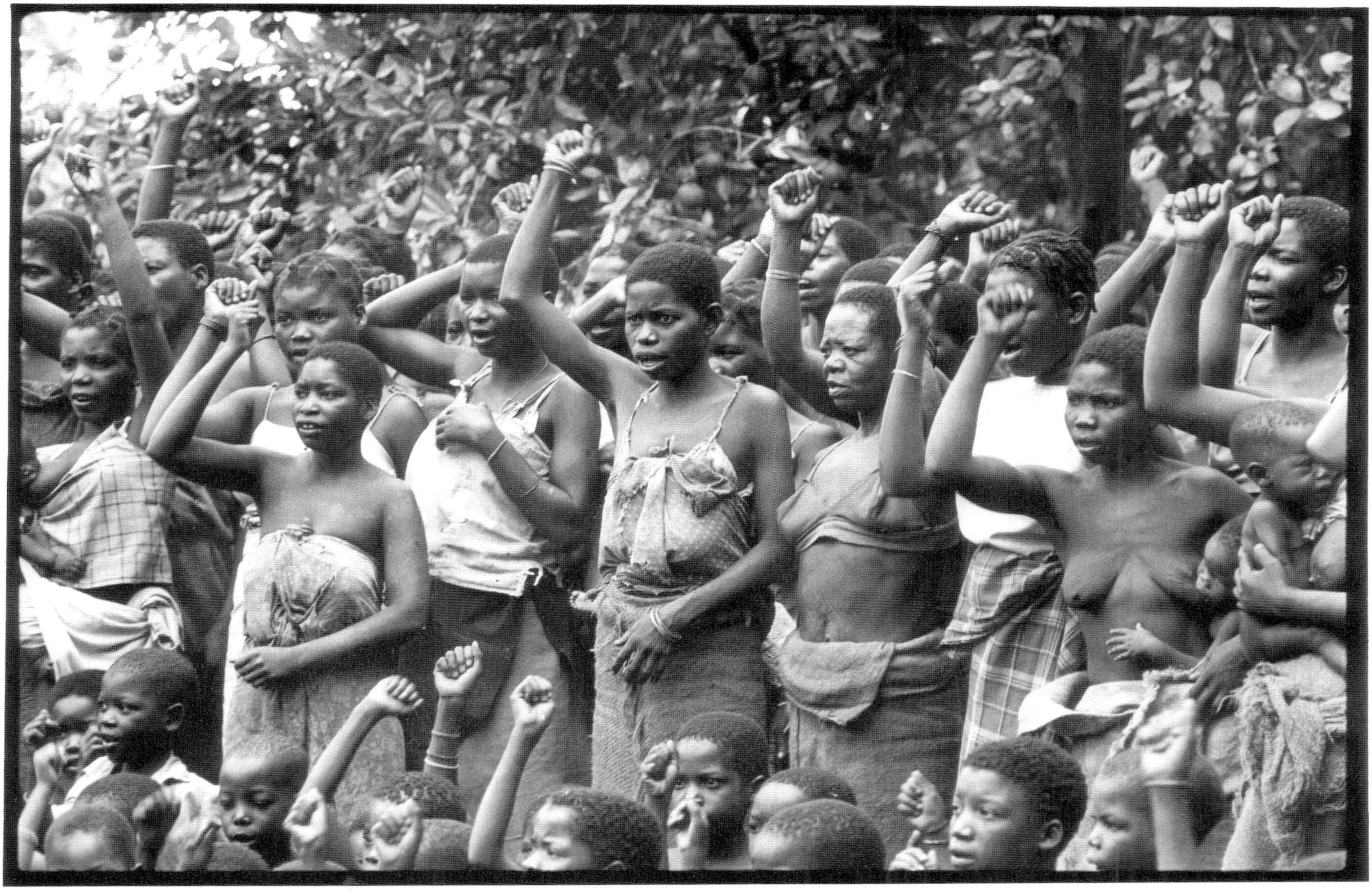

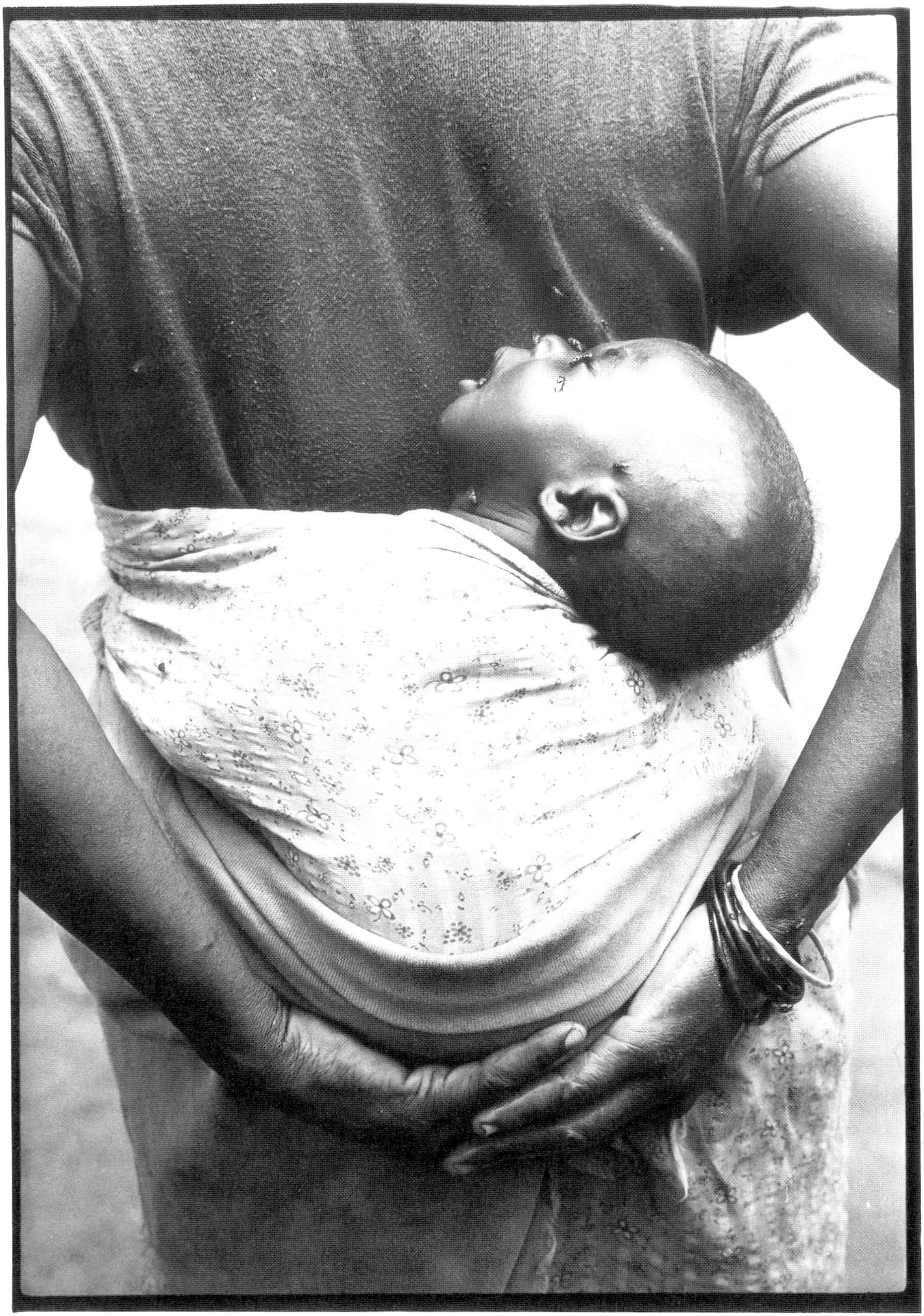

'We have nothing here — we arrived only with what we could carry, what we were wearing when the attacks started. We cannot grow anything here, we have no seed. There were mangoes but they are all finished, only a few coconuts left. We make soup with leaves but it is not enough.'

Refugee, Maganja da Costa

'We left Luabo — the attack started and I said to my husband "Close the door." He came and said "Take the children." I gathered all the children together, I just gathered the children and took one blanket — just one blanket in order to carry the child. The blanket fell down and I carried the child in my arms and just started to run. I ran and returned to take a cloth. I covered the child and started to run again. I jumped up the wall to the beach and then I called for my husband. My husband did not answer. I went up to Chucolone, but he did not appear. I was looking for my husband but did not see him. And then I ran to the land and I saw the bandits again and I started to run again. My little boy was saying "Mummy come here, mummy come here". I went to Chucolone and then to Hapitine at night with the children. I slept for two nights, in the bush, with the children; without anything, without cloth, without anything. I took straw to cover us.

There we are sleeping outside with the children, with plenty of mosquitoes, we don't have anything. You see how this child has become? The child was always keeping well. Now, as he has to sleep outside with mosquitoes — it is not possible. Therefore the child is sick — sick.'

Mozambique refugee

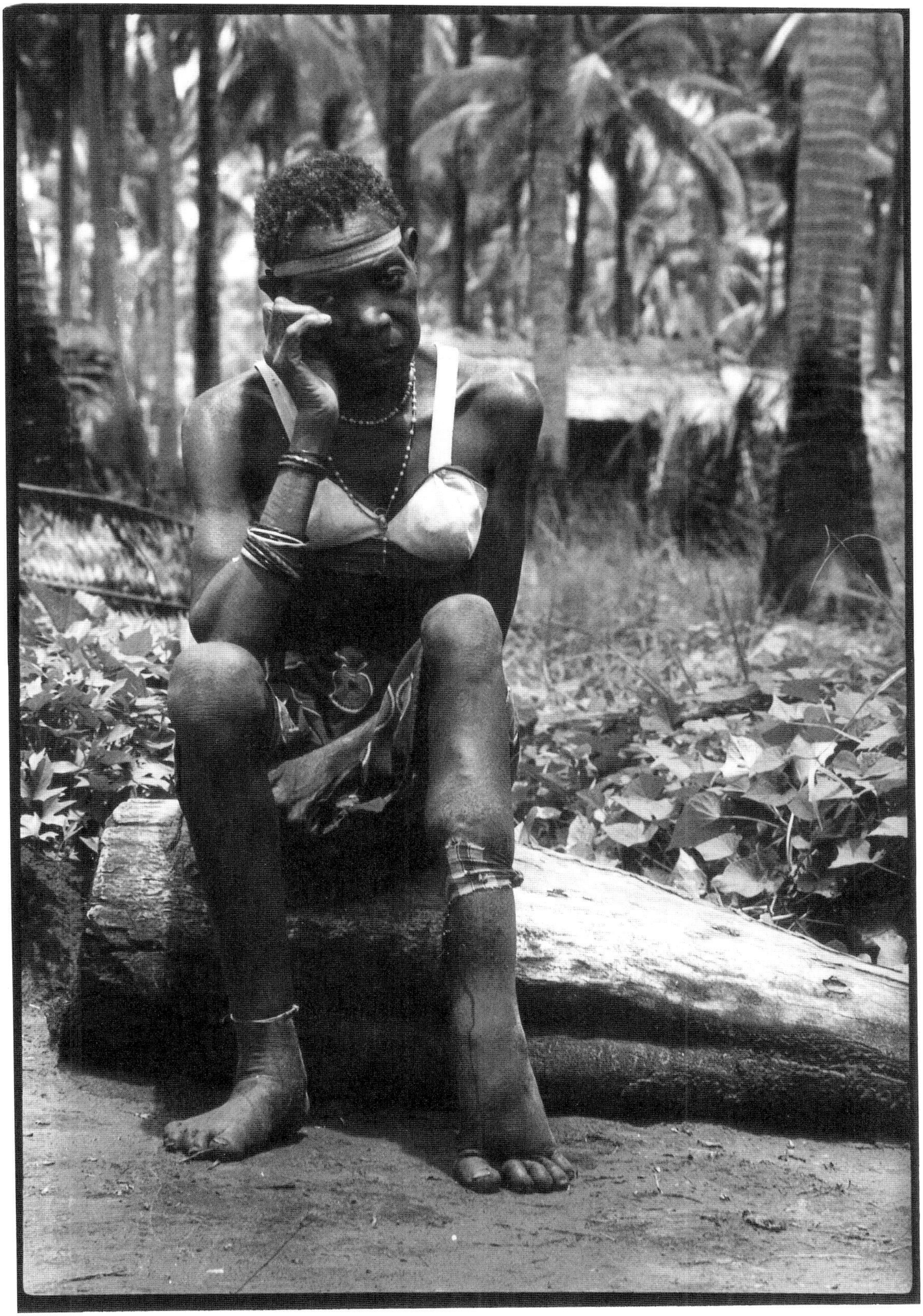

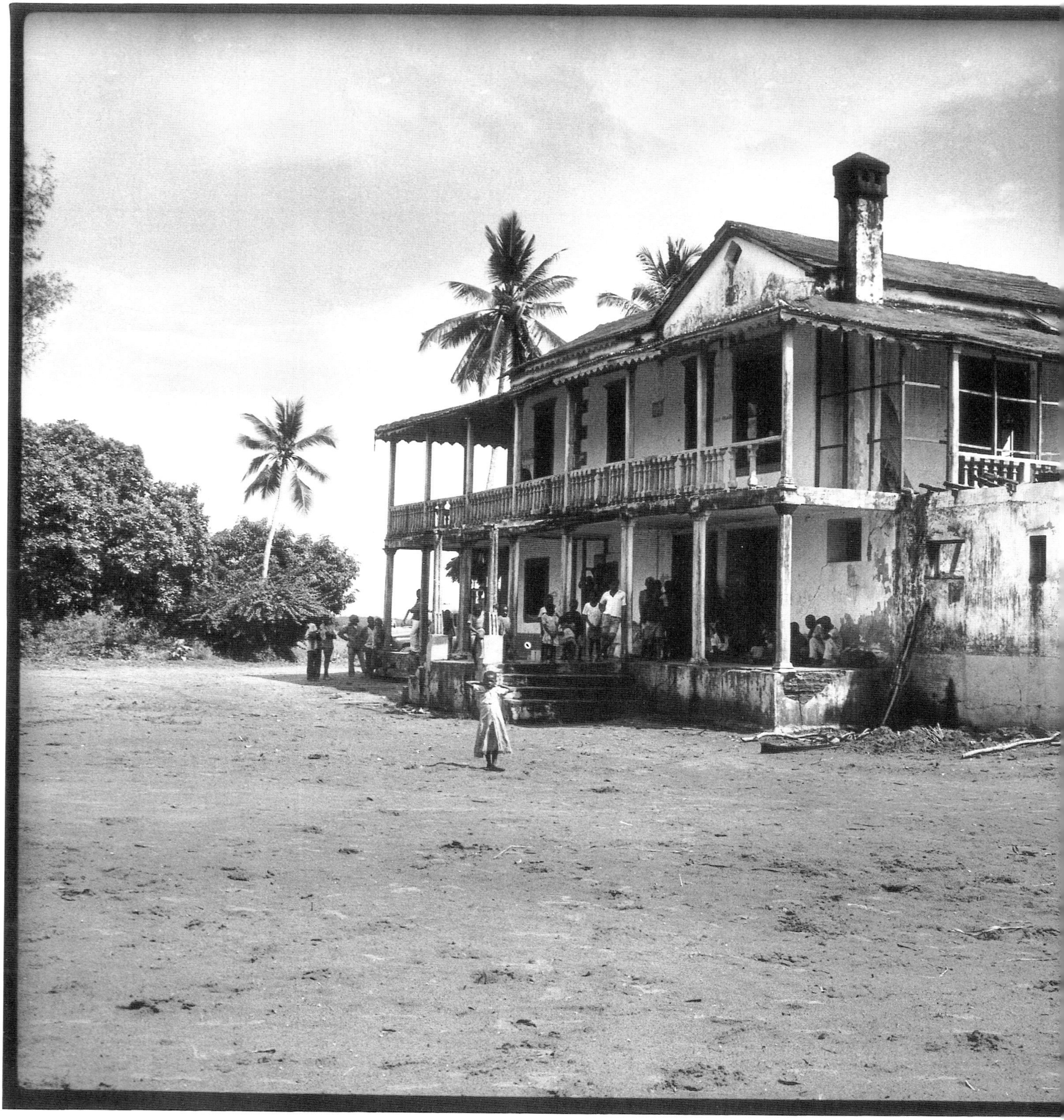

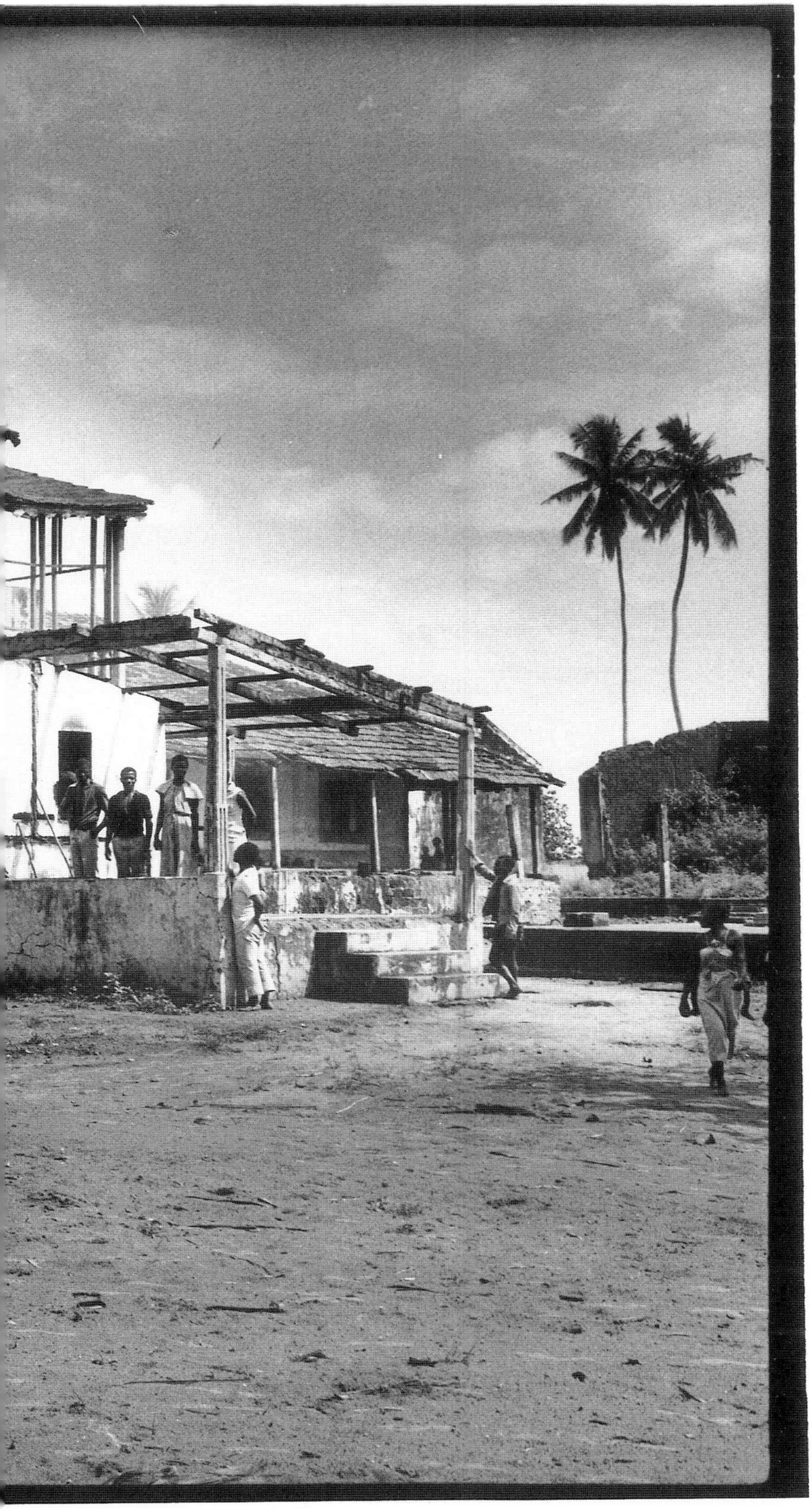

At this house on a former Portuguese sisal estate in Quelimane province, thousands of people displaced by fighting are arriving, hoping for food, shelter and medicine. There are very few supplies of any kind. Ramshackle shelters give little protection from heat and rain. Even at a large camp like this, the refugees need guarding from armed attack.

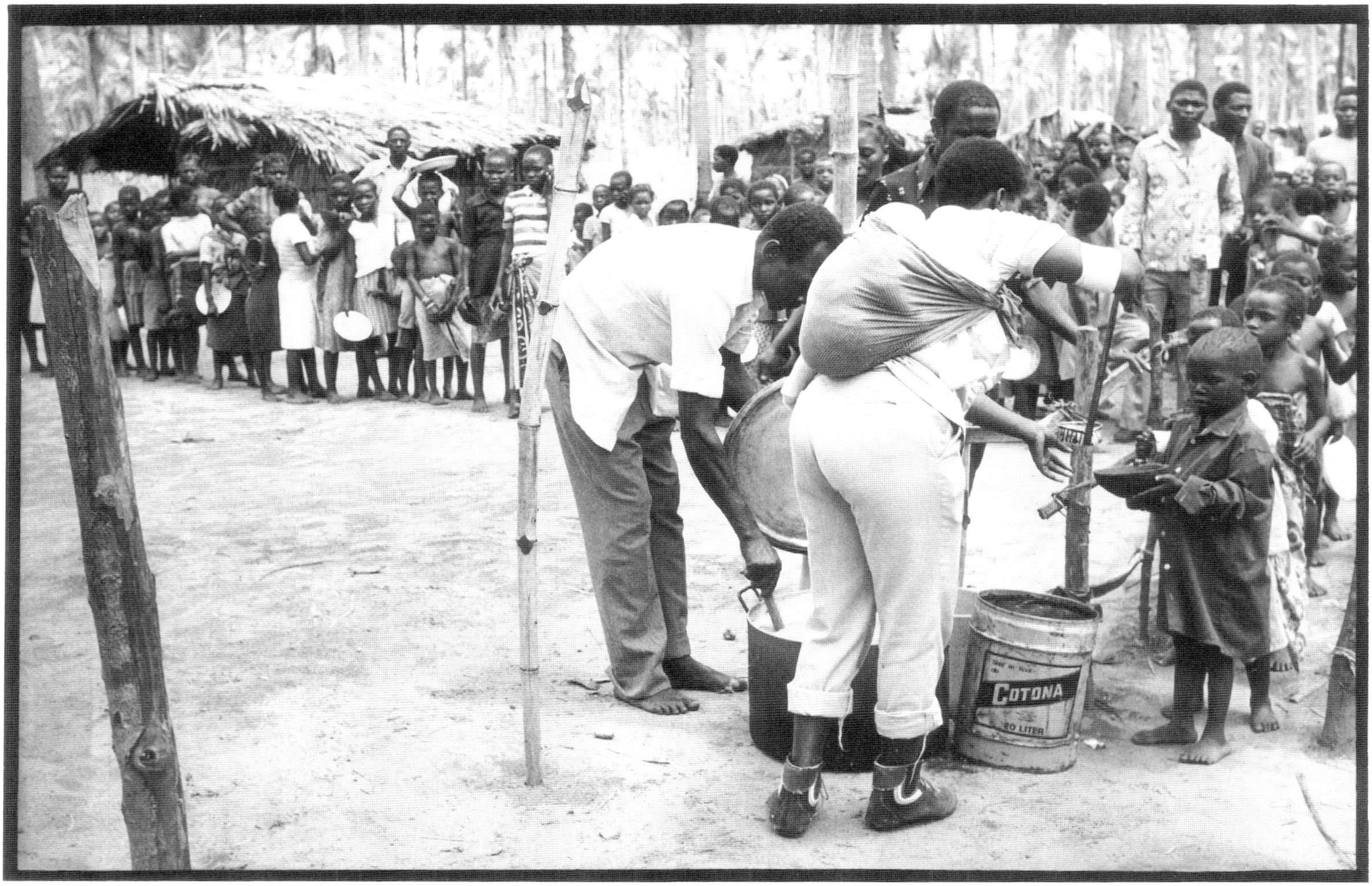
COTONA
20 LITER

At large remote camps such as this, the refugees are not safe from MNR bandit attacks.

Armed Frelimo guards patrol the camp and watch over children as they eat watery soup.

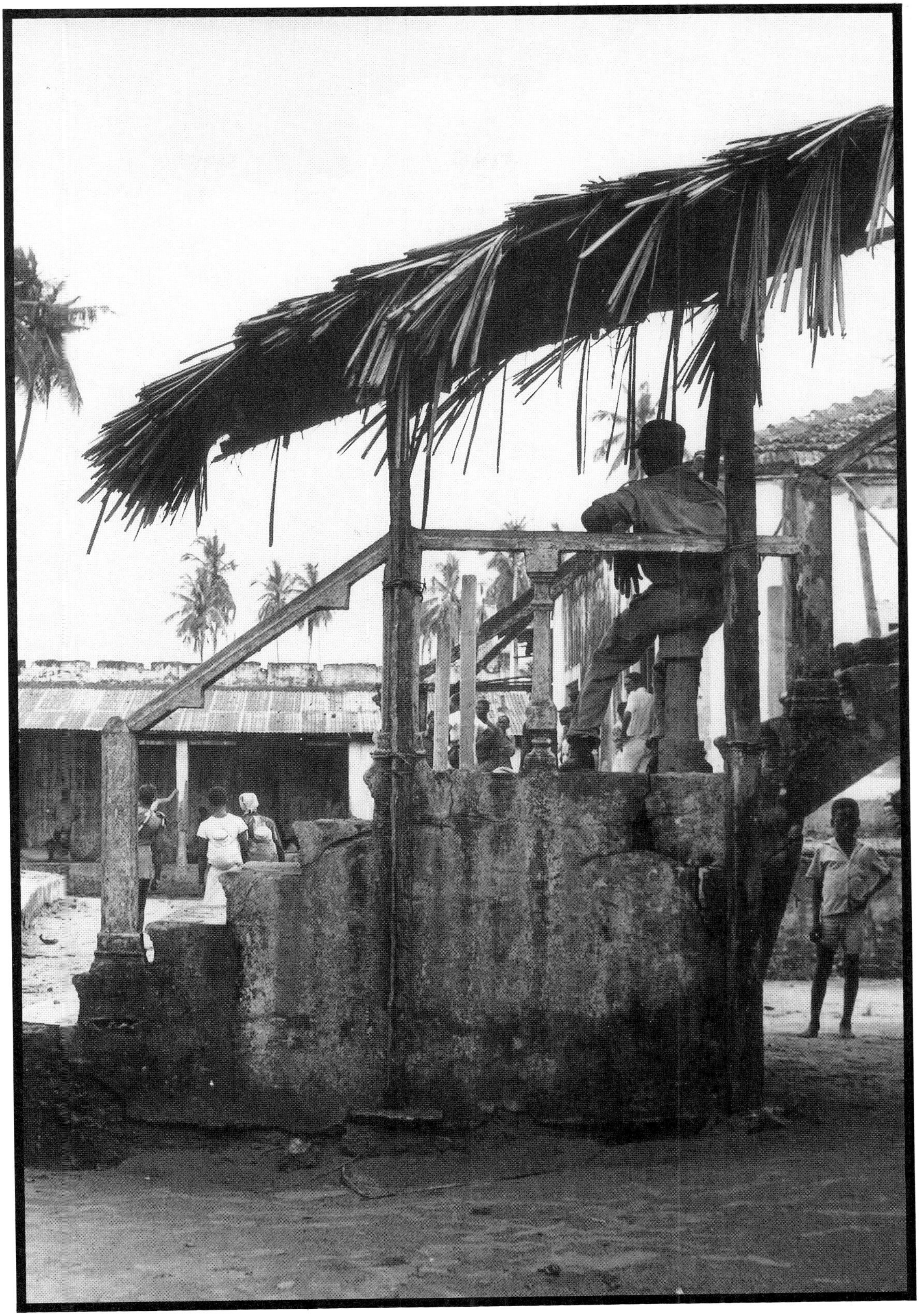

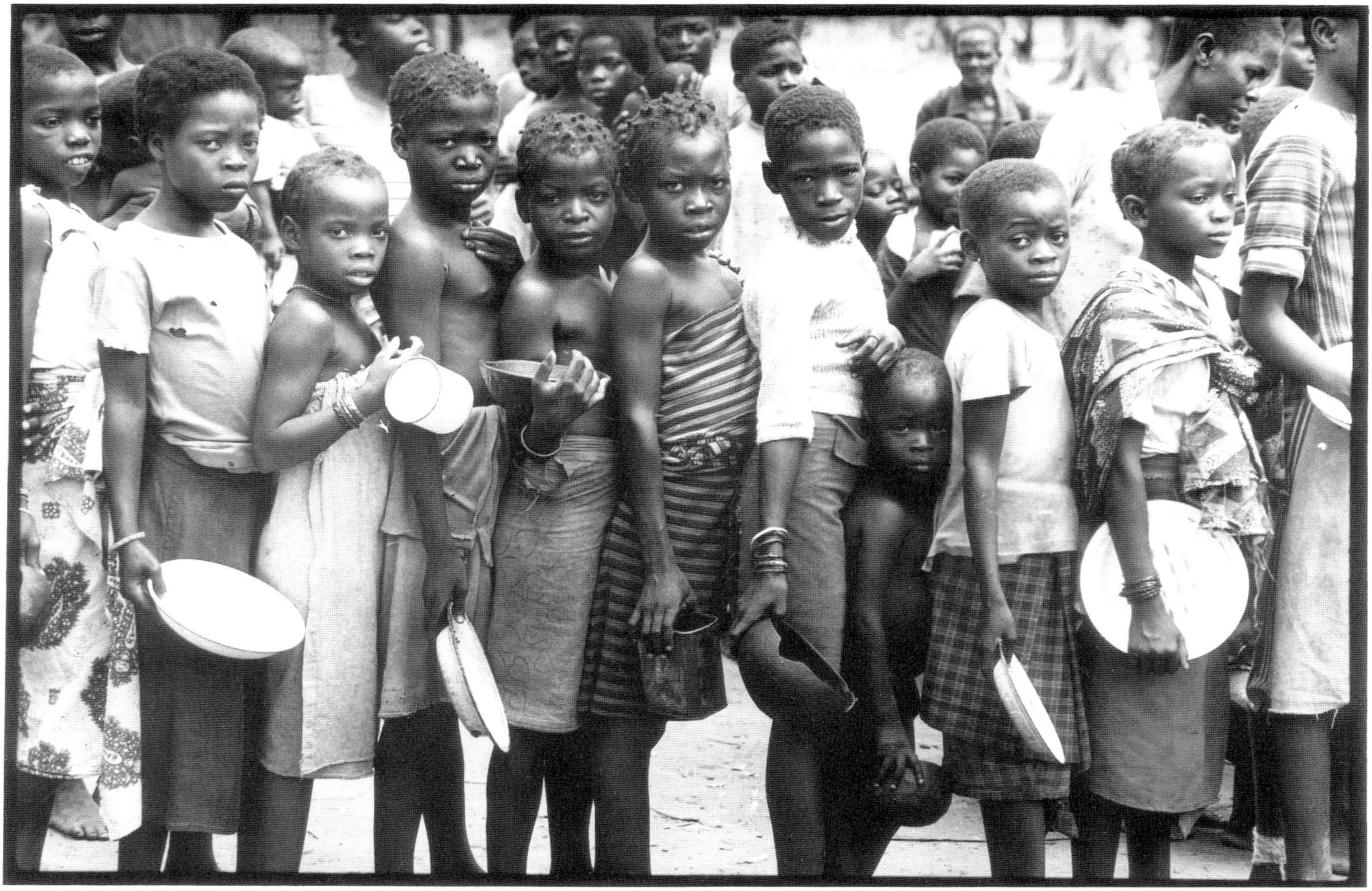

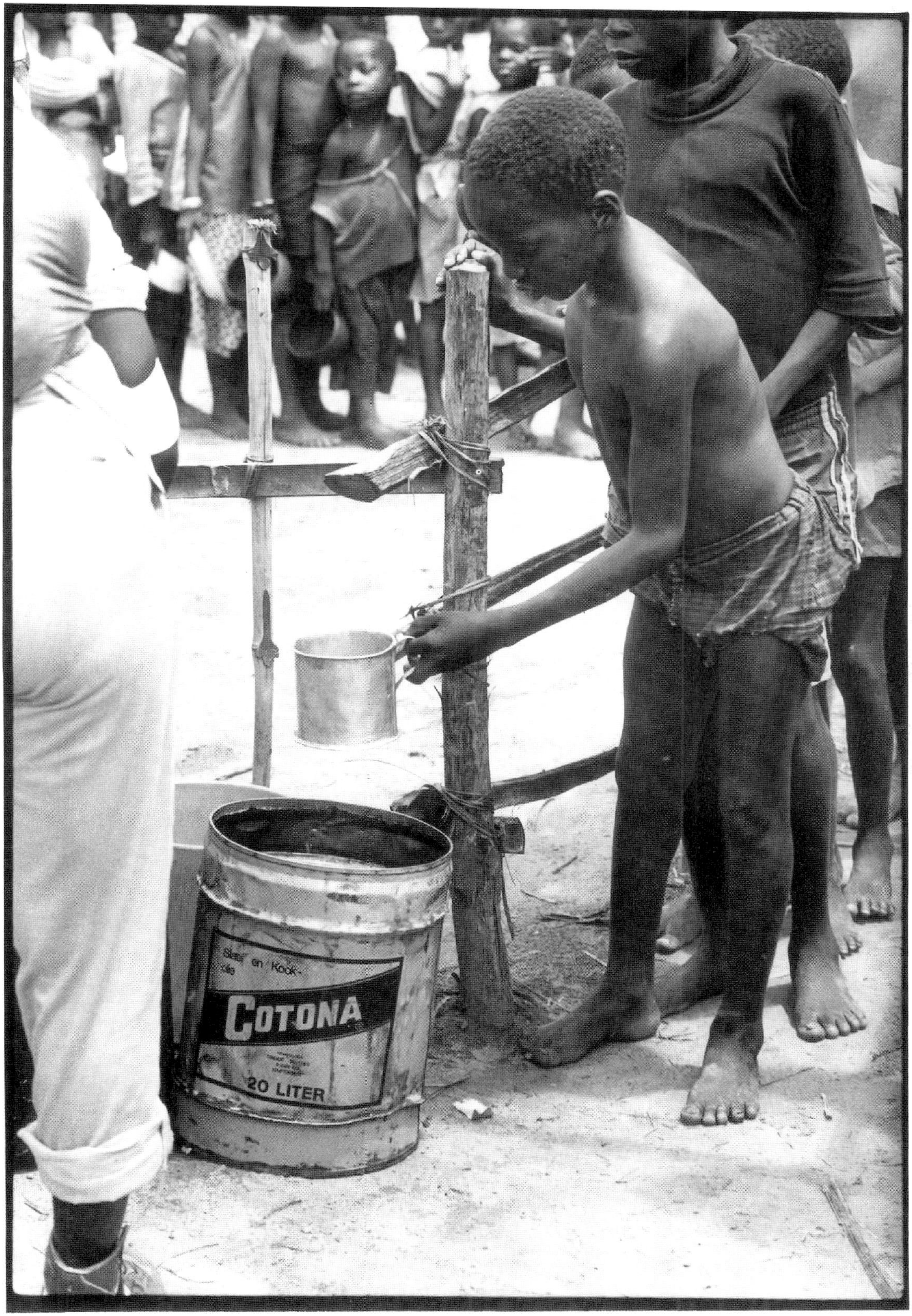
Slaai en Kook-
olie
COTONA
20 LITER

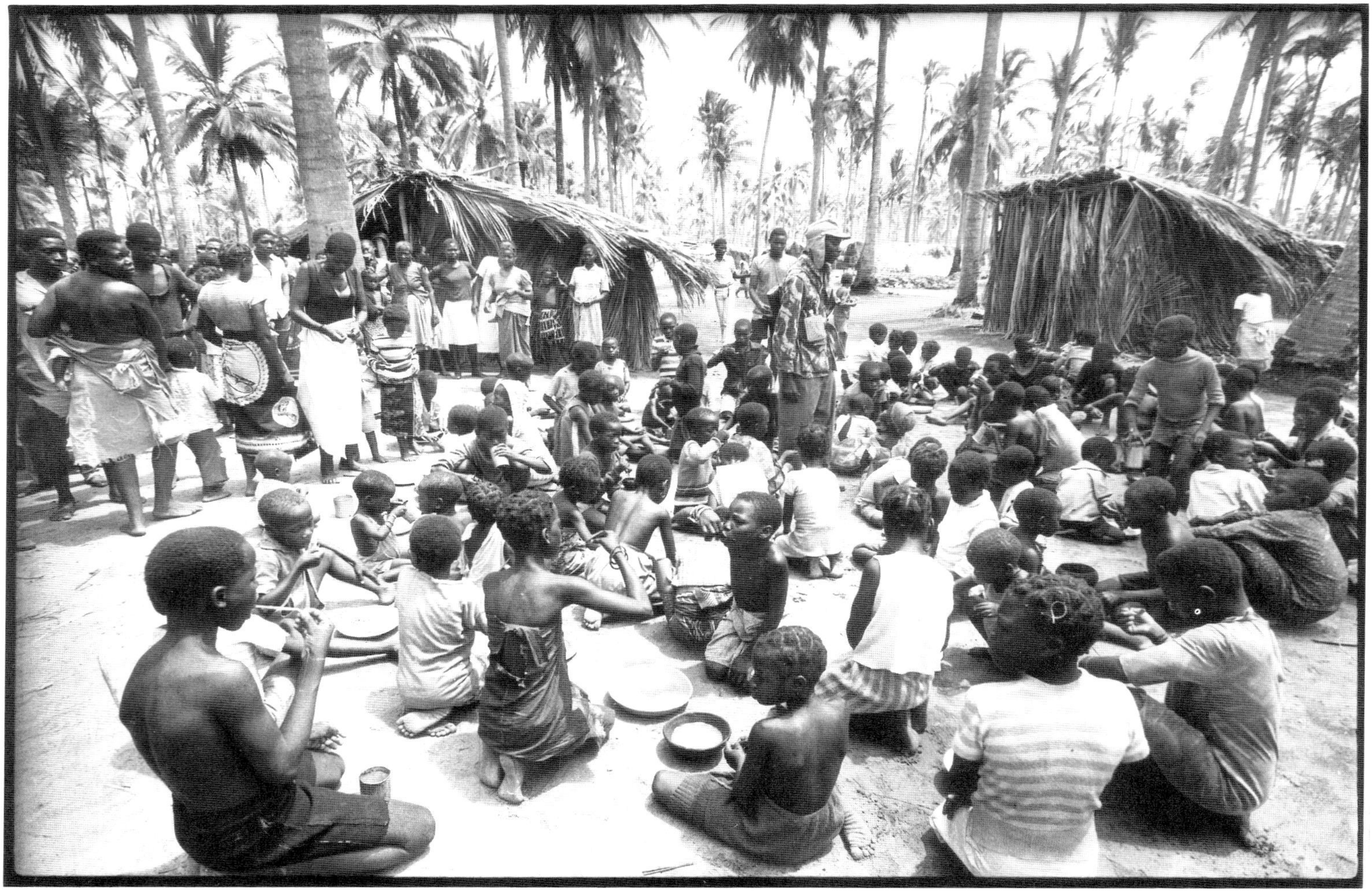

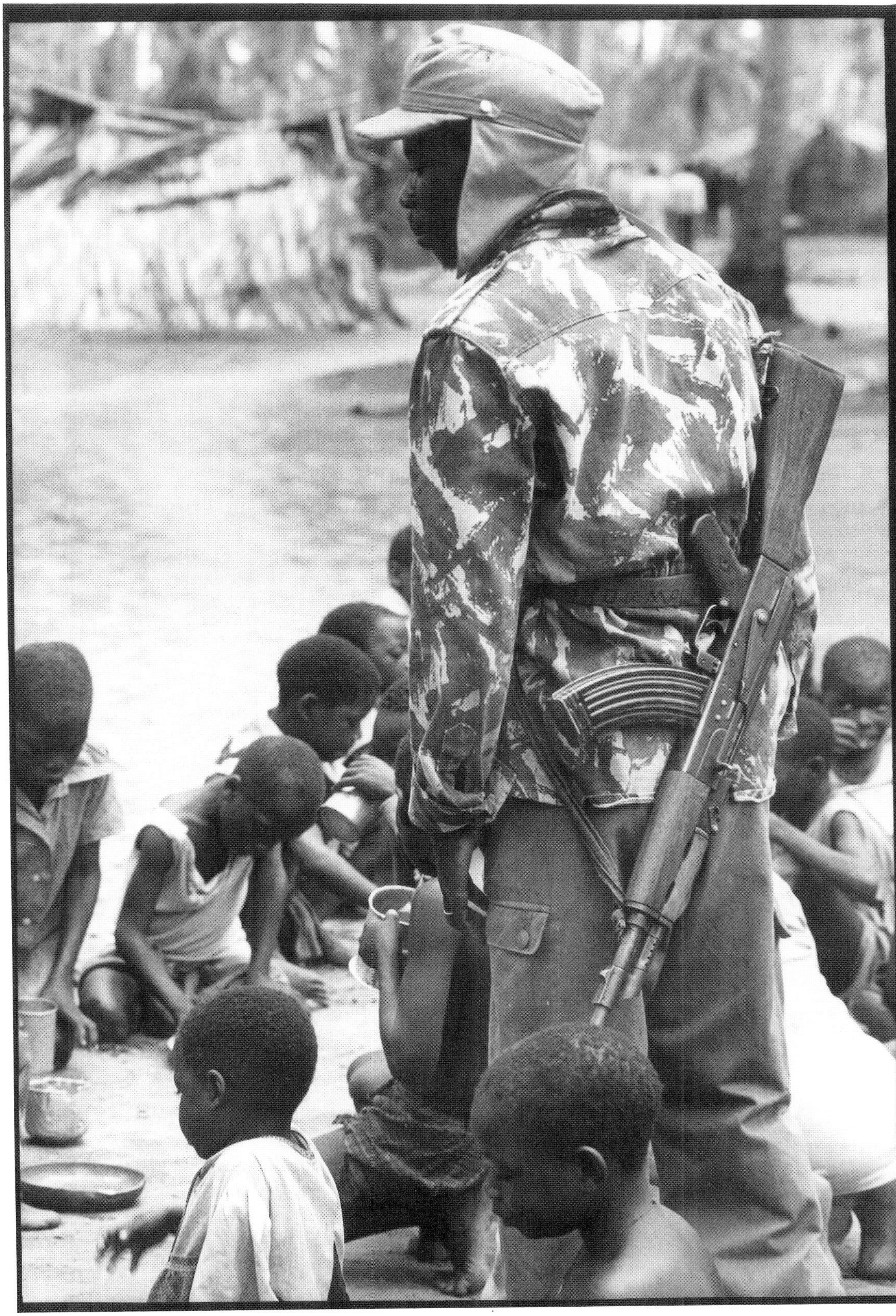

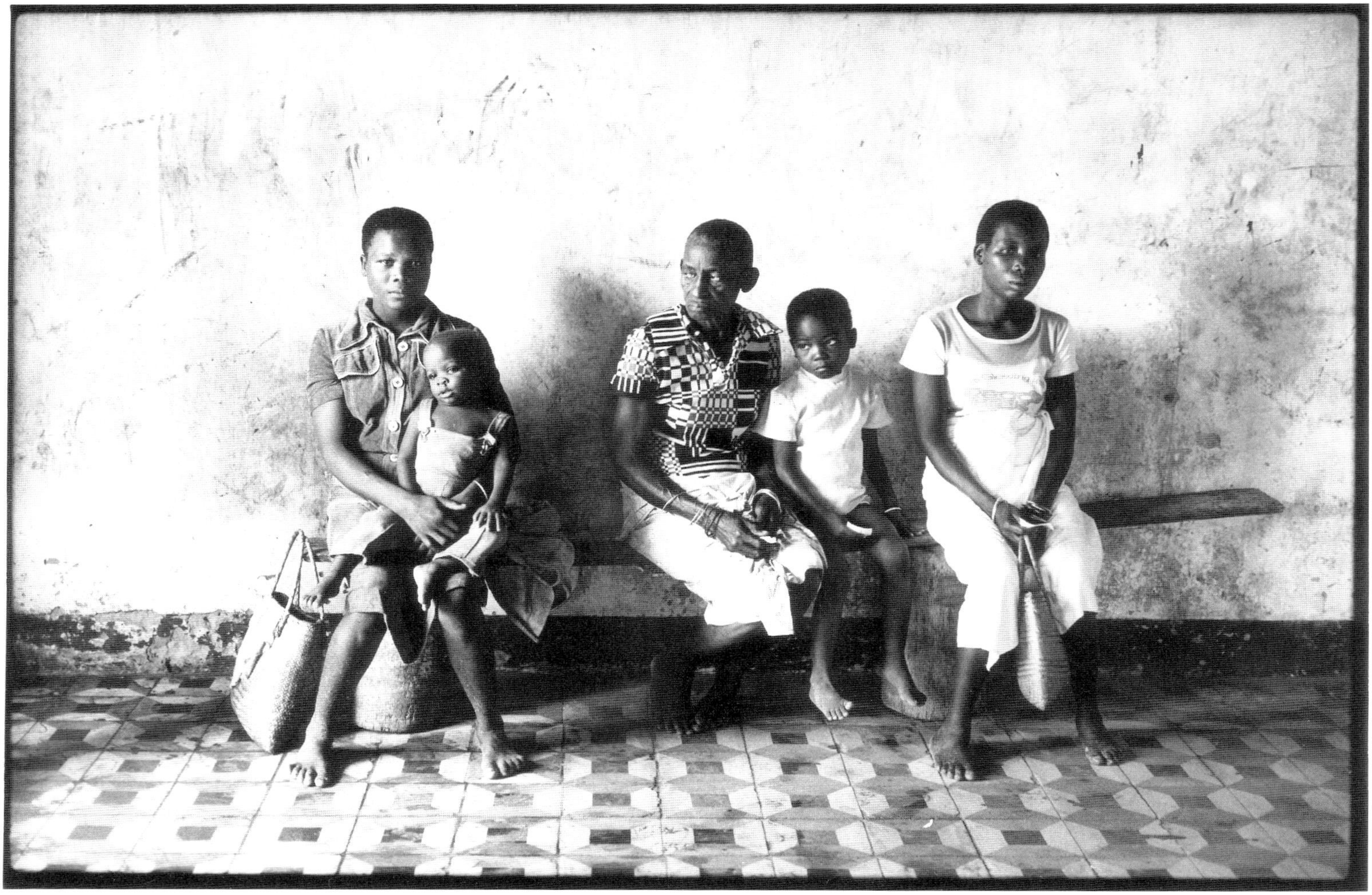

'The armed bandits came and ransacked and set our homes on fire, they took everything that we had, food and clothes. We fled, and we are waiting here for medicine, my boy is very sick. We would like to go back but it is not safe, we must stay here together although we have nothing.'

Refugee, Quelimane

Q — How many people are here in this community? What is the population?
A — There are 2,200, 2,300 and more people arriving every day.
Q — What diseases are you treating?
A — The diseases we have here are many — malaria, tuberculosis, malnutrition, and wounds — abscesses — from armed attacks. There is also a lot of diarrhoea, particularly among the children. I only have the medicines you see here, enough for a few people. It is very hard to get supplies, we need so much.

Refugee health worker, Mozambique

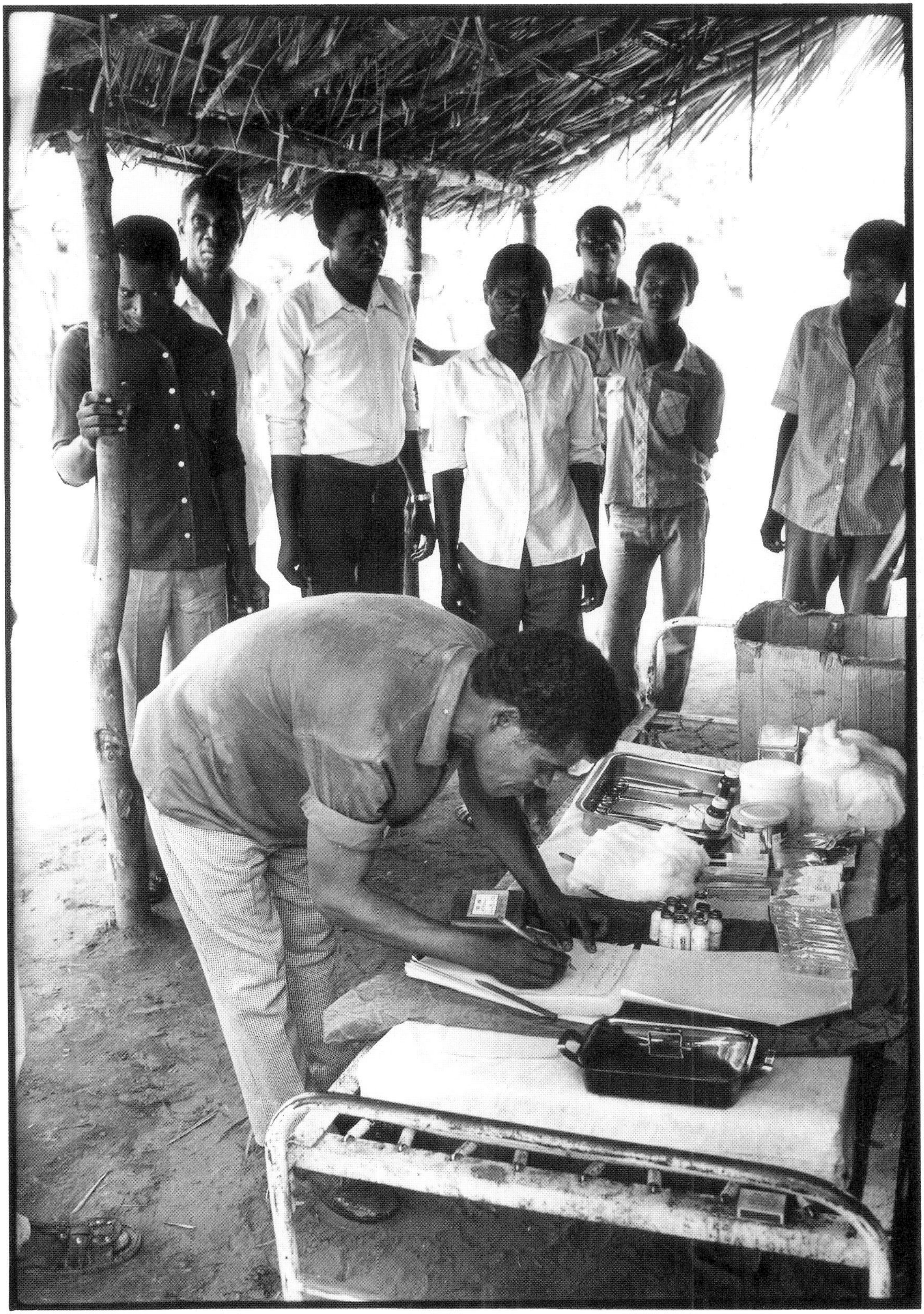

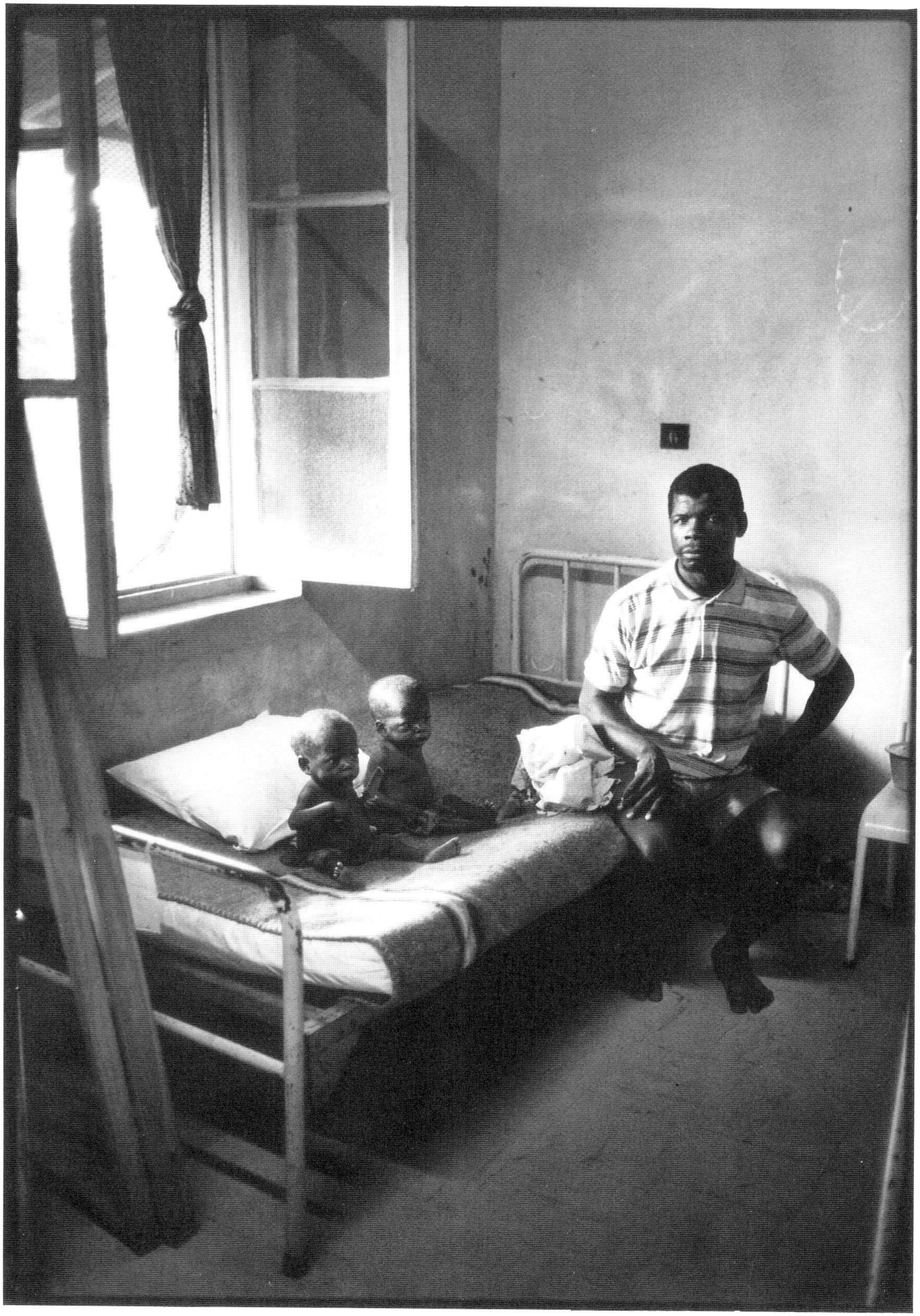

'This is a case of kwashiorkor due to prolonged malnutrition. A very common case here.

These two we love very much because we are treating them for almost one year now. They are twins, almost two years old, but their size and weight is for babies of six months. They were in a very bad condition and we maintained them. They don't have a mother, just a father. Now they are much better, we are looking after them.

Brazilian paediatrician, Quelimane

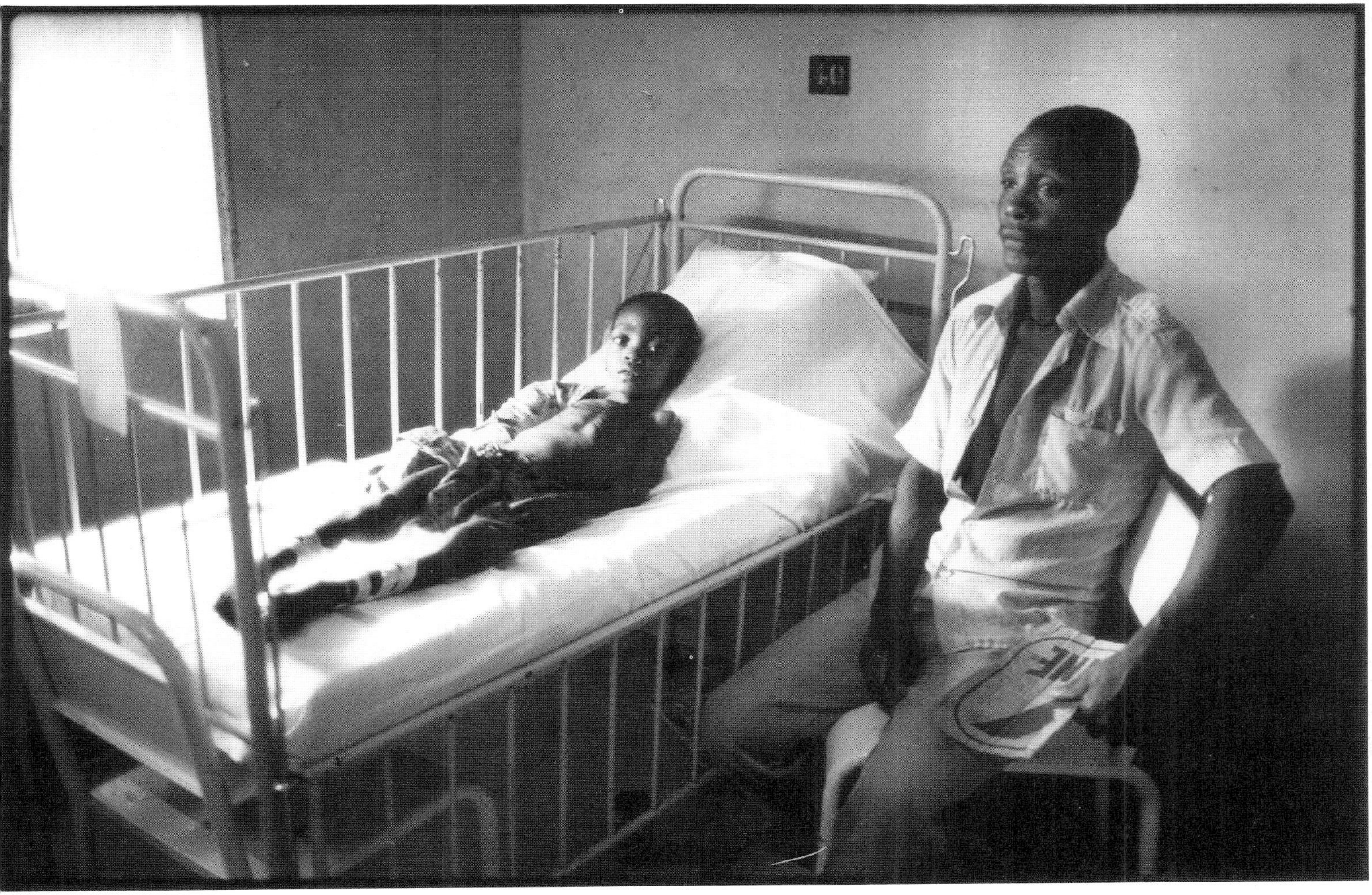

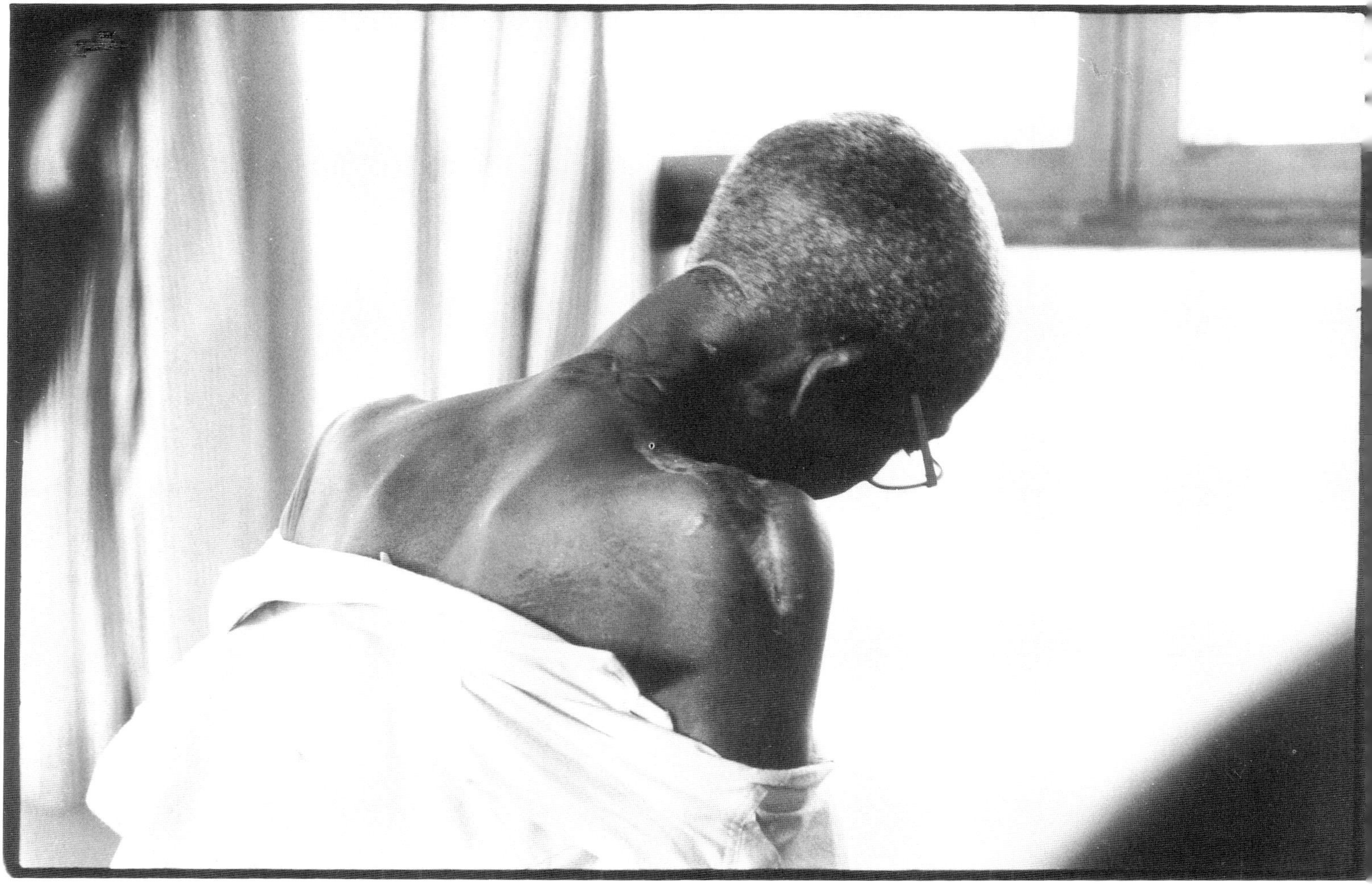

'My name is Raimundo Muchalpa. On the 11th July last year (1986) the armed bandits came to my house and the first thing they did was apologise. They apologised and I thought they were my people, then when I went outside I saw cutlasses, machetes, assagais, and one of them asked: "You are Raimundo Muchalpa, the oldest teacher here?" And I replied Yes. So he said "then it is you who is teaching children to say — "Away with the bandits!" I said: "As you say, and when asked if I was a teacher, shouldn't I have said I was a teacher?" "Seize him" he said and the others seized me. And they directed their rifles on me — three. And the leader said: "Stand up." So I stood up. "You are already a teacher for 35 years then? And you are teaching the children. Take your clothes off — Quickly!" So I took my clothes off. "You know you are going to die because you are a teacher and you are instructing the children." Oh, yes, but why I said? "Because you went to Haputo — stand up." And I stood up. "There — look there". They had a cutlass. What could I do, I had to accept. And then he lifted the sword, and then ... I fell down and I said oh my God. And they said "that is useless, we are not Christians, no use asking God" and they started to cut me first here and here and there. Then they left me behind. From 4.00 am to 11, 12.00 am. I was in the sun and then our troops arrived and they took me straight away to here — to the Central Hospital at Quelimane. Since July, last year up to now, I have been in treatment in the Central Hospital of Quelimane. And that was my story."

Teacher, Raimundo Muchalpa, Quelimane

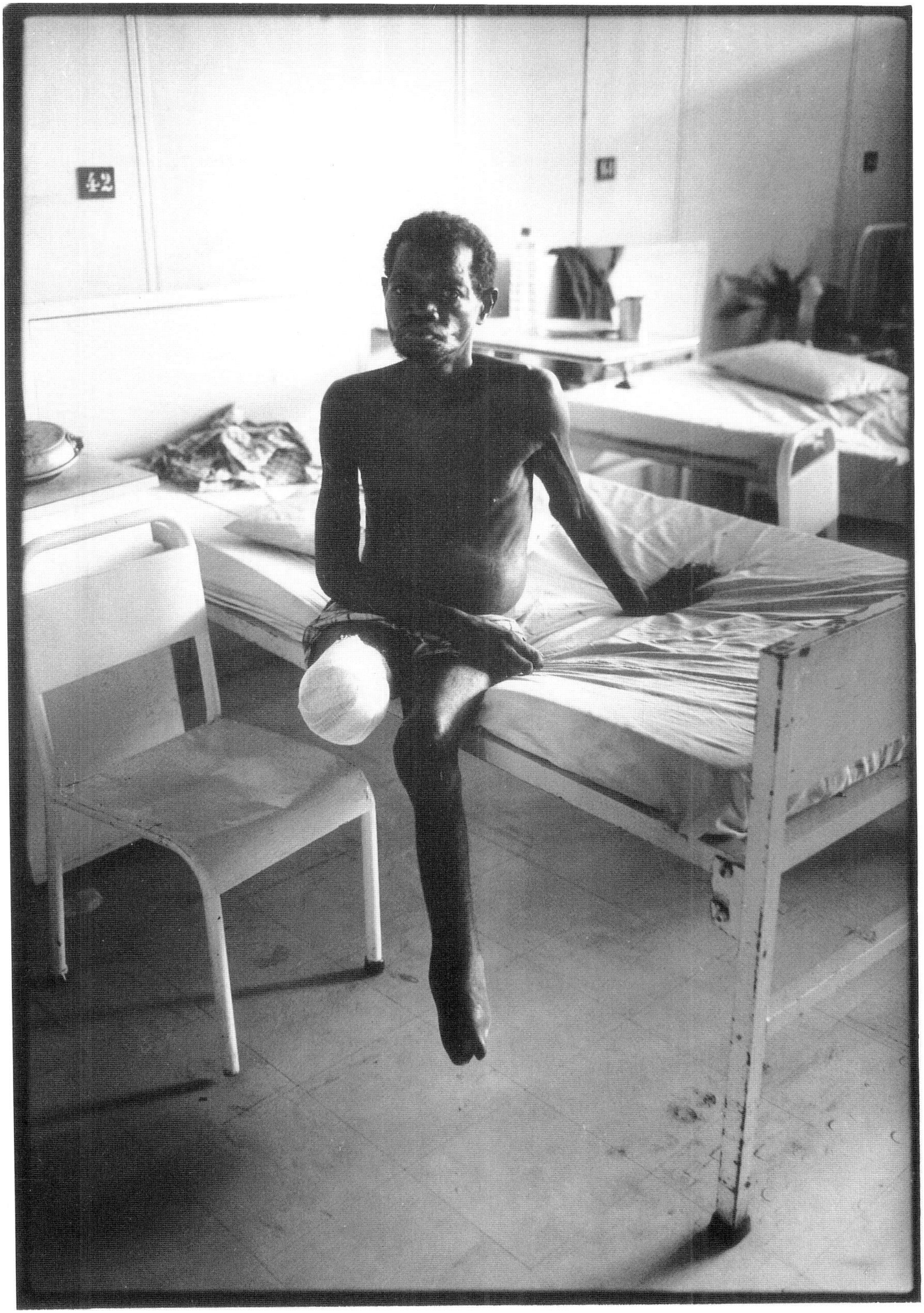

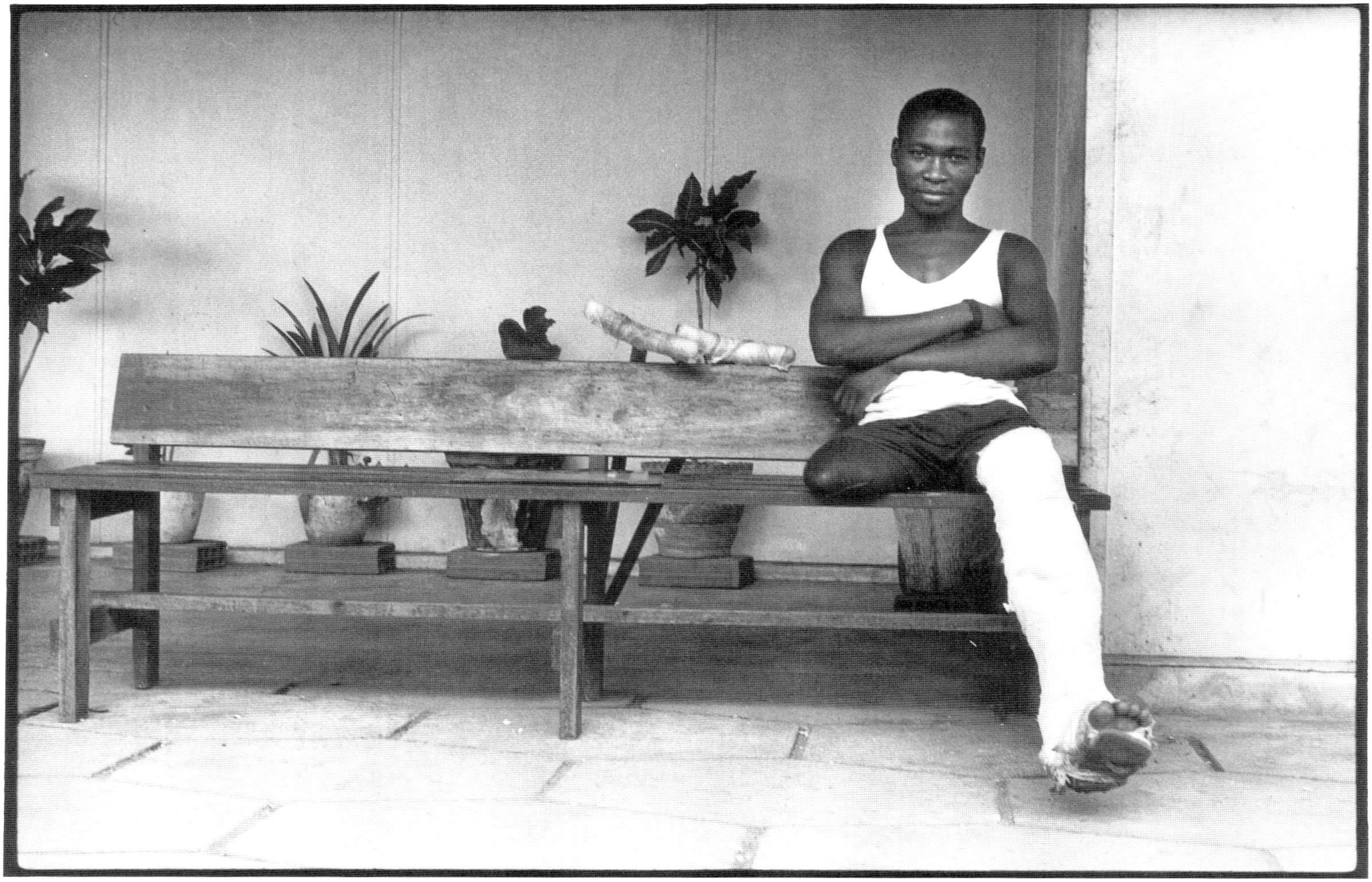

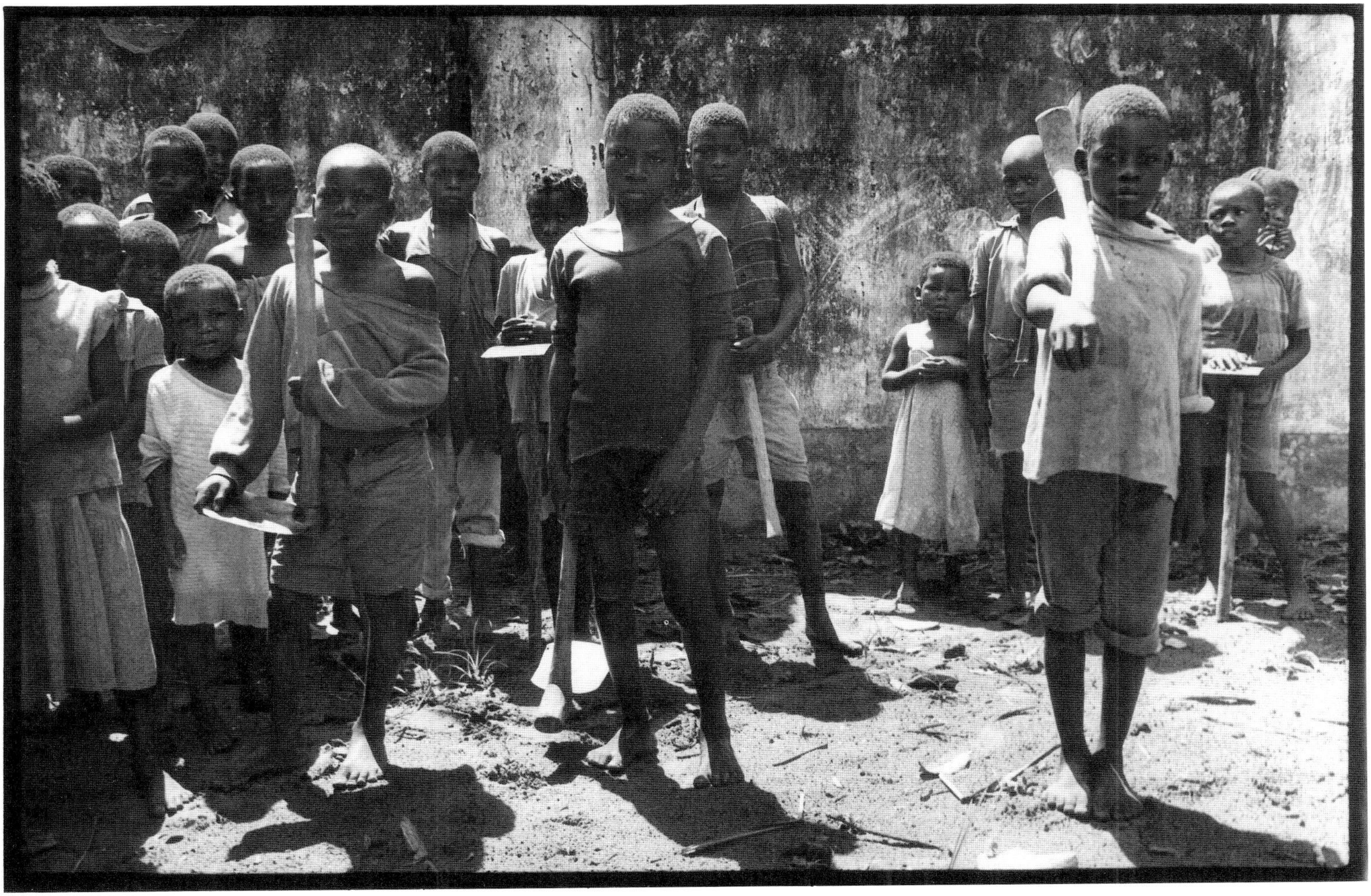

The refugees are living in a lush and fertile area — almost the opposite of the cracked-earth famine regions of north-east Africa. But the result is the same — hunger and starvation. The refugees have nothing to plant, no seeds or crops to sow and only makeshift tools with which to work the land. Mangoes and coconuts were plentiful, but as the only food growing in the region they were eaten months ago. With peace and regular supplies this could return to a prosperous and fertile land.

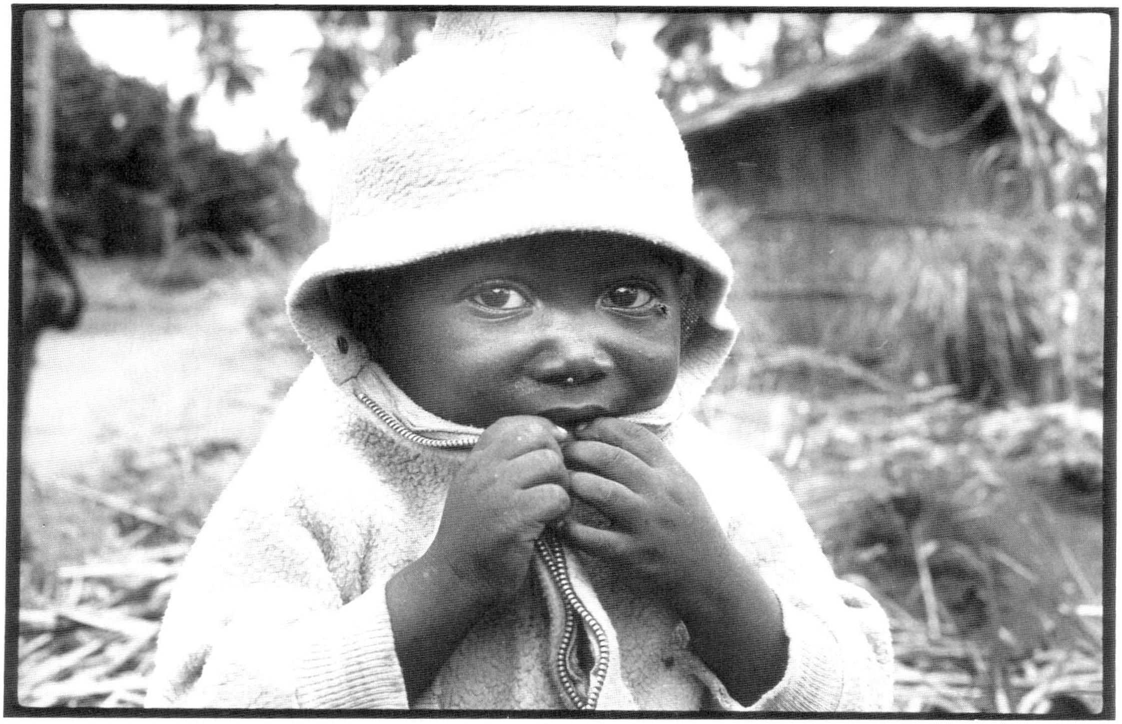

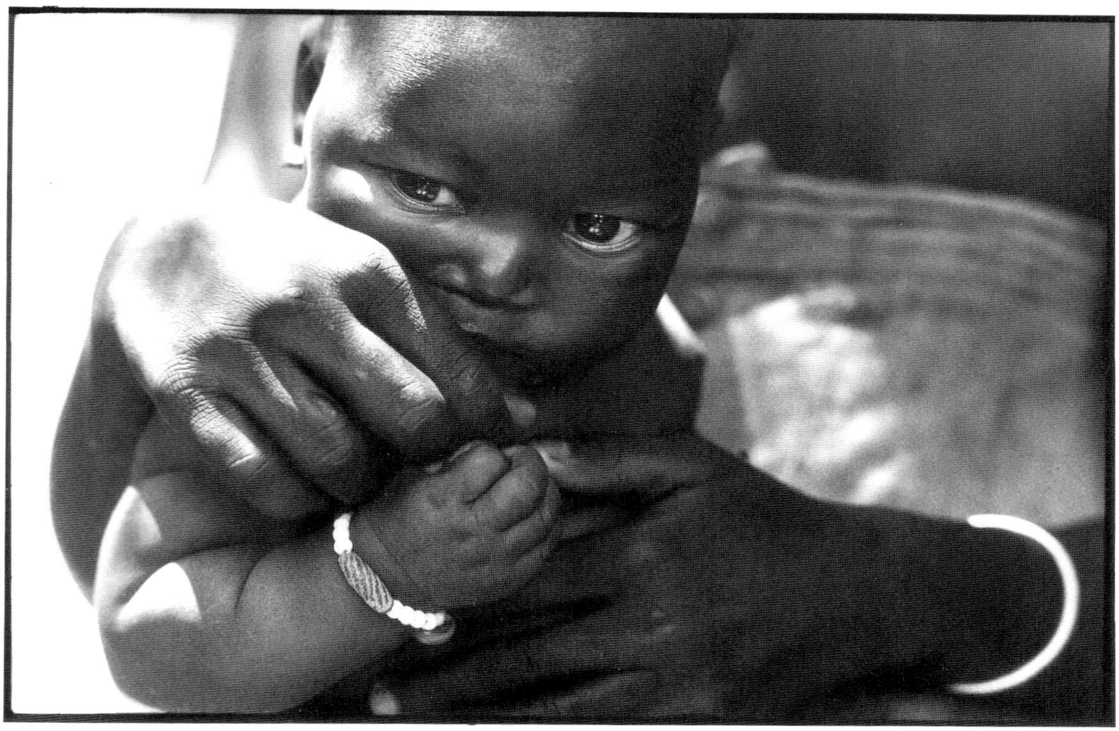

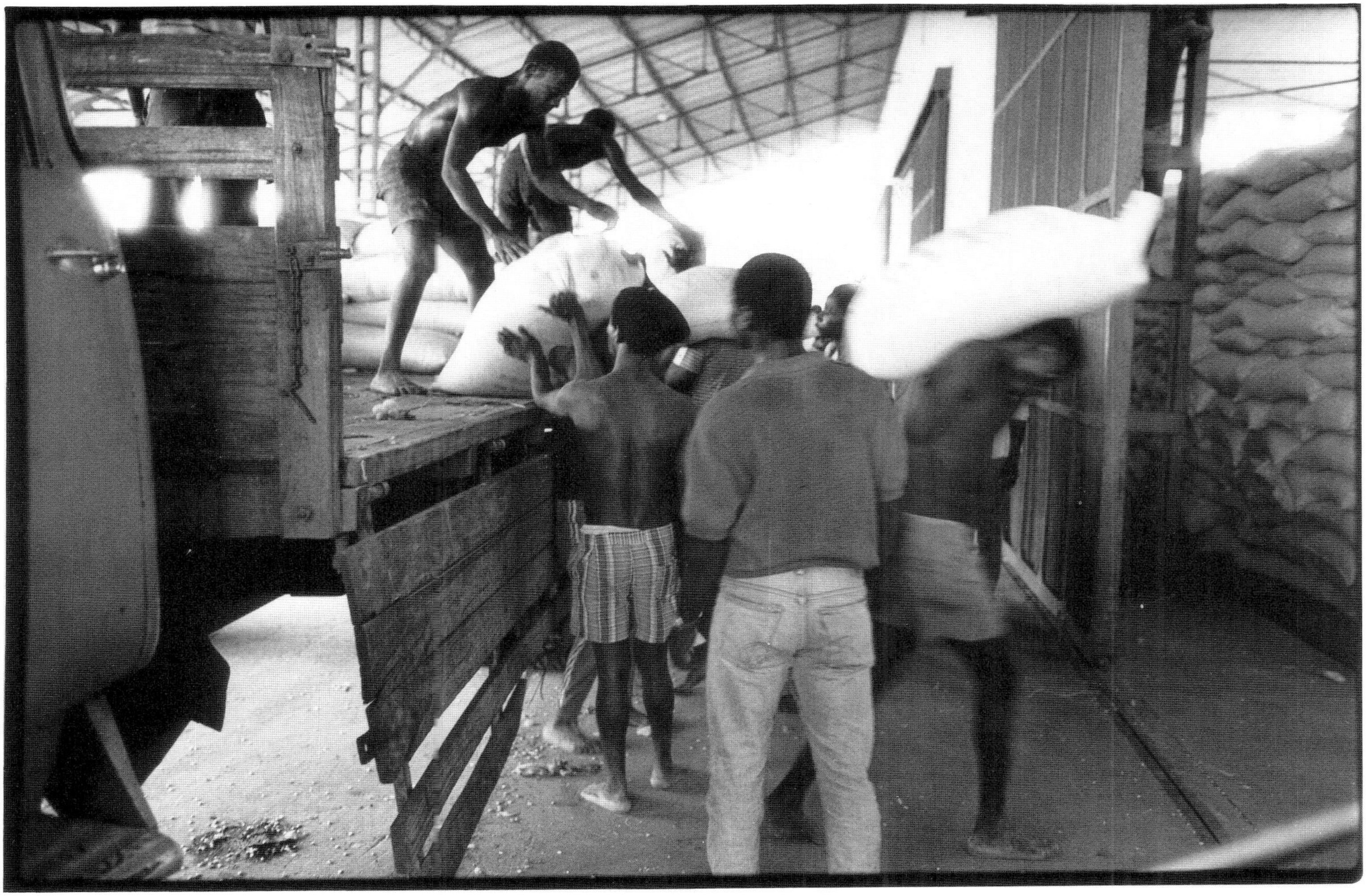

'As a driver of the commercial department of the Natural Disaster Department in Quelimane, I have had many problems going to the camps delivering food to the districts; we are very often exposed to danger, the bandits are always trying to get our goods, and on the way from here to the camp are all the time problems with bandits. Yes, we are afraid because sometimes when they find us they kill us. After each trip we make a report about what happened on the way. When we are attacked, we inform we have been. We must have courage because there are many displaced persons in the district who have fled from the bandits. And the Government is concerned about getting food distributed, because people are starving, people are starving.'

Supplies driver, Quelimane

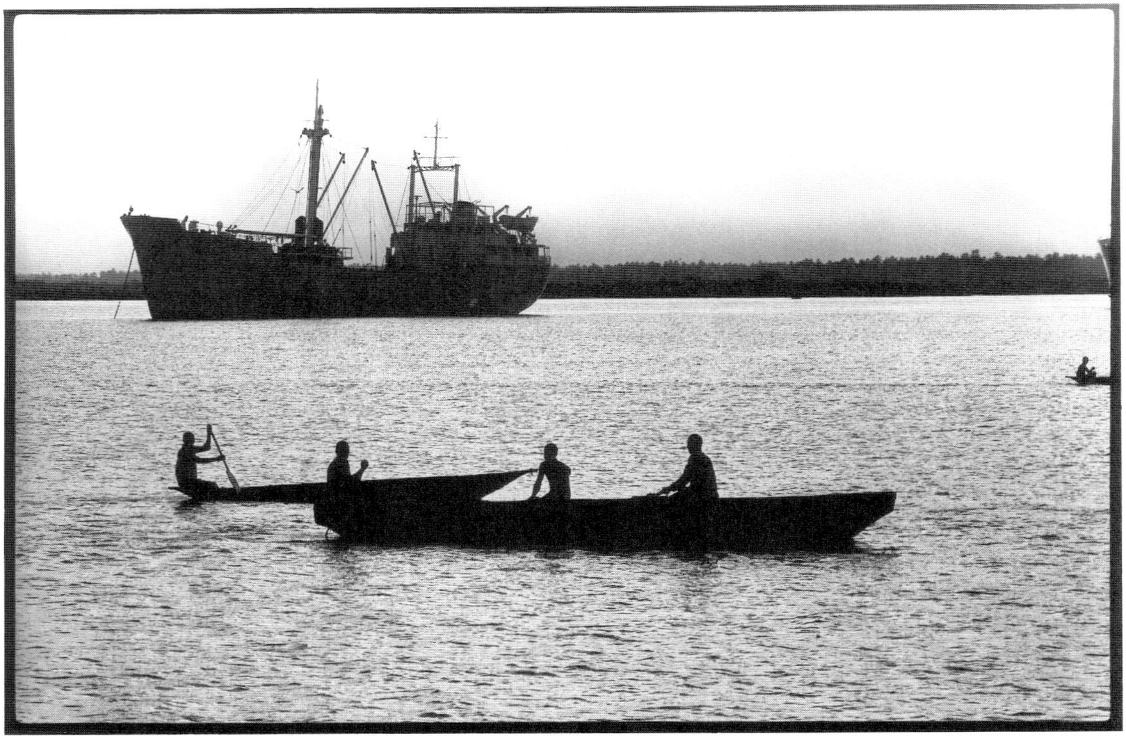

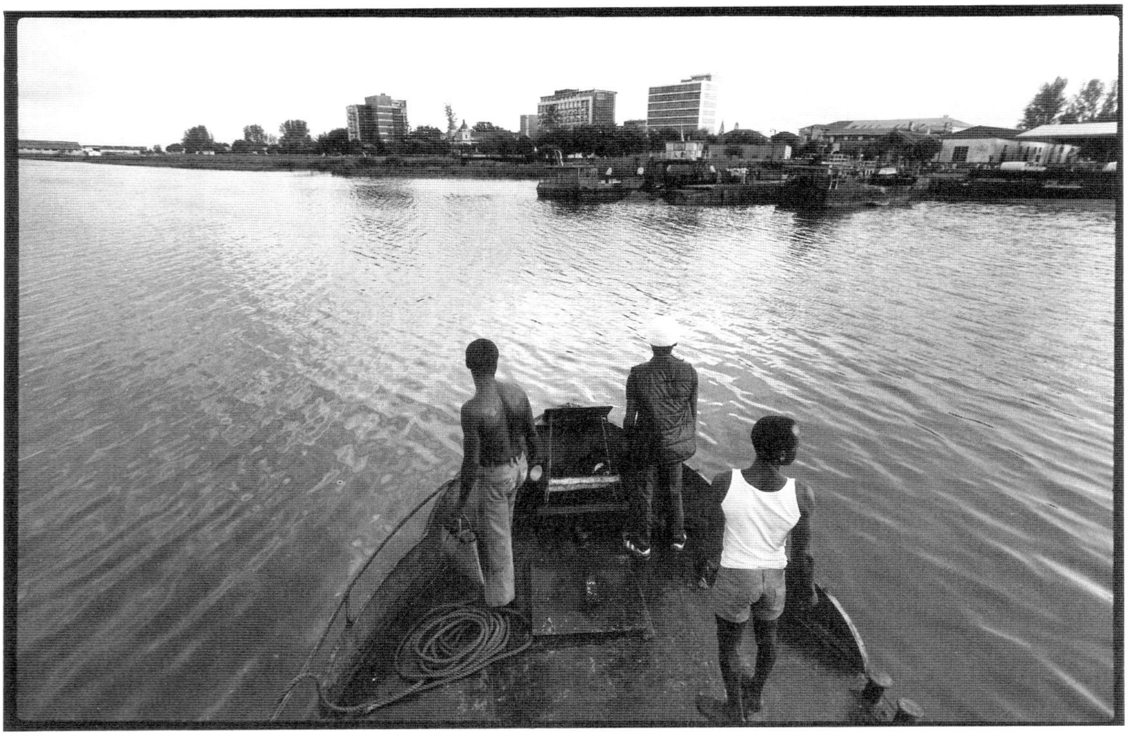

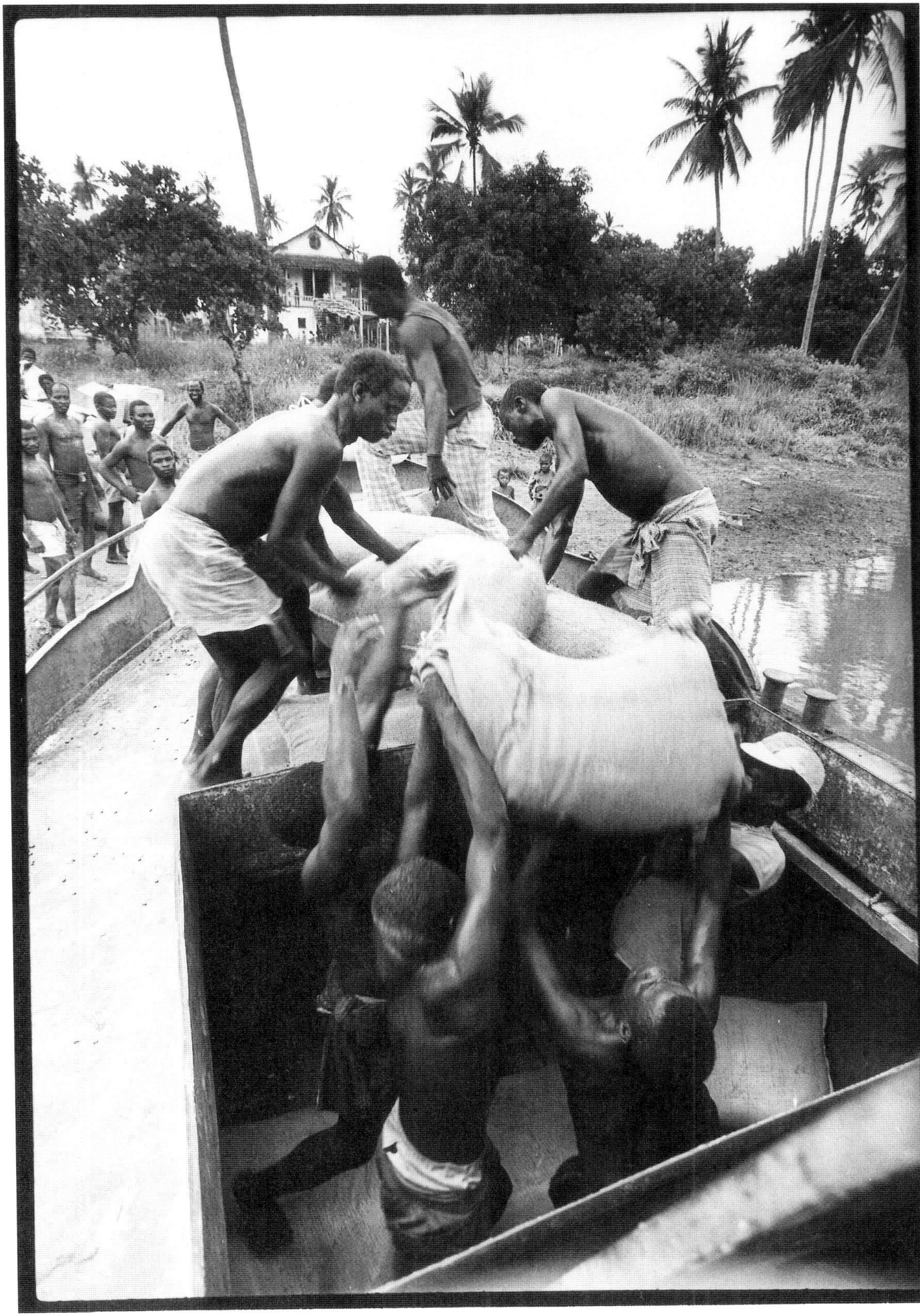

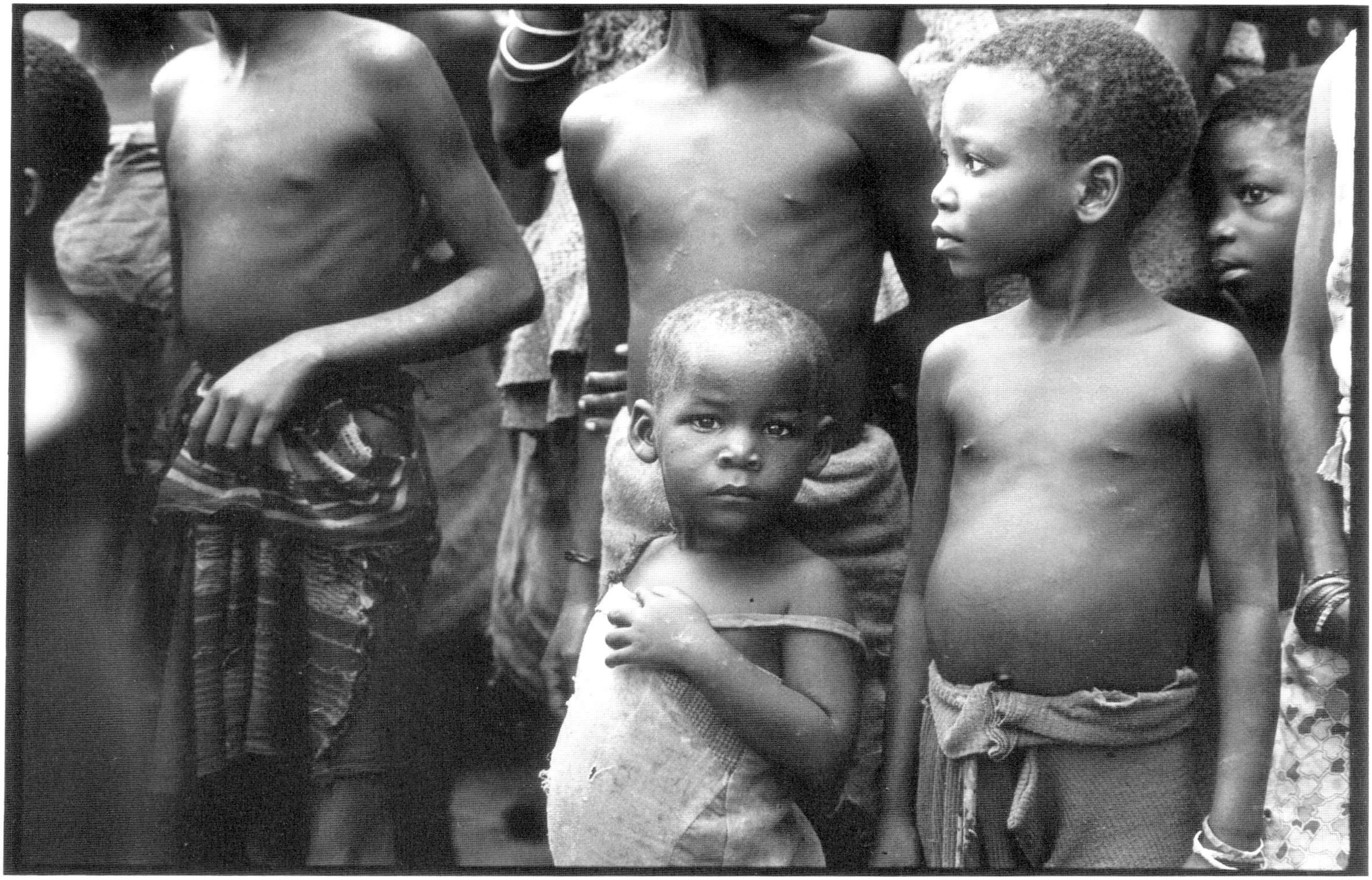

'Most of these children are suffering from malnutrition. Most of them live around the villages and they leave their homes and houses and they can't grow anything here. They have nothing to eat. And with malnutrition, some of these children have TB. It's very easy to get TB with malnutrition. It's getting worse because for two years the situation in this province was really good, and now there's something wrong and the bandits come to this province. And the population, everybody comes to the camps. So we can see that everybody's without food, without clothes, living around camps with hunger. If you want to see we have these guards for the people to protect them from the bandits' attacks.'

Camp governor, Quelimane

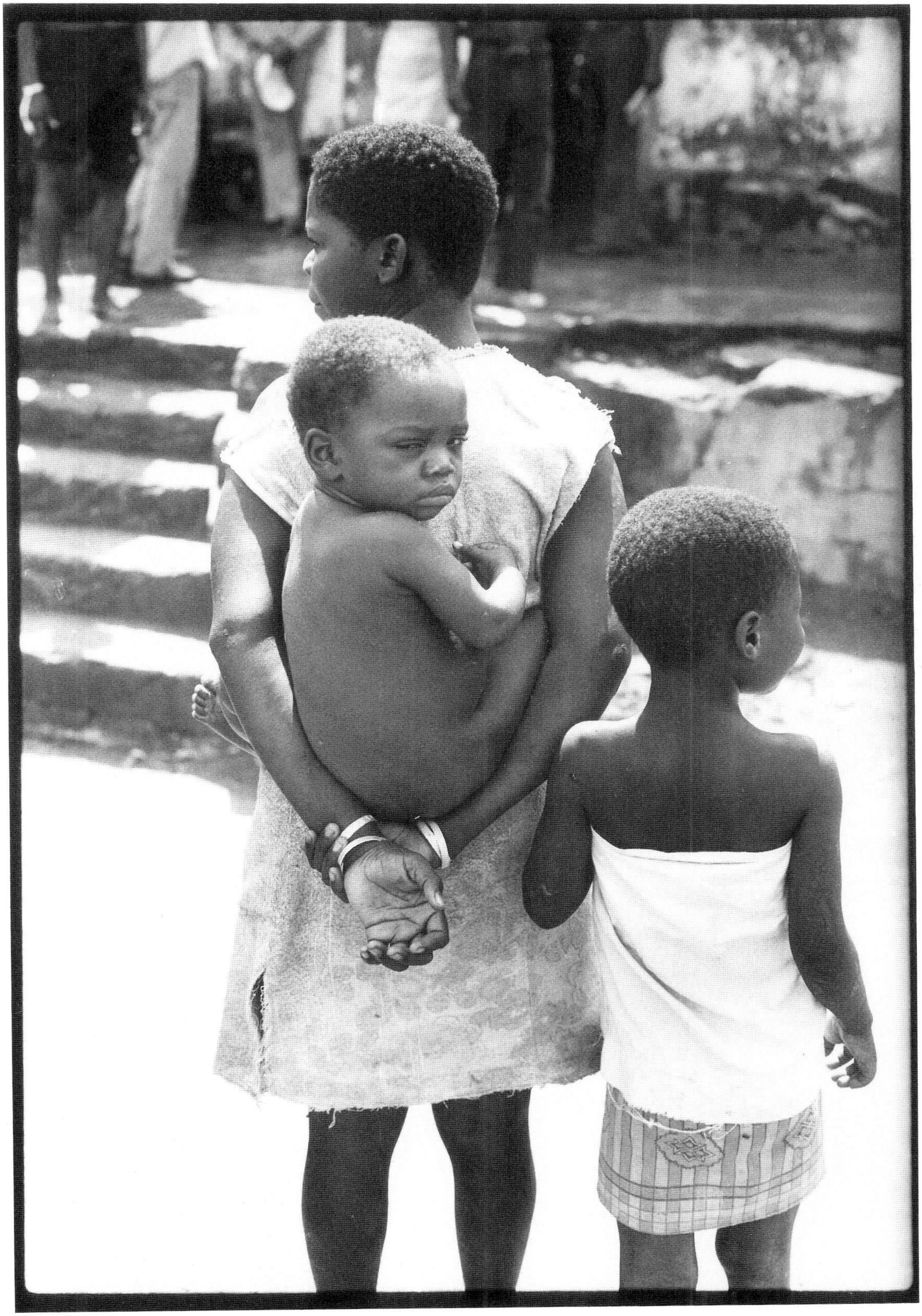

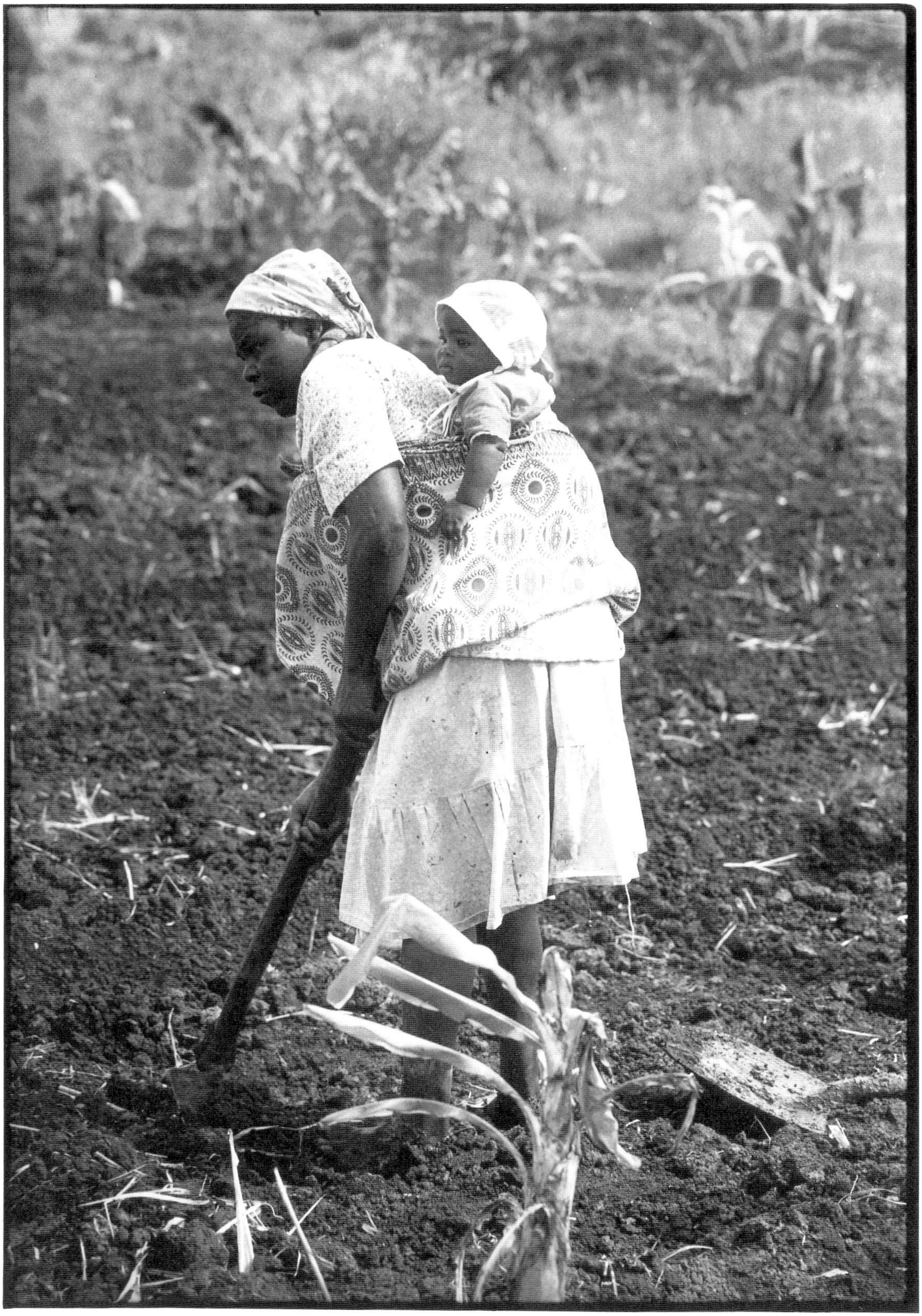

A co-operative 20 km outside Maputo, with five hectares of land. A variety of vegetables is grown here, along with peanuts, beans and manioc. There is also a day nursery (see next picture) for 100 children who attend classes while their parents work in the fields.

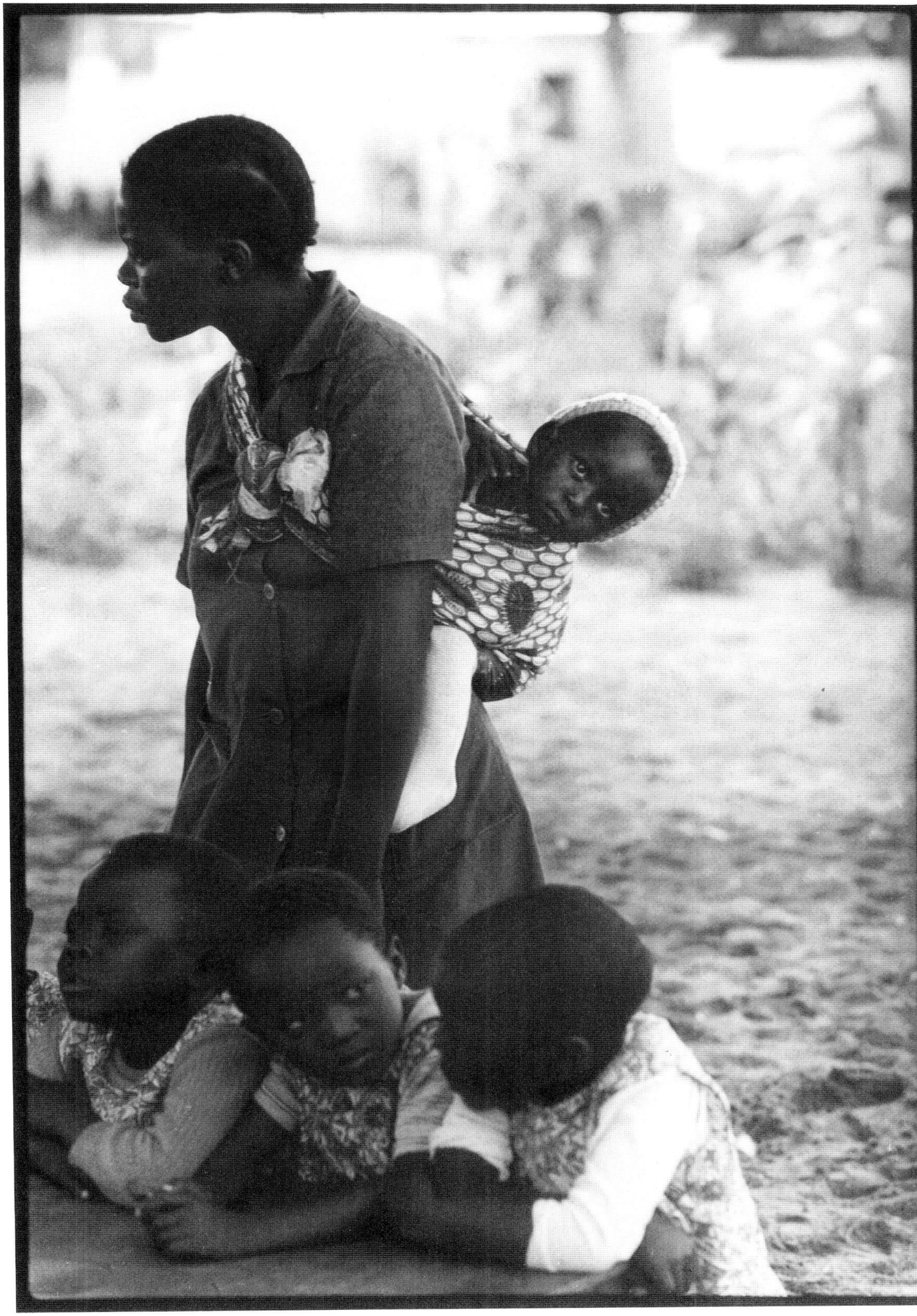

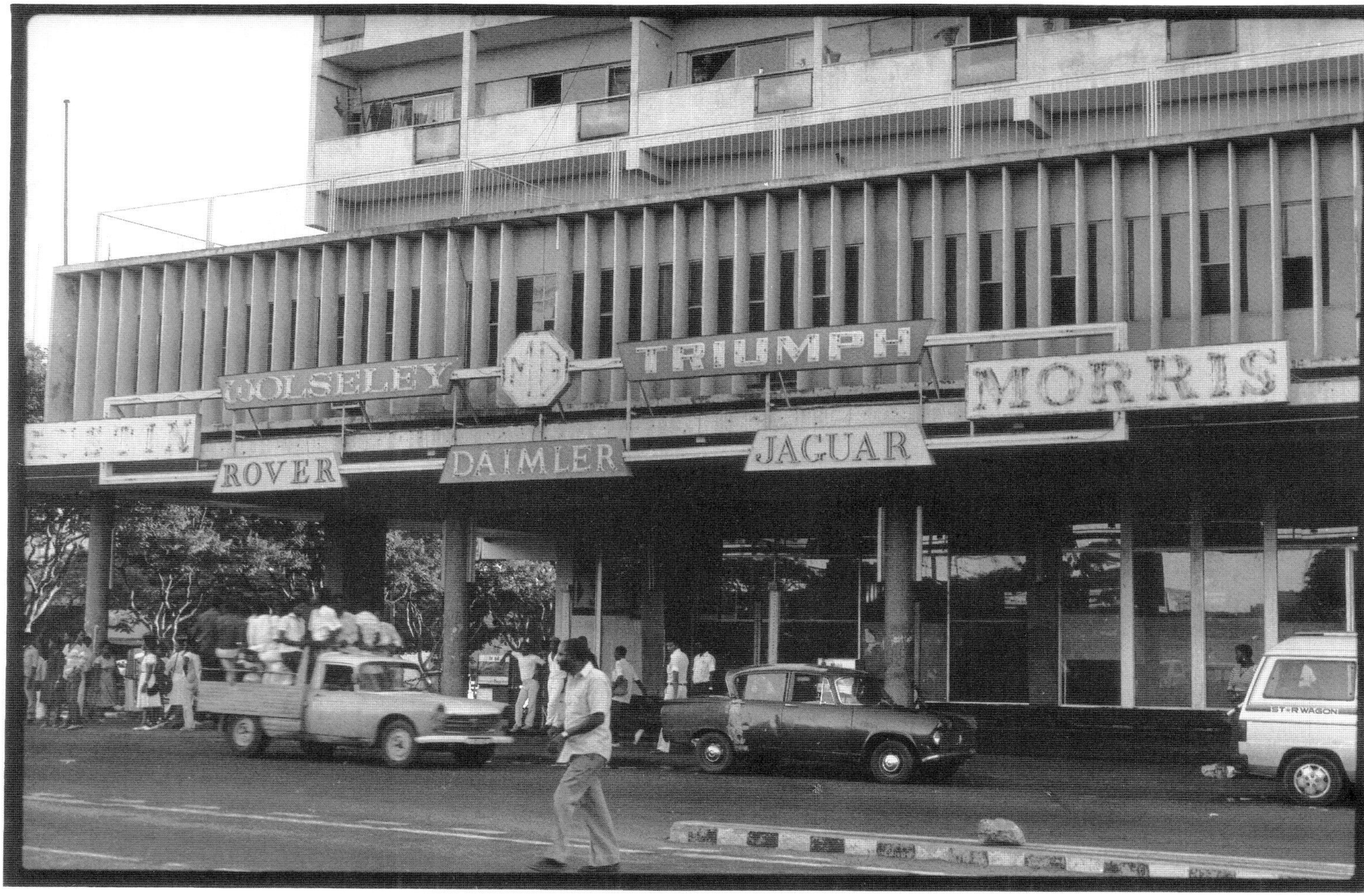

In the Mozambique capital, Maputo, there are signs everywhere of a formerly thriving and prosperous economy — there was extensive foreign investment, including representation from many British firms. This has now all been withdrawn, and only the peeling façades and out-of-date signs remain.

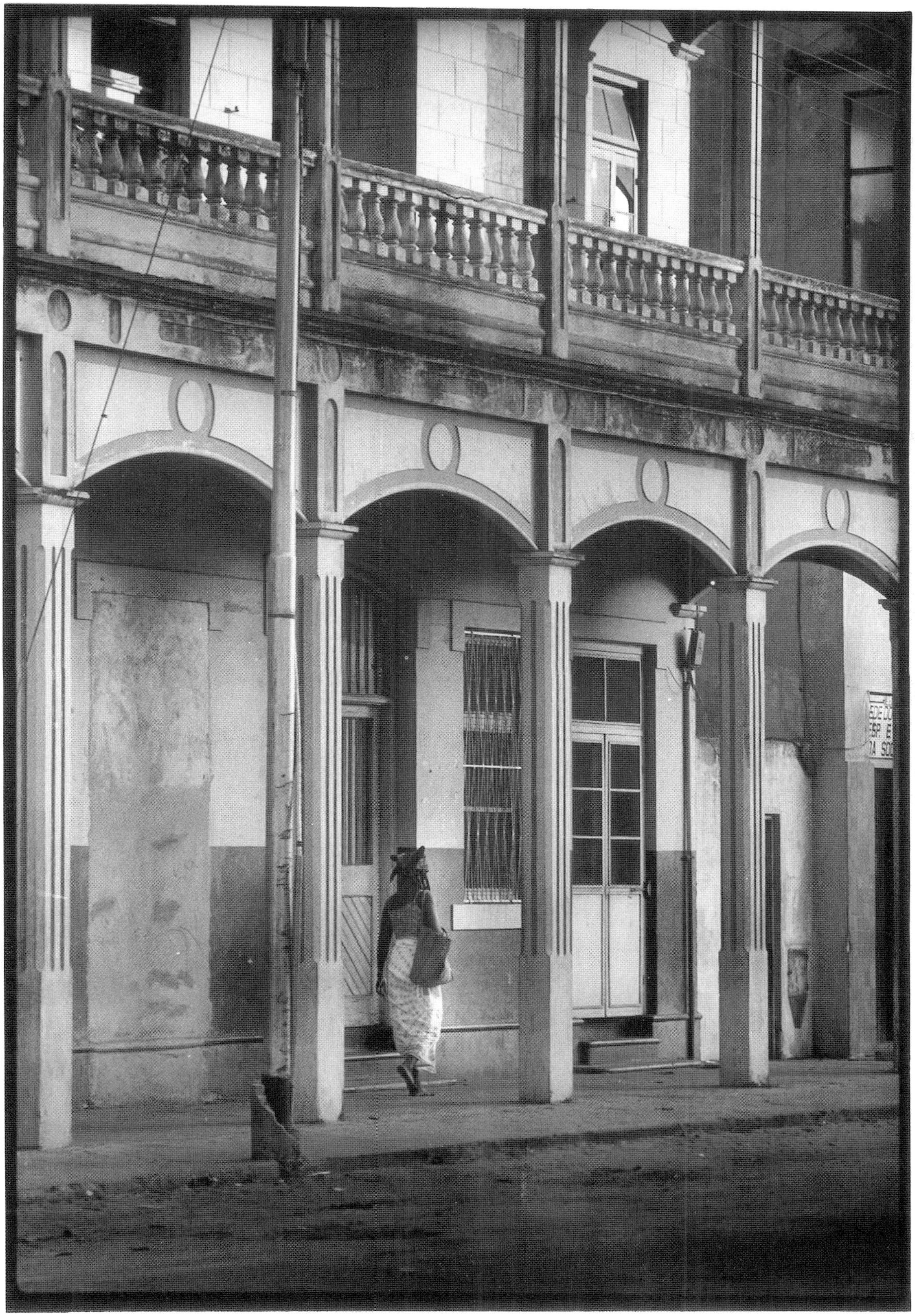

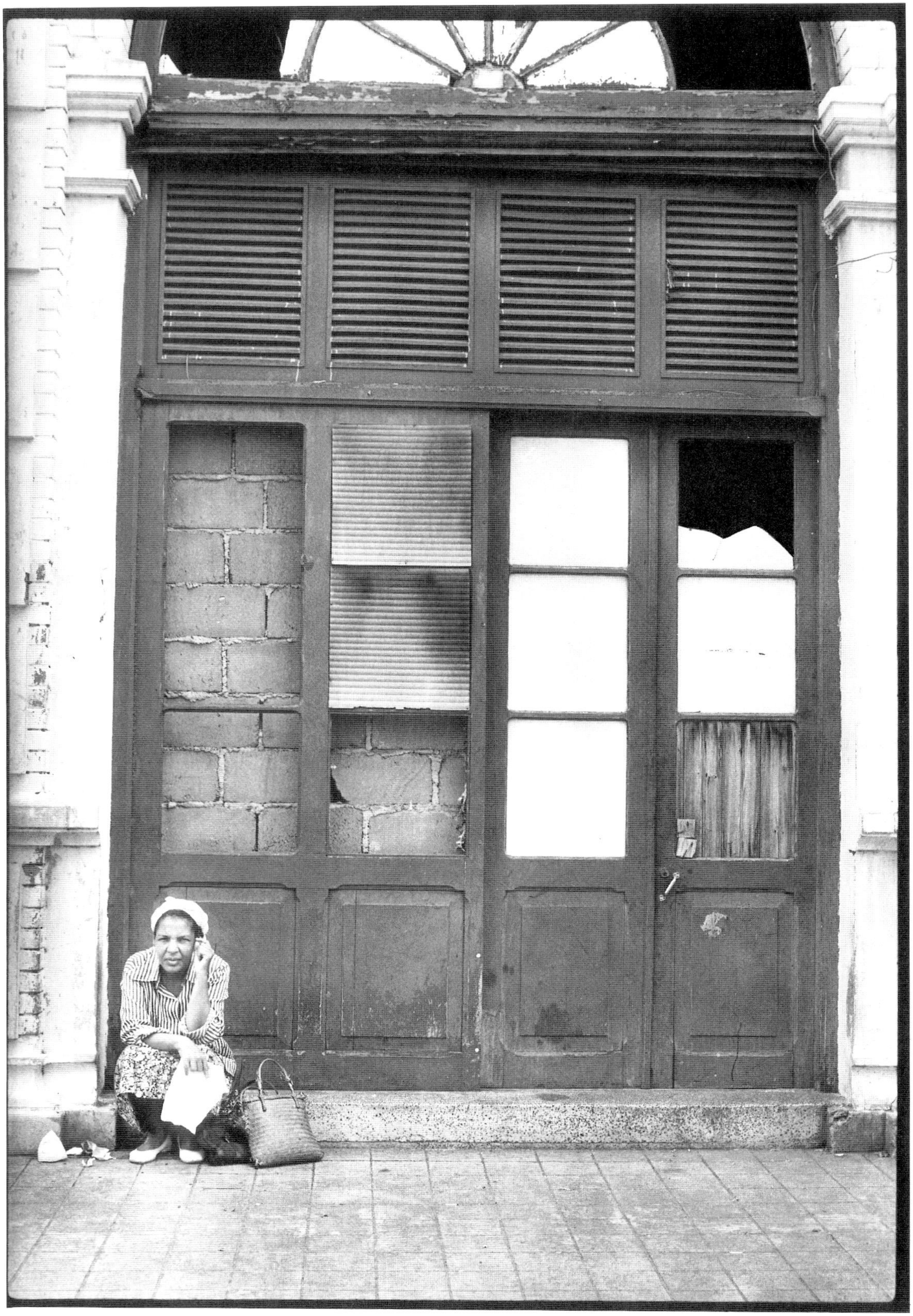

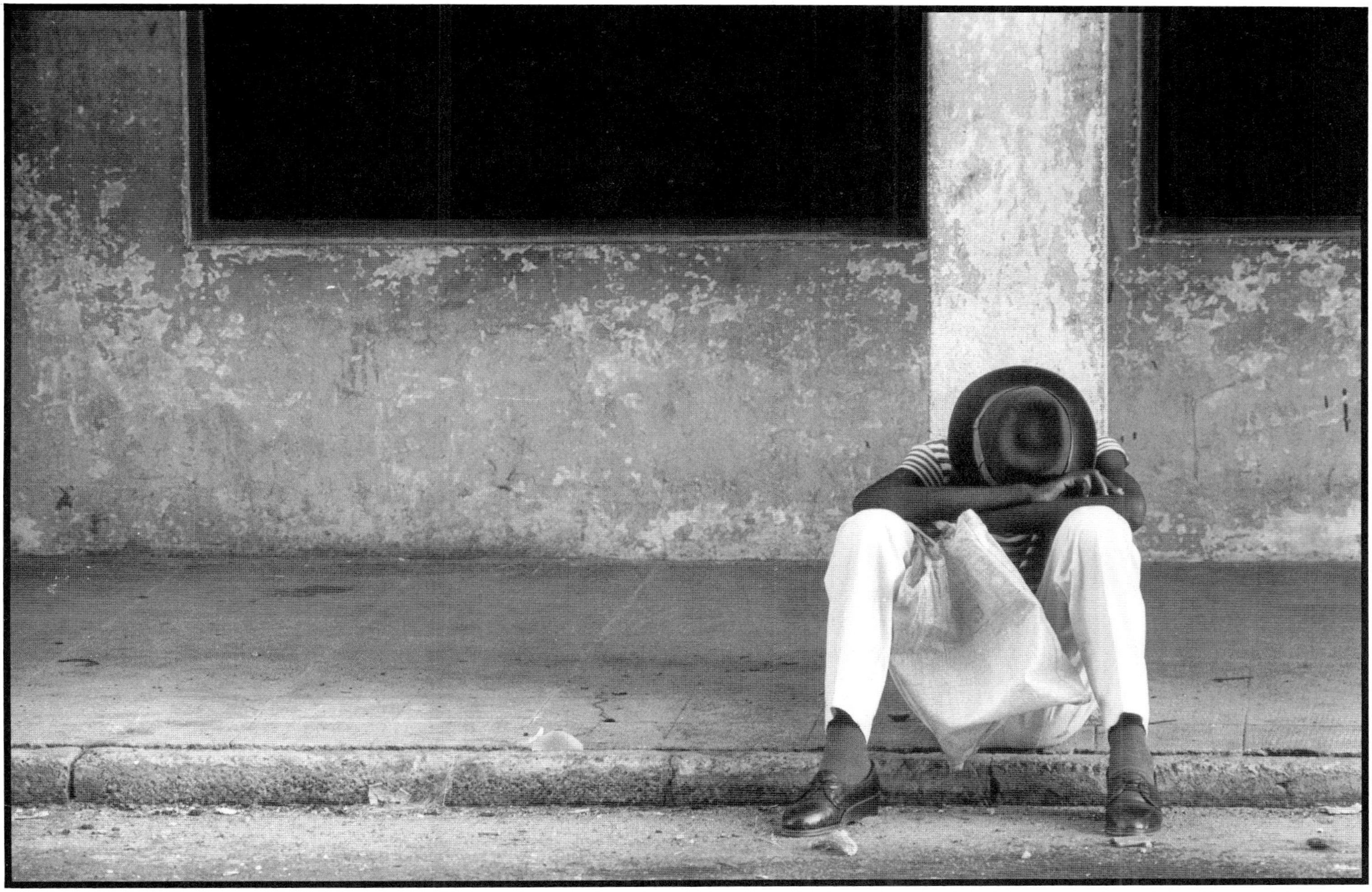

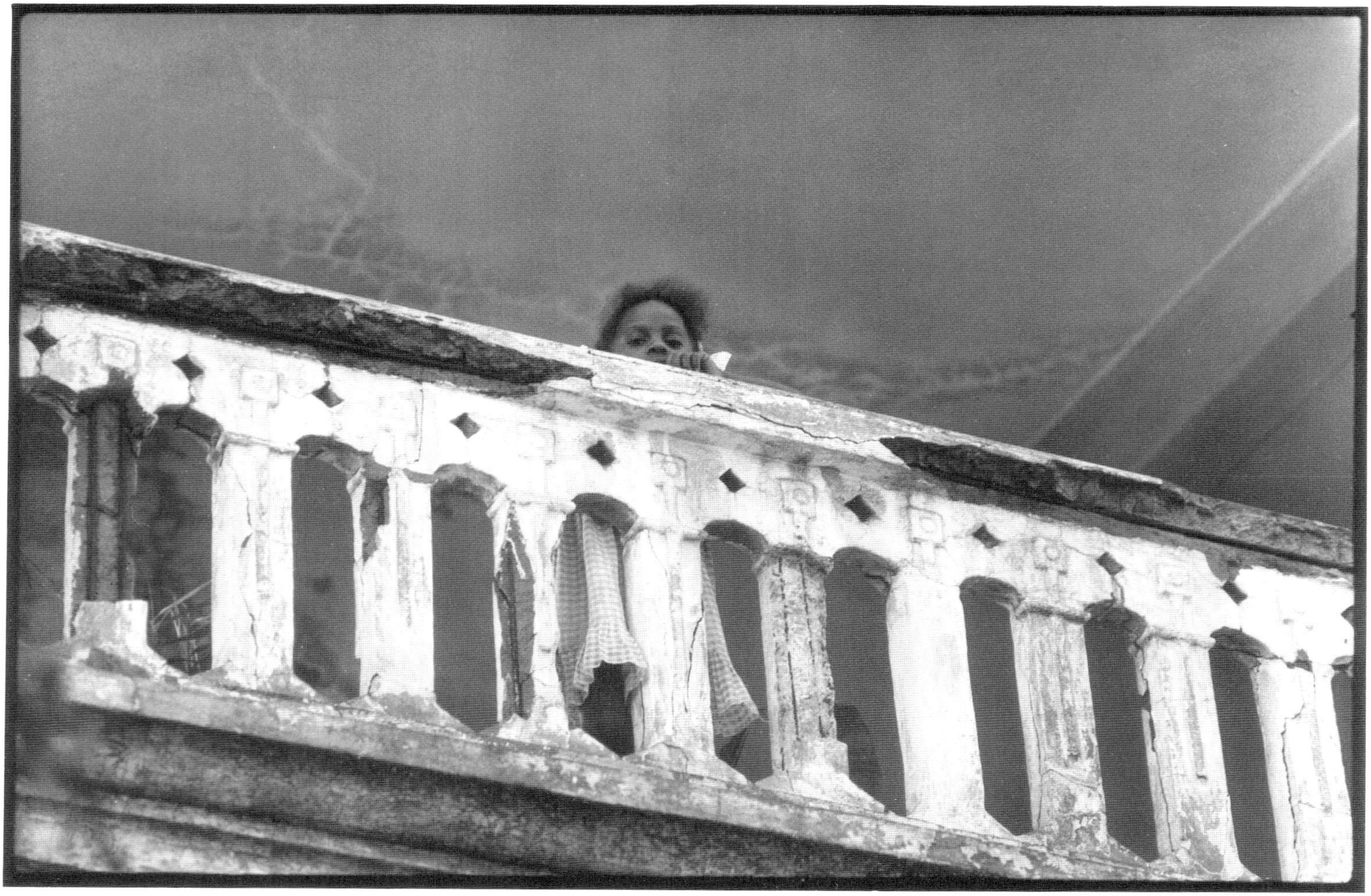

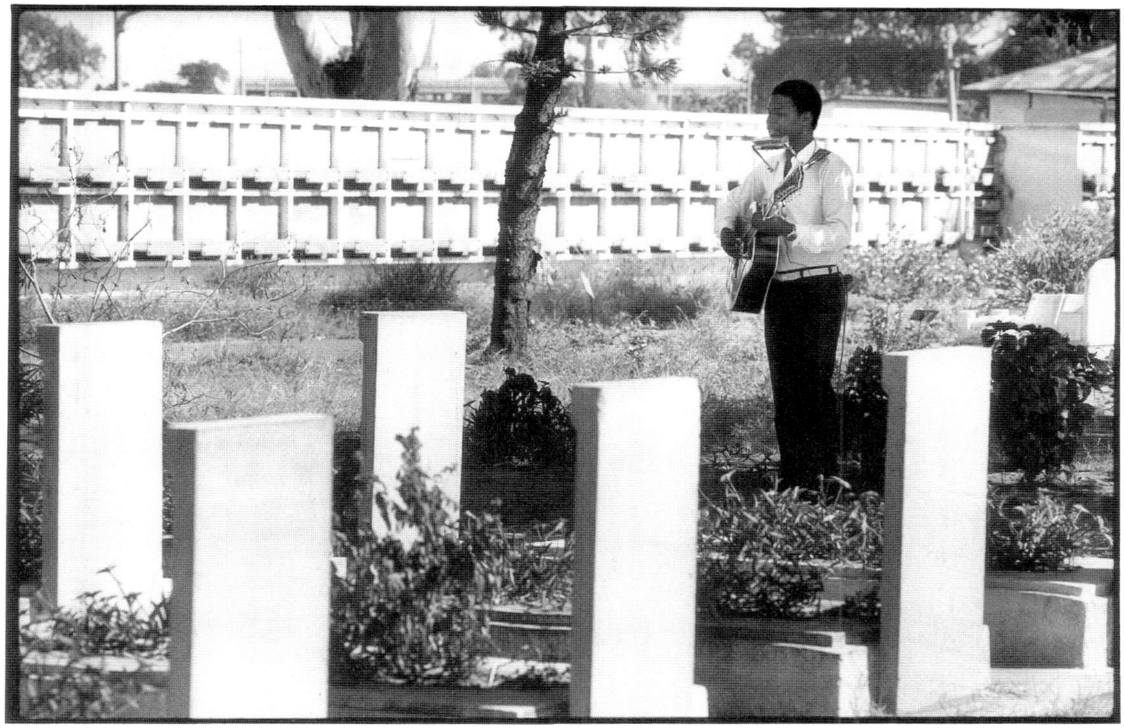

The present South African policy of 'total strategy' was heralded in January 1981 with a bombing raid in the Mozambique capital, Maputo. This was the first official cross-border raid since the invasion of Angola.

Yana is a popular Mozambican singer — he is standing here among the graves of victims of the 1981 raid, singing a song he wrote about the attack, 'Let Them Come'.

'It was at day-break, the 30th of January 1980 a commando of "Boers" arrived
priceless mercenaries who lose a thumb for two rands
who lose an arm for ten
who lose a foot for twenty and when he loses his head, how much do they pay him?
Who is suffering? Who is crying? Who is in mourning?
I am asking, you are asking, he is asking, we are asking, all of you are asking . . . they don't ask!
Who is suffering? Who is crying? Who is in mourning?

These mercenaries entered here, somebody opened the
door for them in exchange for a "Marlboro", in
exchange for a bottle,
in exchange for a pair of "cigars".
In exchange for fantasies, lives are lost, houses
are lost, revolutionaries are lost;
but as we already know they want something from us:
Let them come let them come.

Let them come
Let them come
Let them come, let them come'

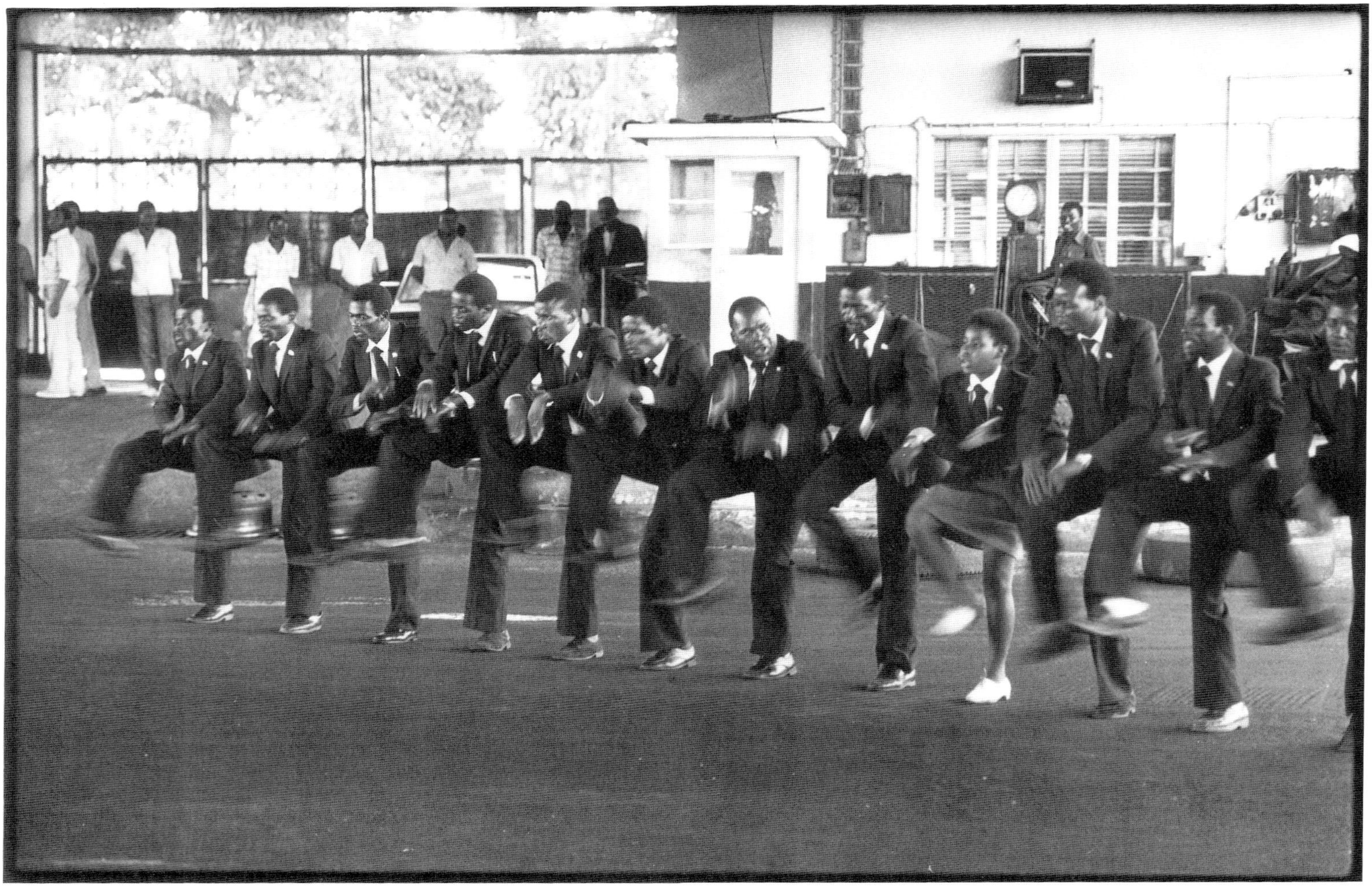

This is a choir of the Mozambique bus drivers union, TPU. Their song and dance routines, called Makwela, are very popular throughout the country, as they tour Mozambique giving performances. Recently the group on tour was attacked by bandits — 16 of them were killed.

Beira Corridor

'I think it's worth defending. If we're serious in our attempt to have an economic saving to this part of the world, we've got to be prepared to pay for it.'

Dennis Norman, Chairman of Beira Corridor Group

'Well, I think really effective counter measures which could be taken are developing the alternative routes to the sea using Mozambique, like the Beira corridor, and not only concentrating on the Beira corridor because that also can be a mistake if we did that, but also to try and rehabilitate the Chicualcuala line. I understand the British have put some money towards the Chicualcuala line. I think there's going to be some dramatic changes and I think the main thing is to concentrate on developing alternative routes and alternative markets, seeking markets where we can export our goods and also seeking sources where we can import the raw materials that we need in this country, and I think that is being done now.'

Nathan Shamuyarira, Minister of Information, Zimbabwe

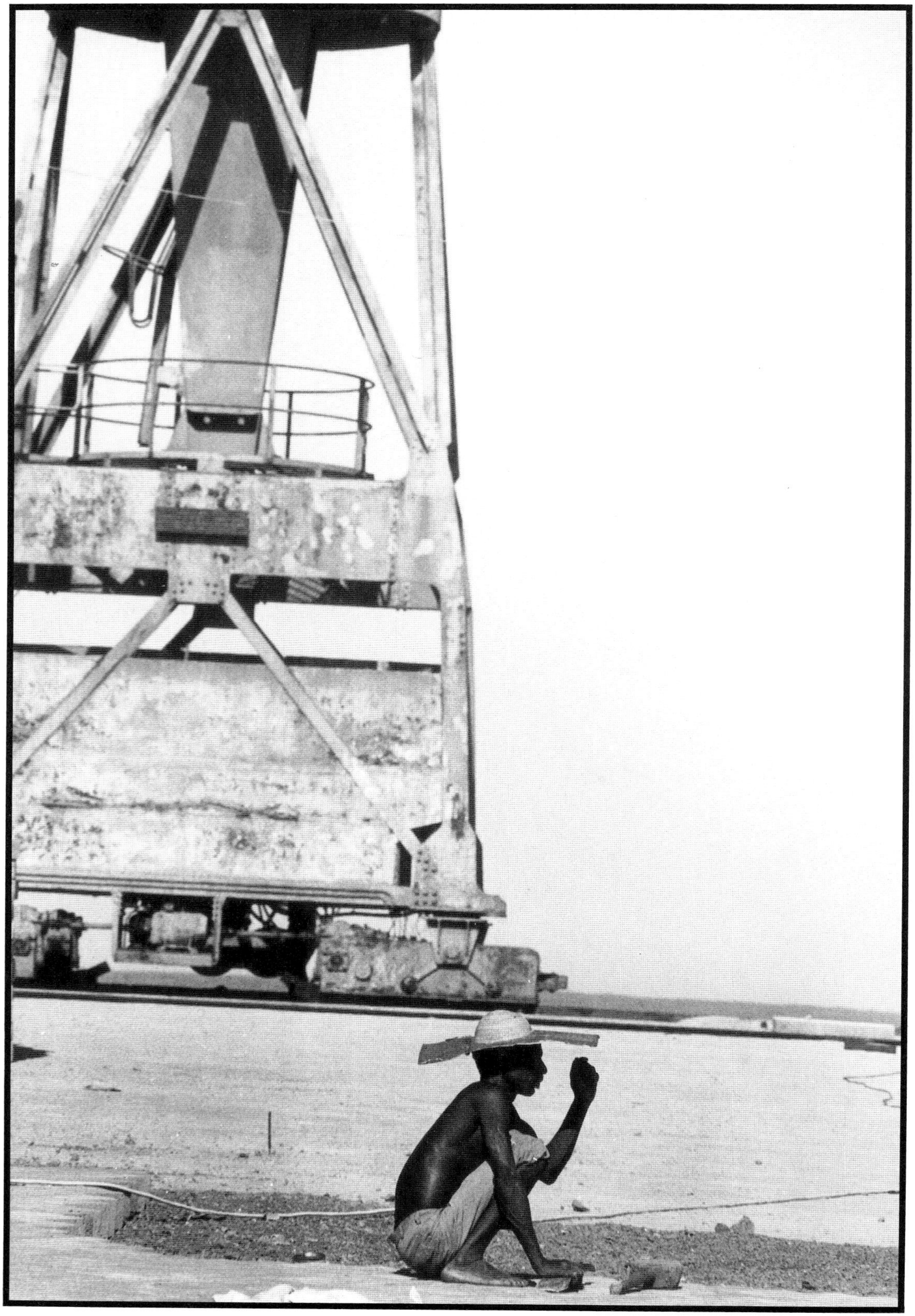

With the aid of EEC and international finance, the Southern African Development Co-ordination Conference (SADCC) is attempting to rehabilitate Beira port. SADCC is the grouping of Frontline States seeking to reduce economic dependence on South Africa.

Part of South Africa's long-term strategy has been to remain the dominant economic and political power in Southern Africa. SADCC is one way in which the Frontline States can resist.

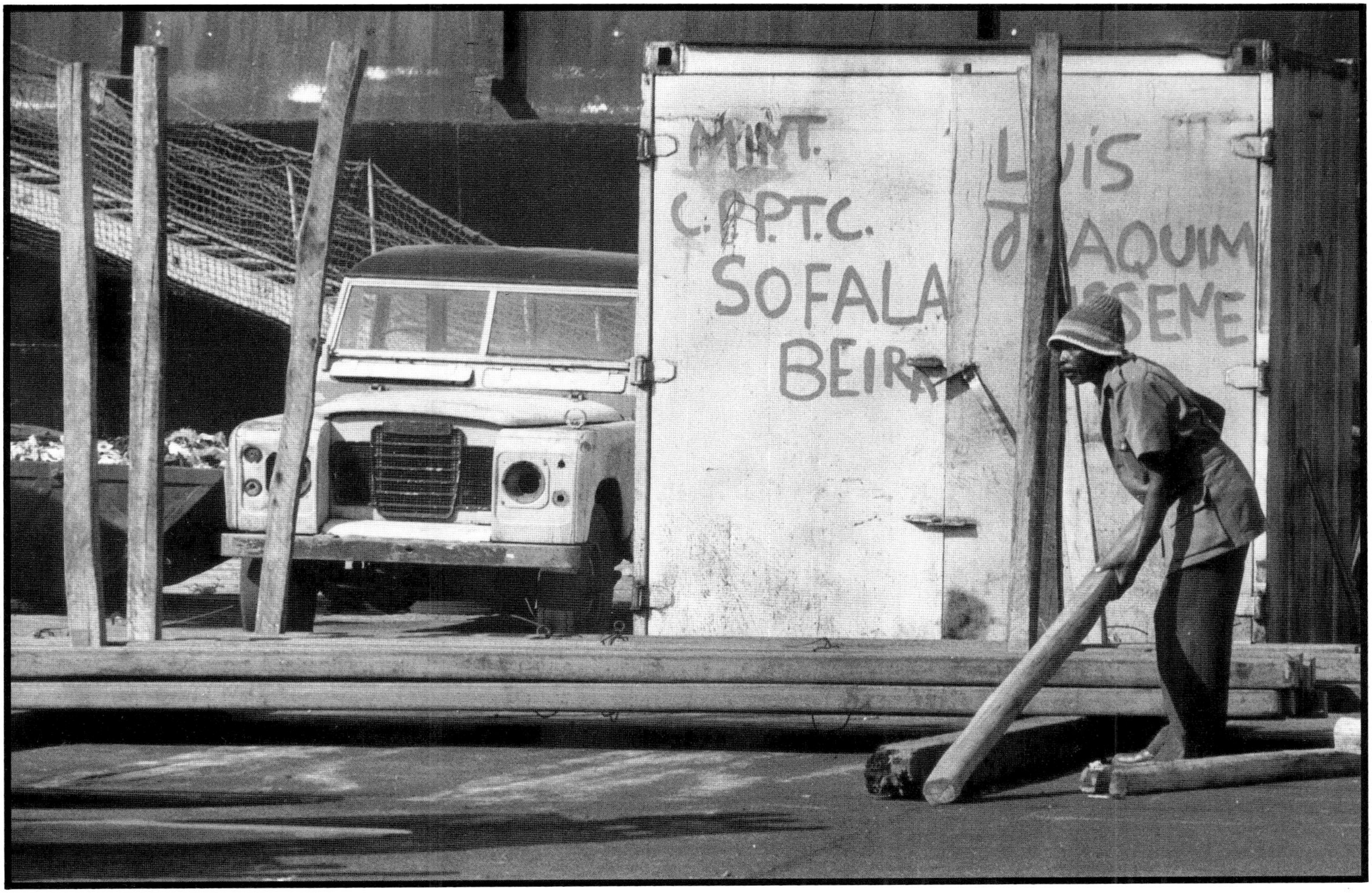
C.P.T.C.
SOFALA
BEIR

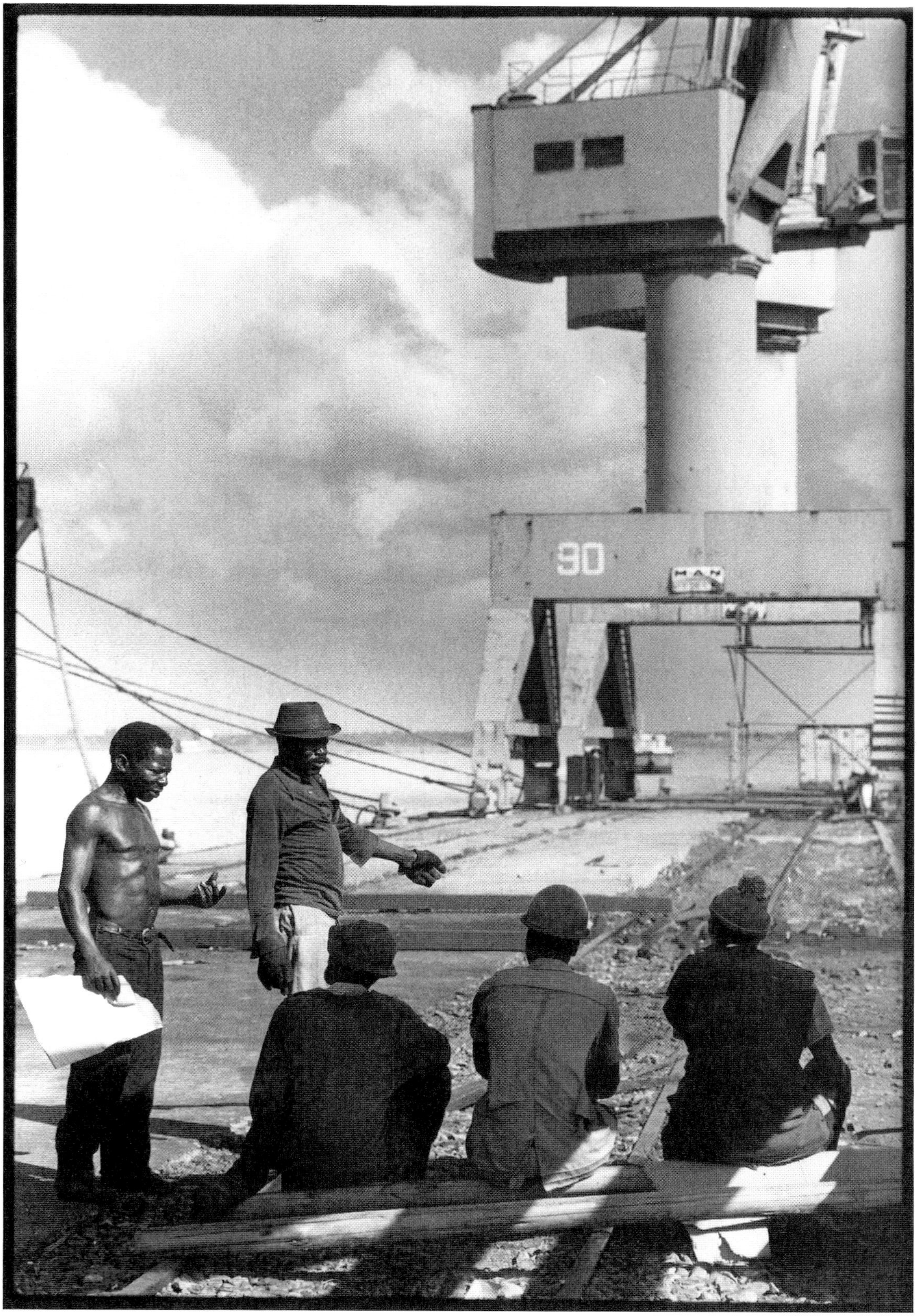
90
MAN

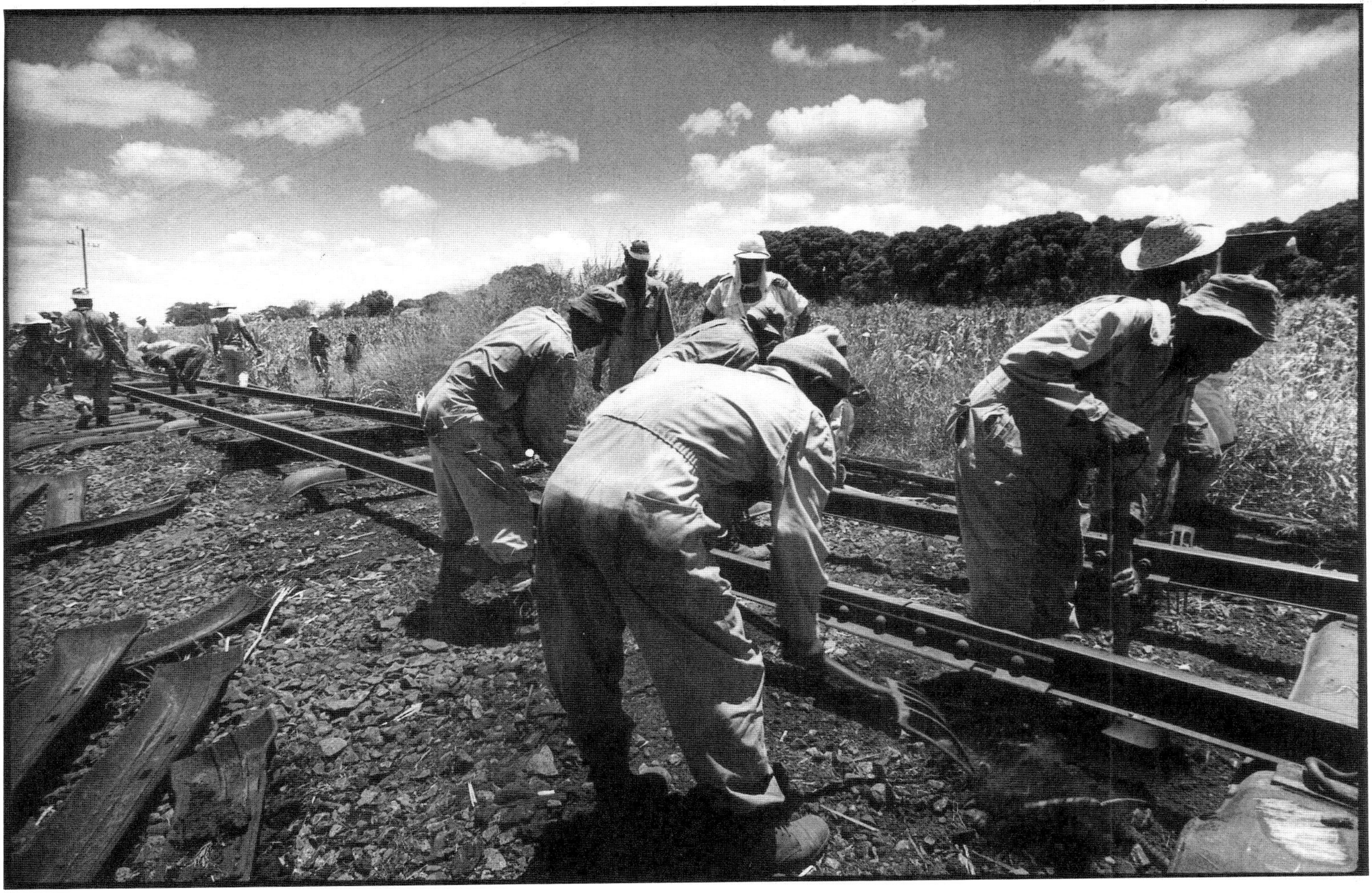

‘We are helping the Mozambicans because they cannot afford to maintain the railways here. These bandits which are being sent by South Africa want to destroy this railway, but due to the fact that we have the army protecting us along the line, they won’t be able to destroy the line. We want our country to develop, we want to be able to export the minerals from our country to France, Italy and West Germany.’

Gang Foreman

‘We are working here with Zimbabwe Railways for the rehabilitation of the Beira corridor line, in conjunction with Mozambican personnel. The Zimbabwe security forces are manning the length of the line, along with Frelimo men. But it is a difficult situation, very difficult.’

Joe Meyers, Zimbabwe National Railways

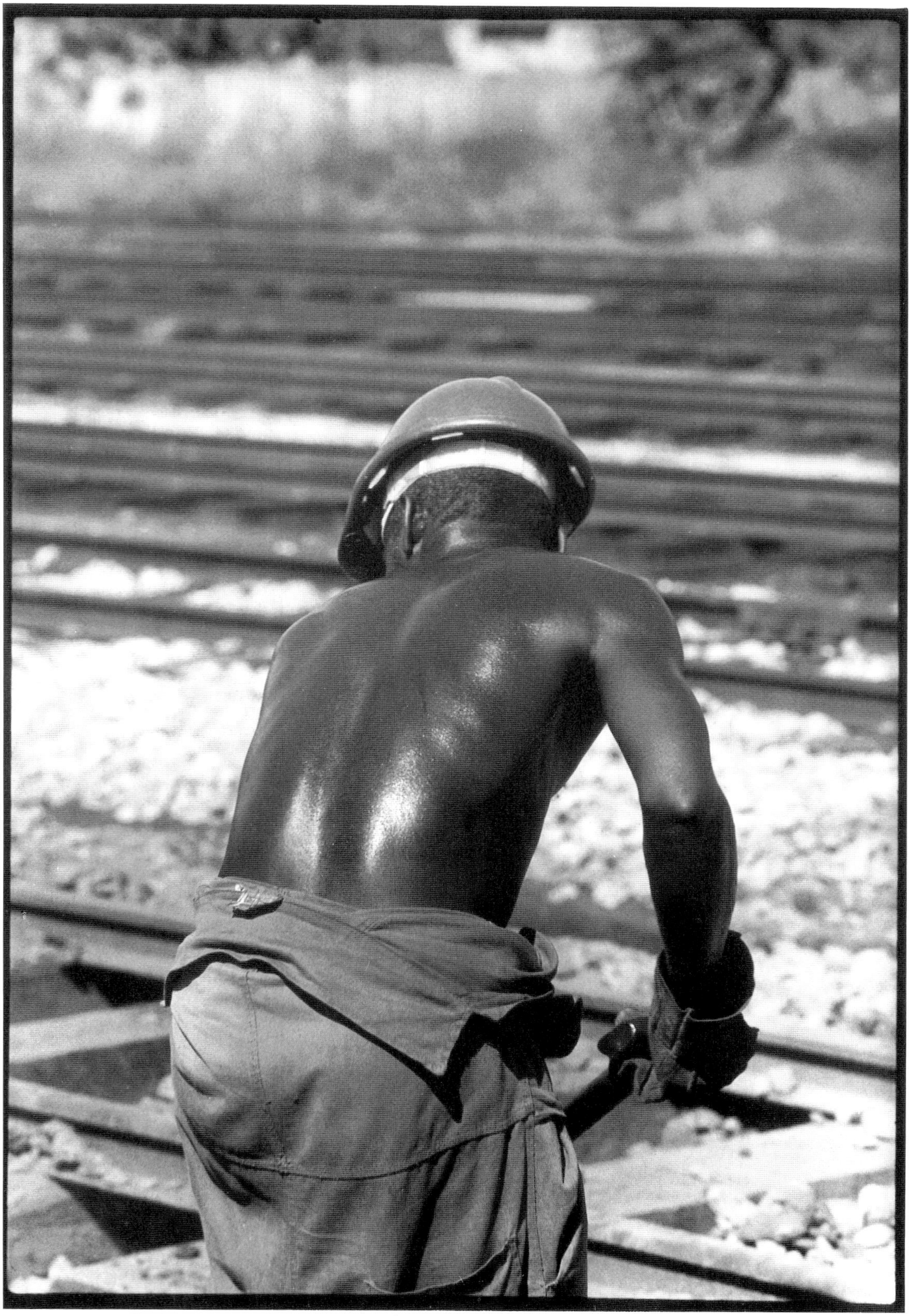

'I have been guarding this part of the Beira line at Almada for three years, a little bit more. I haven't seen my family for two years, I don't know how they are, what's happened to them. I have a boy, I don't know anything of my family for two years. It is very hard to get food here, I haven't had anything to eat for three days. The bandits destroy the line therefore we are here at this position as armed forces.'

Frelimo soldier, Almada, Beira line

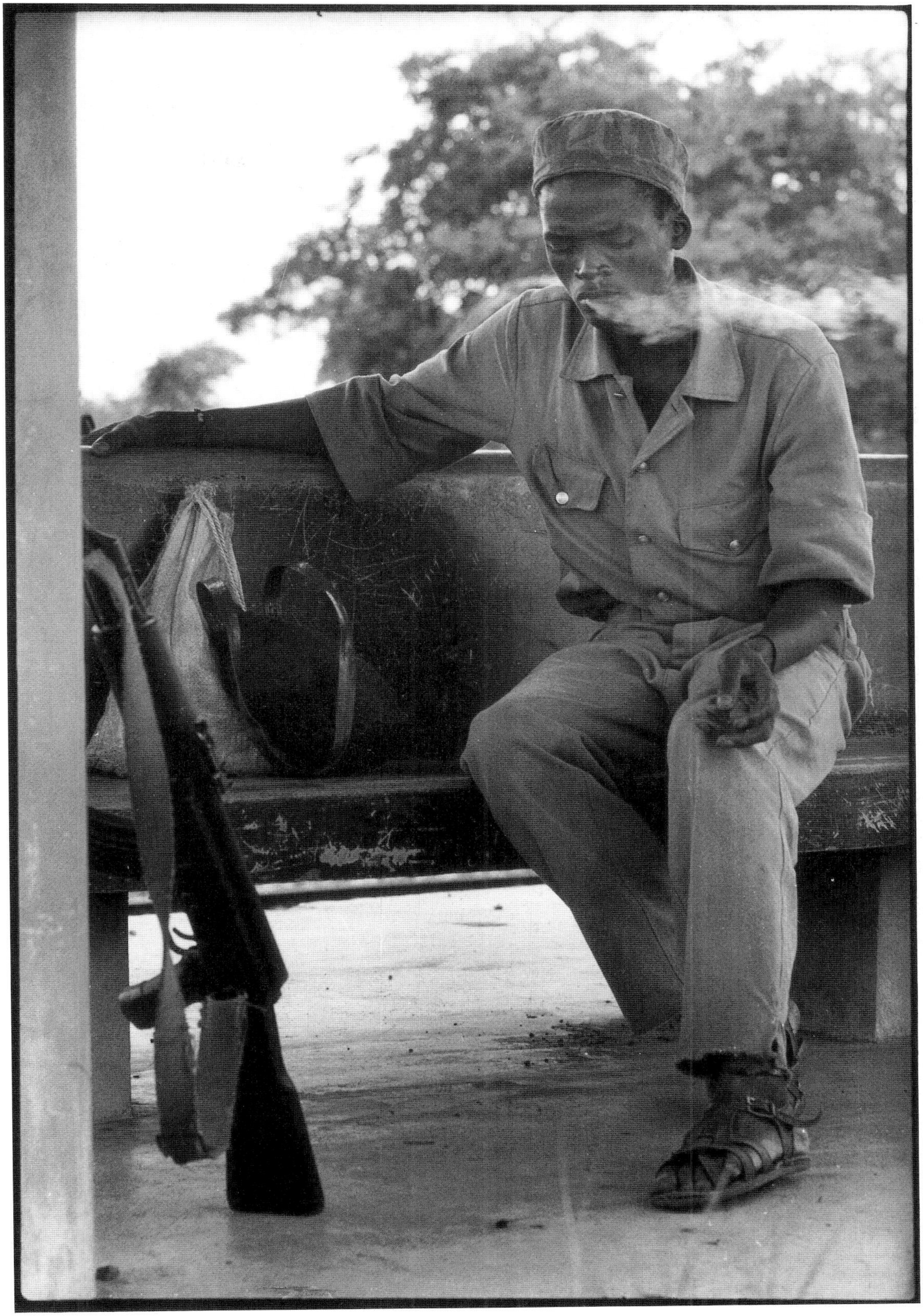

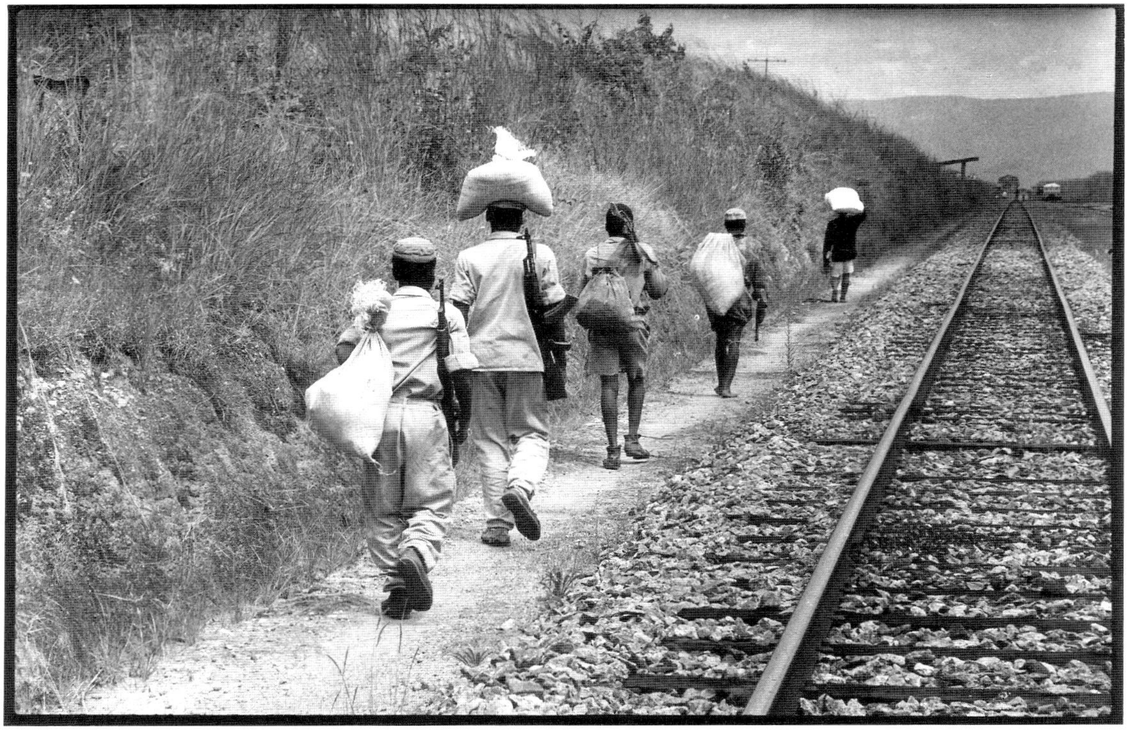

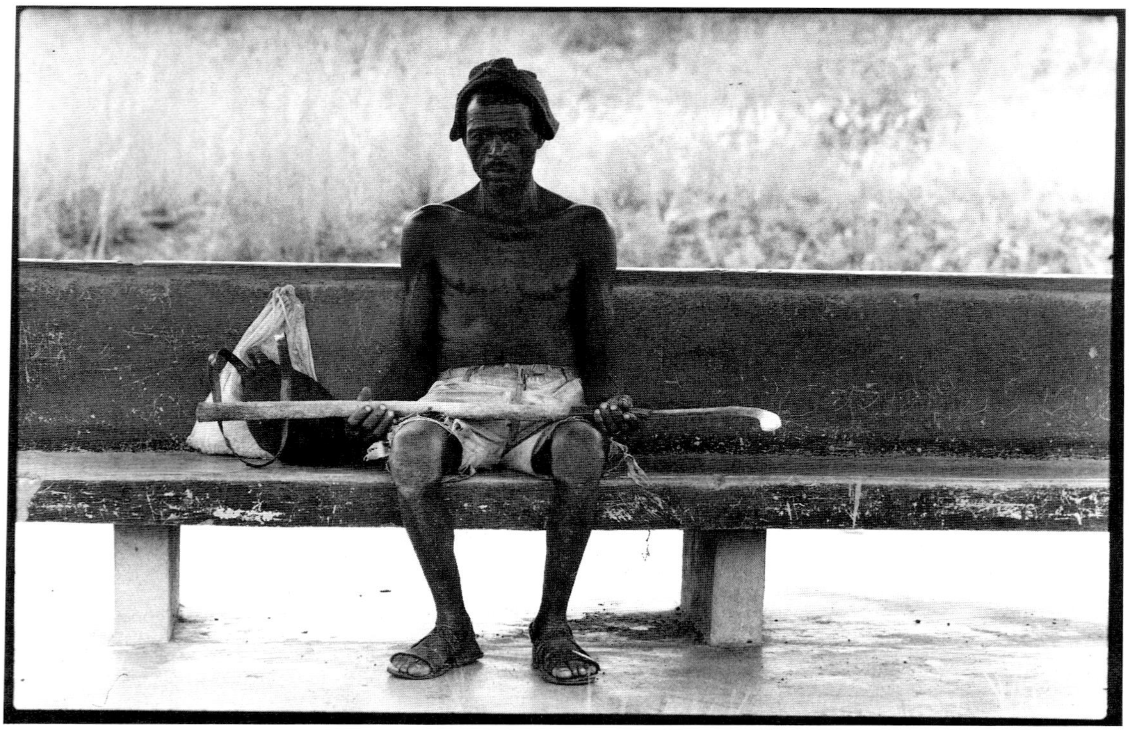

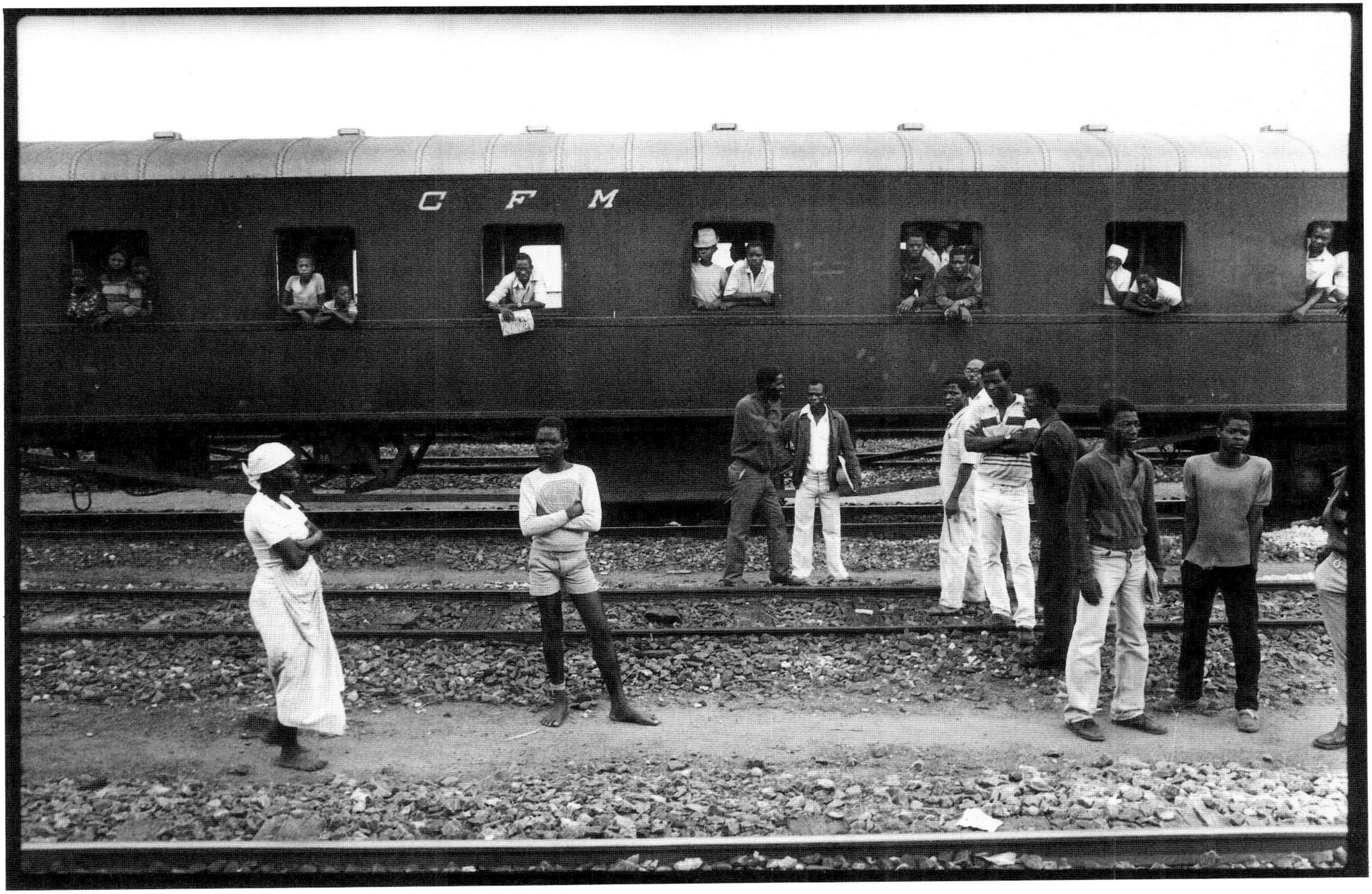

The Beira railway line is a favourite target of frequent MNR attack. Despite the long-term presence of Frelimo guards, it is impossible successfully to guard its entire length. The attacks do not destroy the line — they are small explosions which temporarily disable it, but the effect is immense in a country where communication and travel are always difficult. When the track is blown up, the trains stop and passengers have no option but to wait.

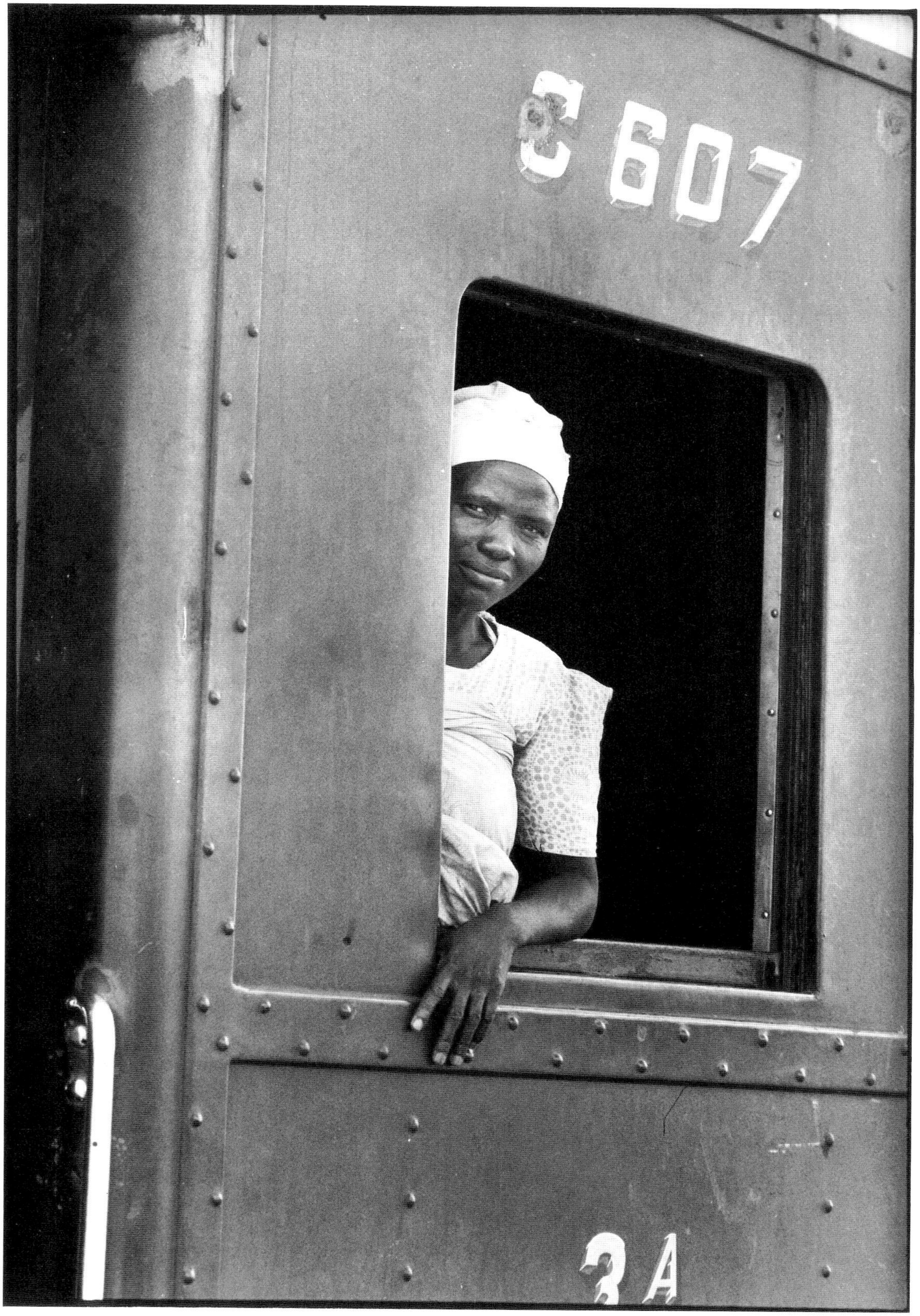
607
3A

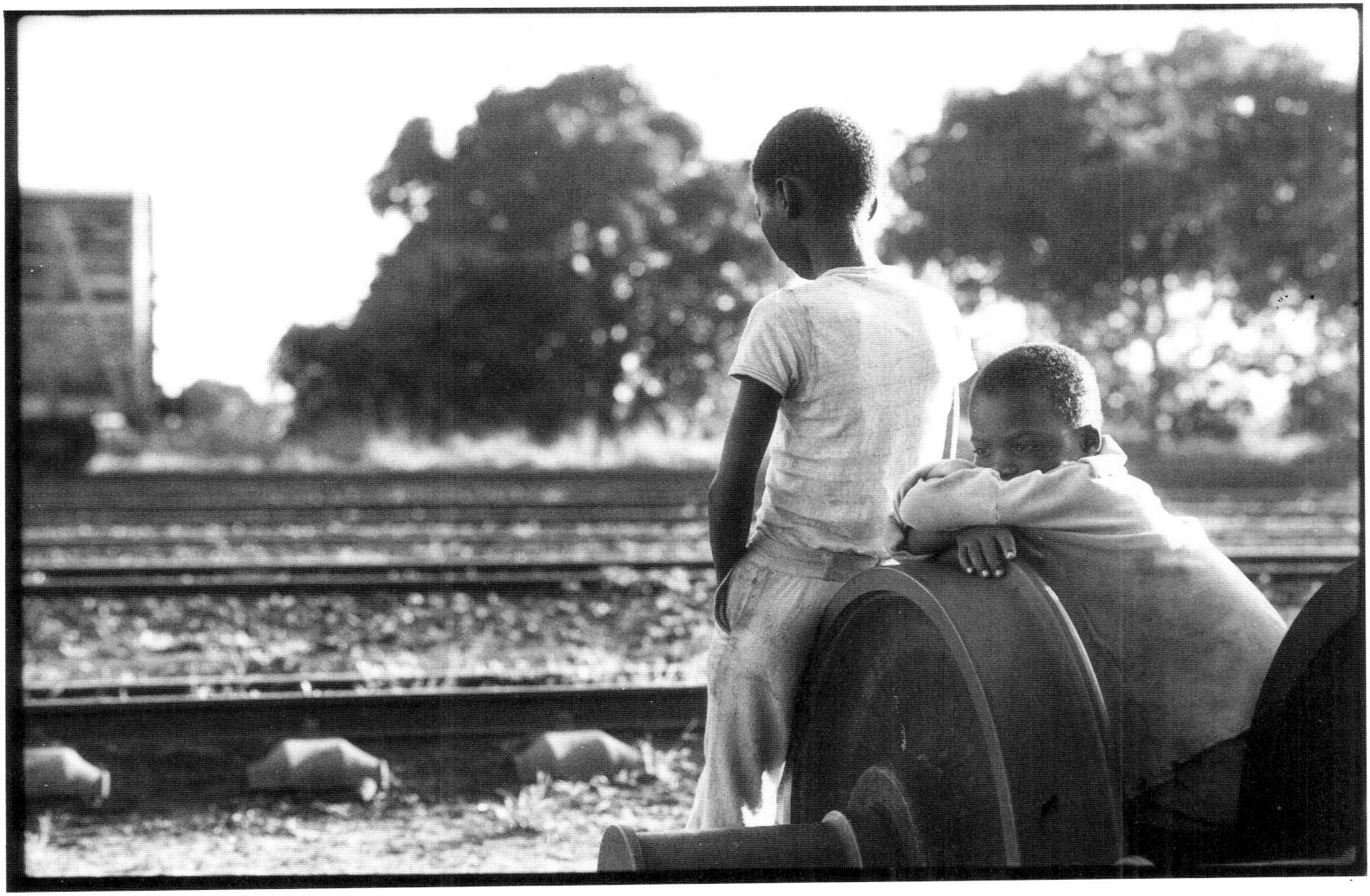

Zimbabwe

'If the situation was different we would have used our money for capital development for the better living of our people, but we are forced by circumstances now to go for militarisation.'

Emerson Munangagwe, Minister of State, Zimbabwe

Zimbabwe and its neighbour Zambia are both landlocked countries. Their exports are almost totally dependent upon access to the coast. The shortest route for Zambia's copper belt is the Benguela railway line, west through Angola; for Zimbabwe, routes east through Mozambique — the Chicualcuala railway link to Maputo and the rail, road and pipeline link to Beira. Due to sabotage of these routes, the only alternatives available in recent years are South African ports and railways at the additional cost of over 300 million dollars per year. Of all Zambia's and Zimbabwe's links to the outside world, South Africa has allowed only one to remain open, Beit Bridge. This is the bottleneck through which all bulk traffic must pass. It represents a powerful economic weapon, and, as South Africa has already demonstrated, they can close the line at will — as they did for a period in 1982, cutting virtually all trade to and from Zimbabwe. The saving to the Zimbabwe steel industry, which is forced to ship 95 per cent of its production via South Africa, would be enormous if it could ship directly through Mozambique.

But the MNR continue to sabotage the Beira line. Zimbabwe and Mozambican railways are working together to rehabilitate the Beira corridor. With the aid of EEC and international finance, SADCC is seeking to reduce dependence on South Africa by rehabilitating Beira Port. Part of South Africa's long-term strategy has been to remain the dominant economic and political power in southern Africa.

'Well, we had hoped that with independence and the end of the war, the security problem would cease. Unfortunately that wasn't the case, immediately after the war we had a great deal of banditry which operated not only in the rural areas but also in the towns. In recent years, the banditry in the towns has ceased. It has continued in the rural areas on an on-and-off basis. We've had farmers attacked in their homesteads, murdered, ambushes on roads, ambushes at set points like cattle dips, buildings burnt and destroyed and this did cause a great loss of confidence and a considerable number of farmers left the land, either permanently or to try and operate from town.

I don't know who the people attacking the white farmers are, and there's no way we can find out. They certainly are established locally, they are able to operate locally, but who controls them, we don't know and we have no way of finding out. The attacks culminated about two years ago after a series of murders in the Matabeleland area, we had to withdraw all the farmers from there. This obviously was very detrimental and after discussions with the government we were able to establish farm militia, i.e. we were able to give farmers guards on their farms and since then morale has improved considerably and we are getting a return of people to the land.'

E.W. Kirby, Chmn Comm. Farmers Union, Matabeleland, Zimbabwe

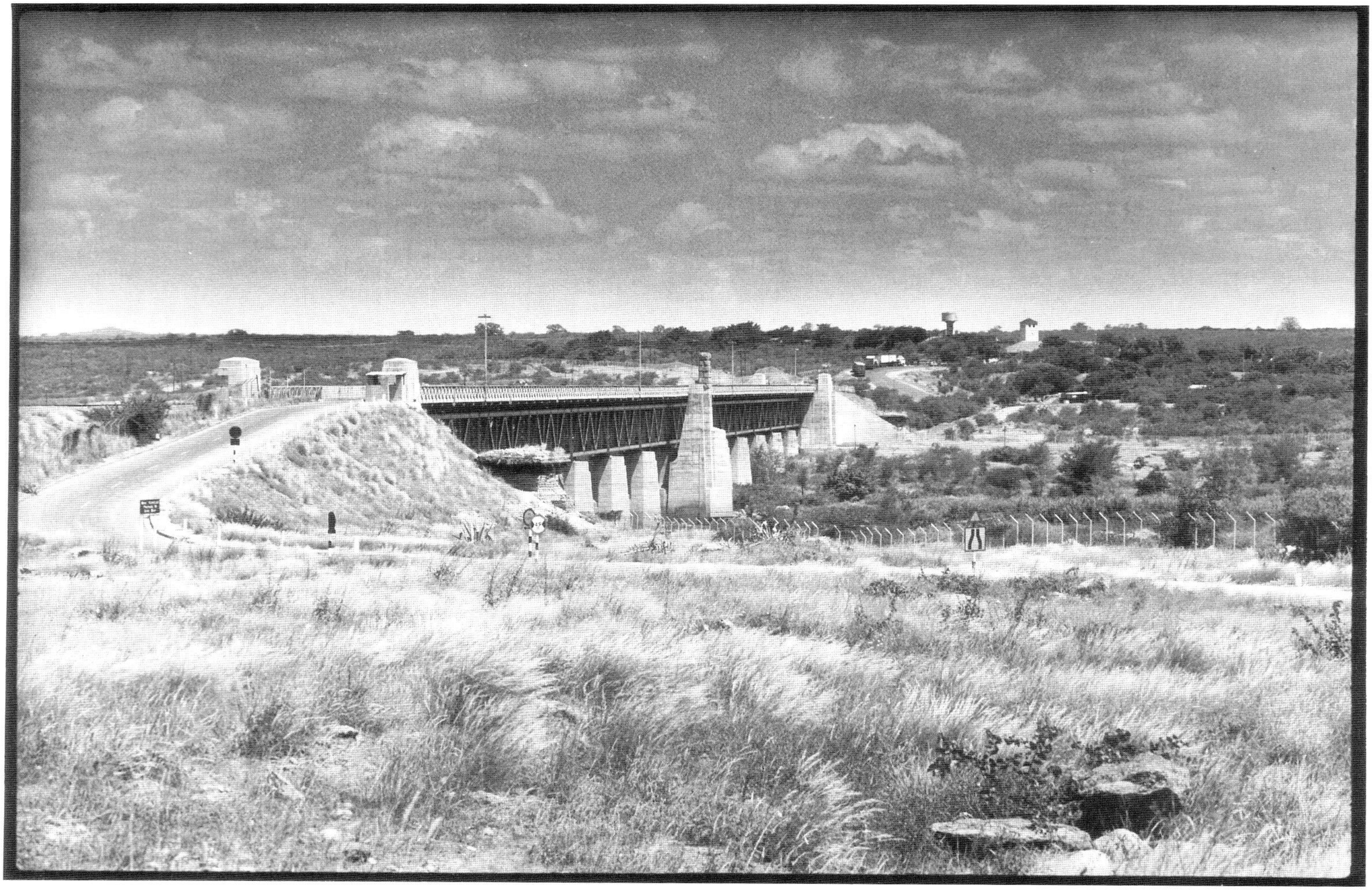

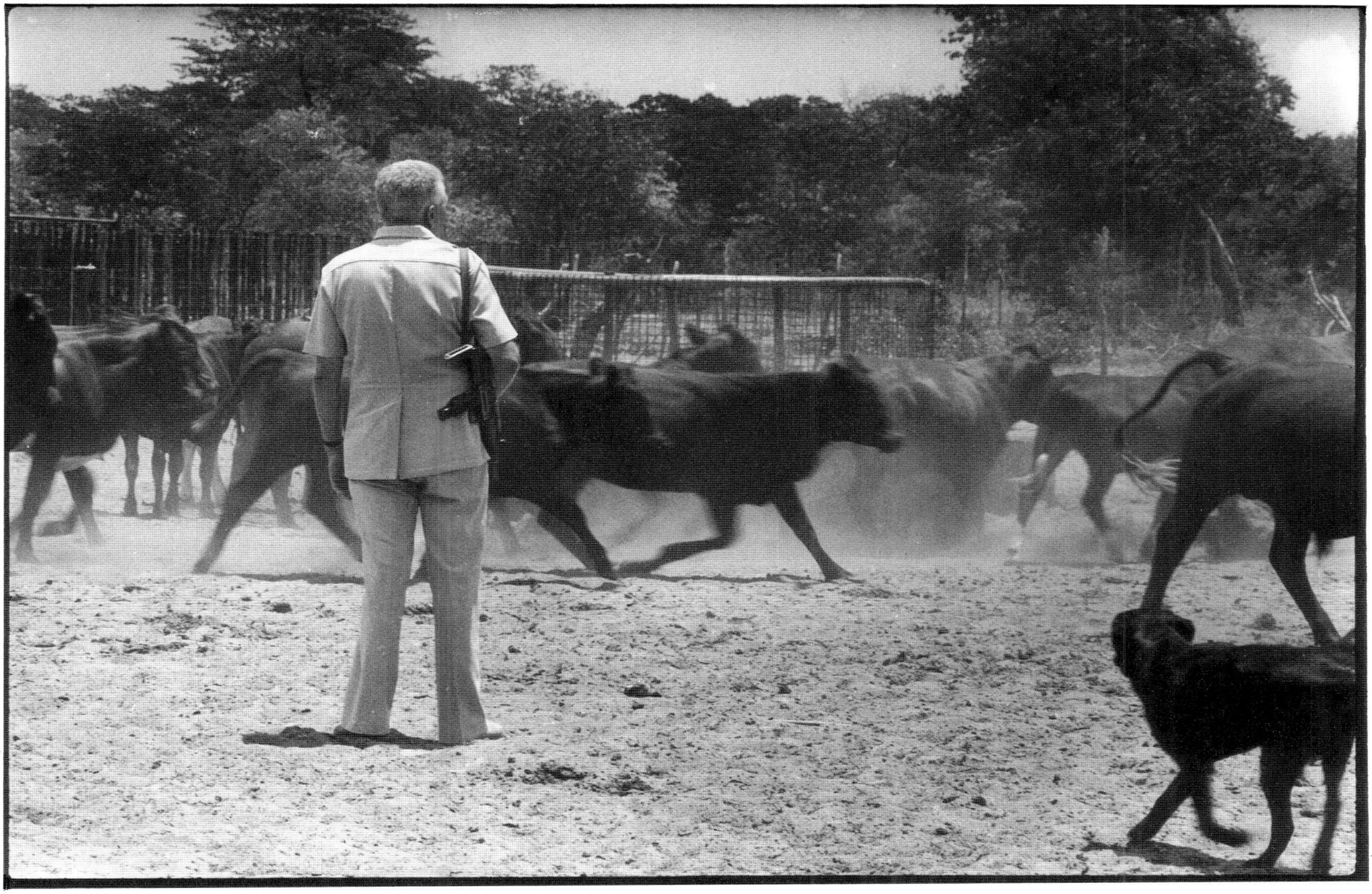

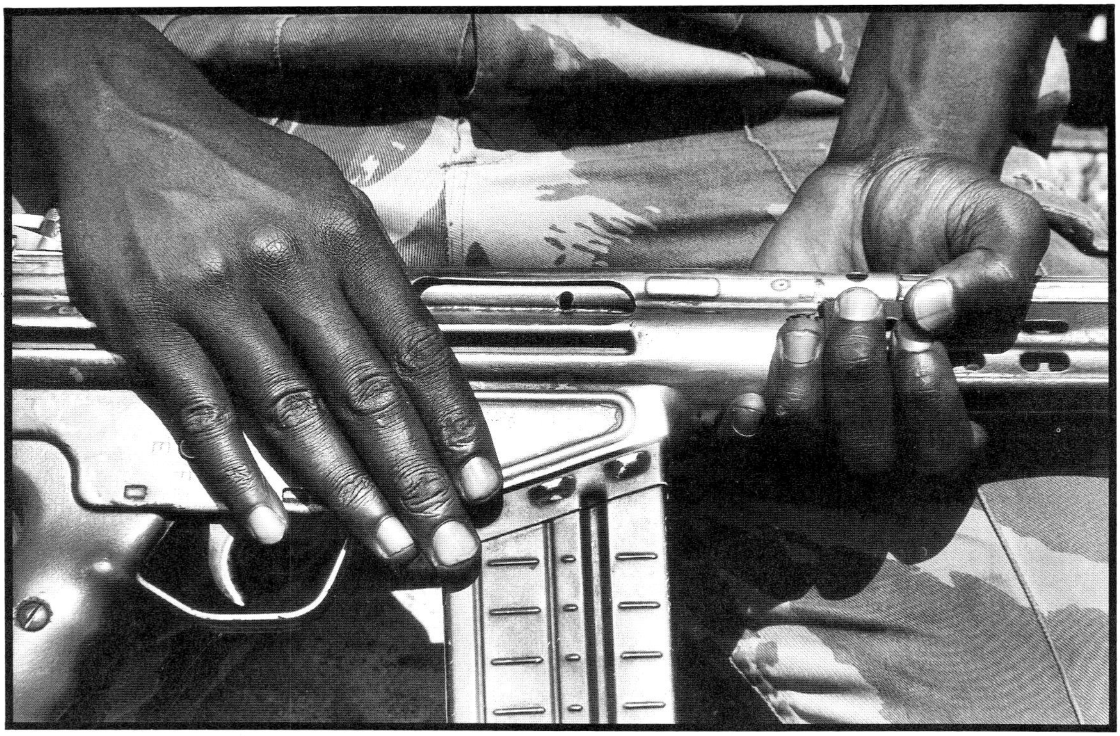

The large farms in Matabeleland are heavily protected. E.W. Kirby, the Chairman of the Commercial Farmers Union for the region, inspects his cattle with a machine gun over his shoulder (see preceding picture). His farm is also protected by armed guards.

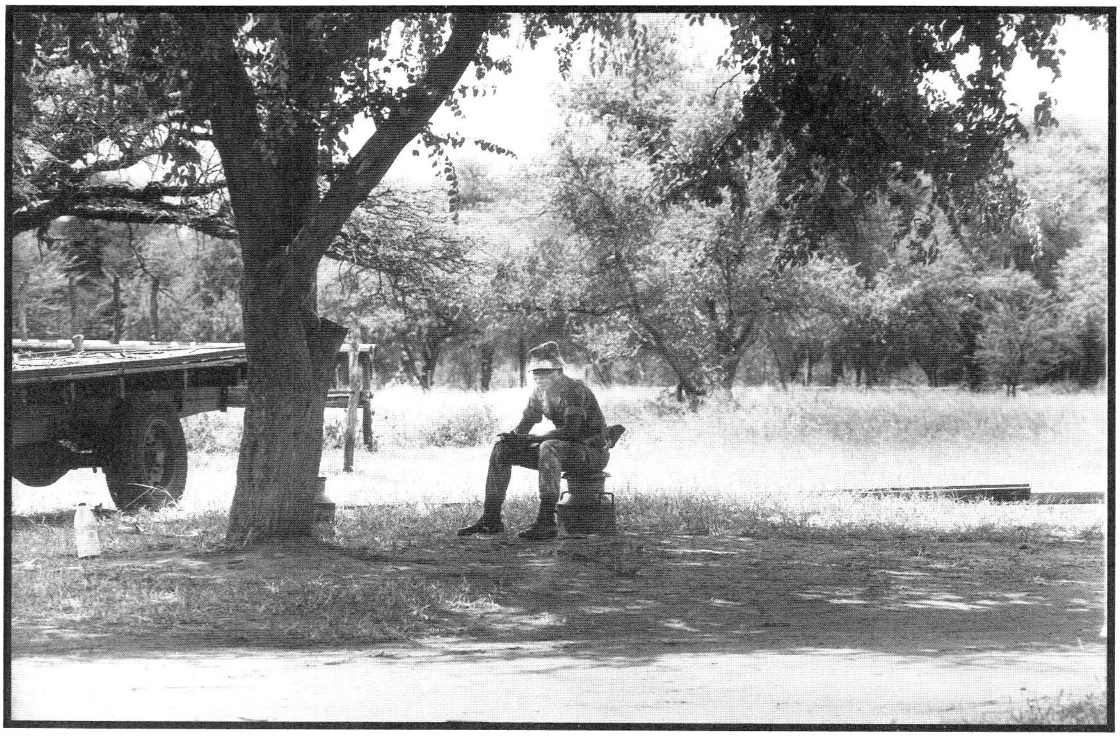

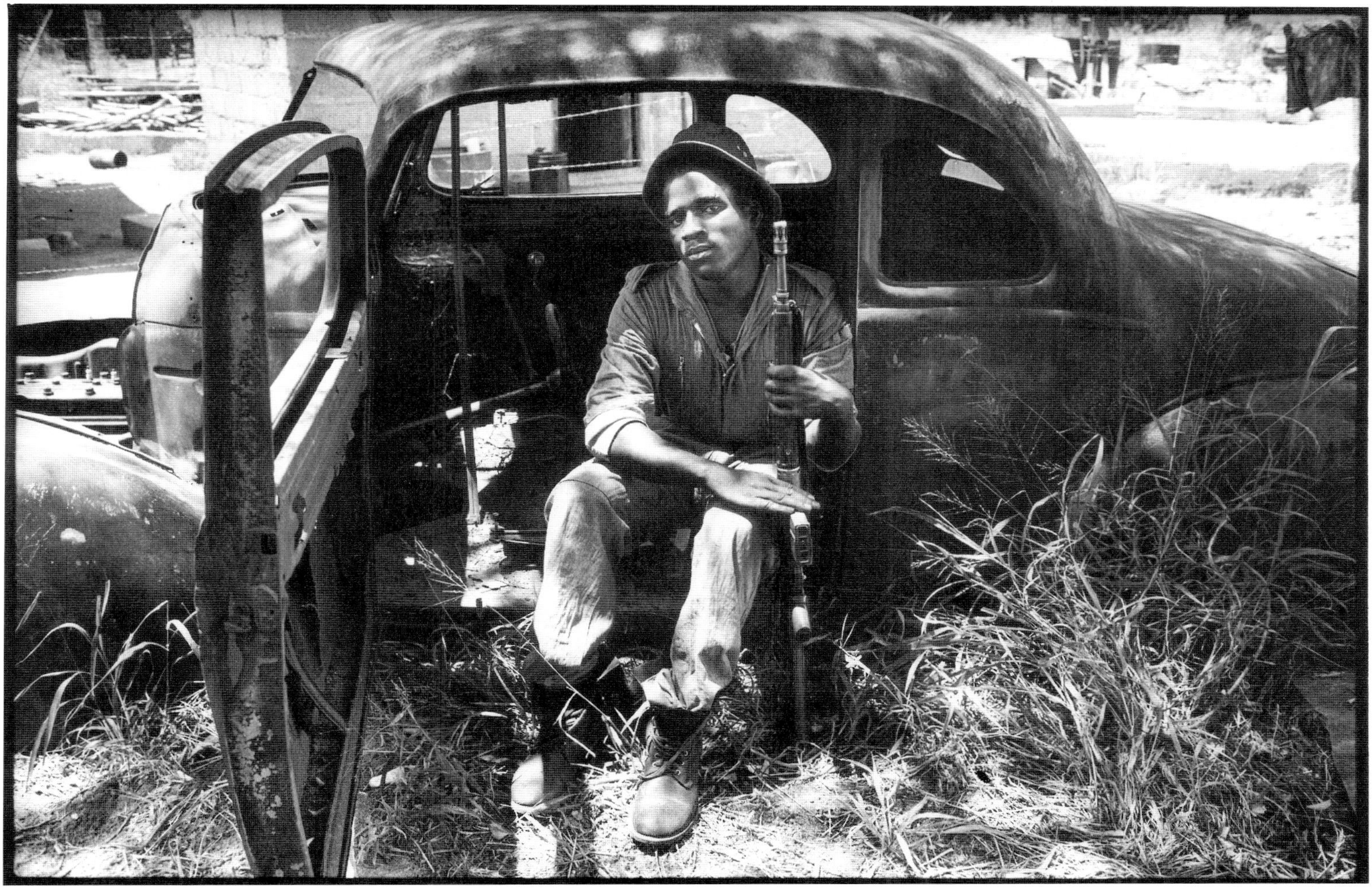

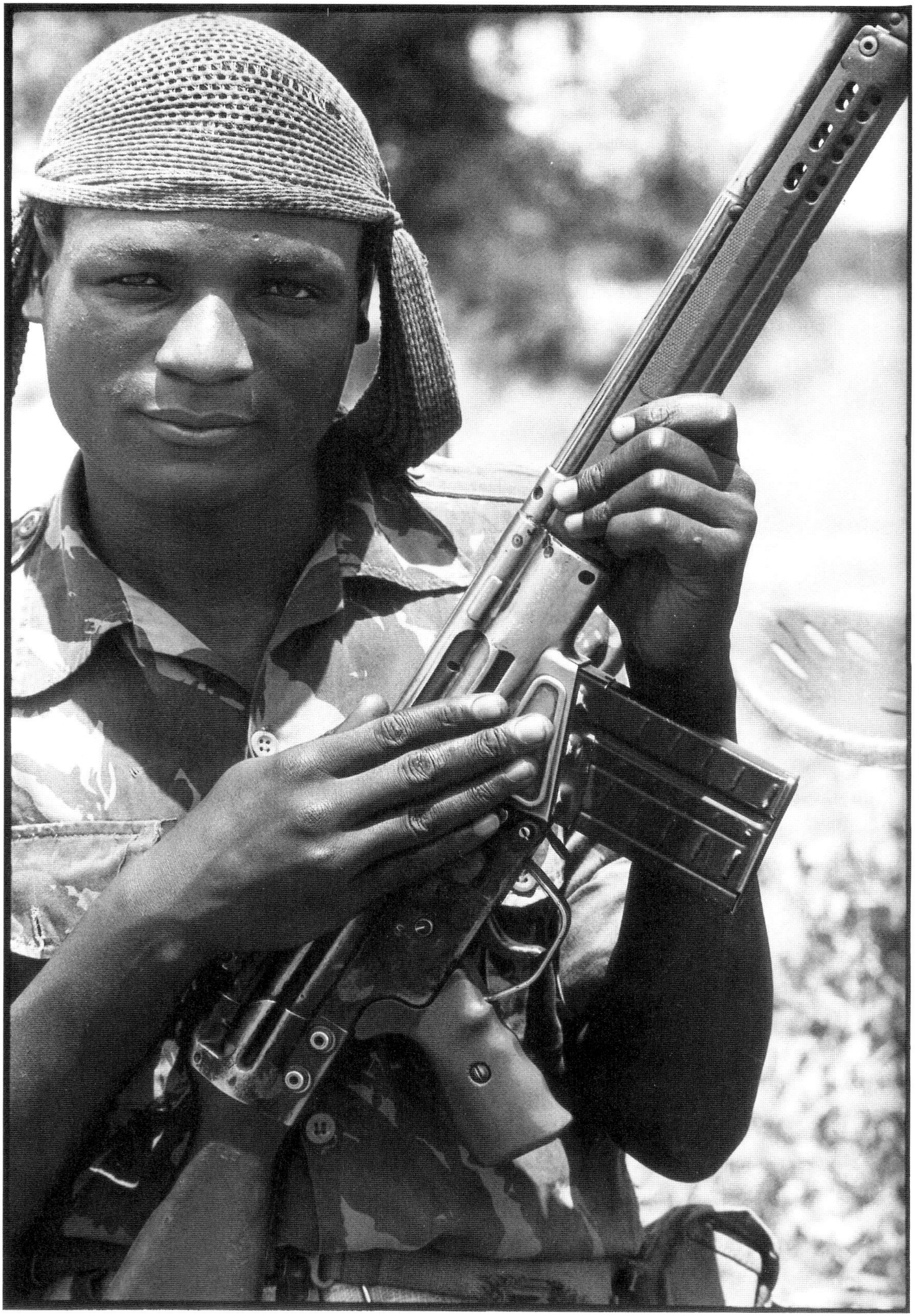

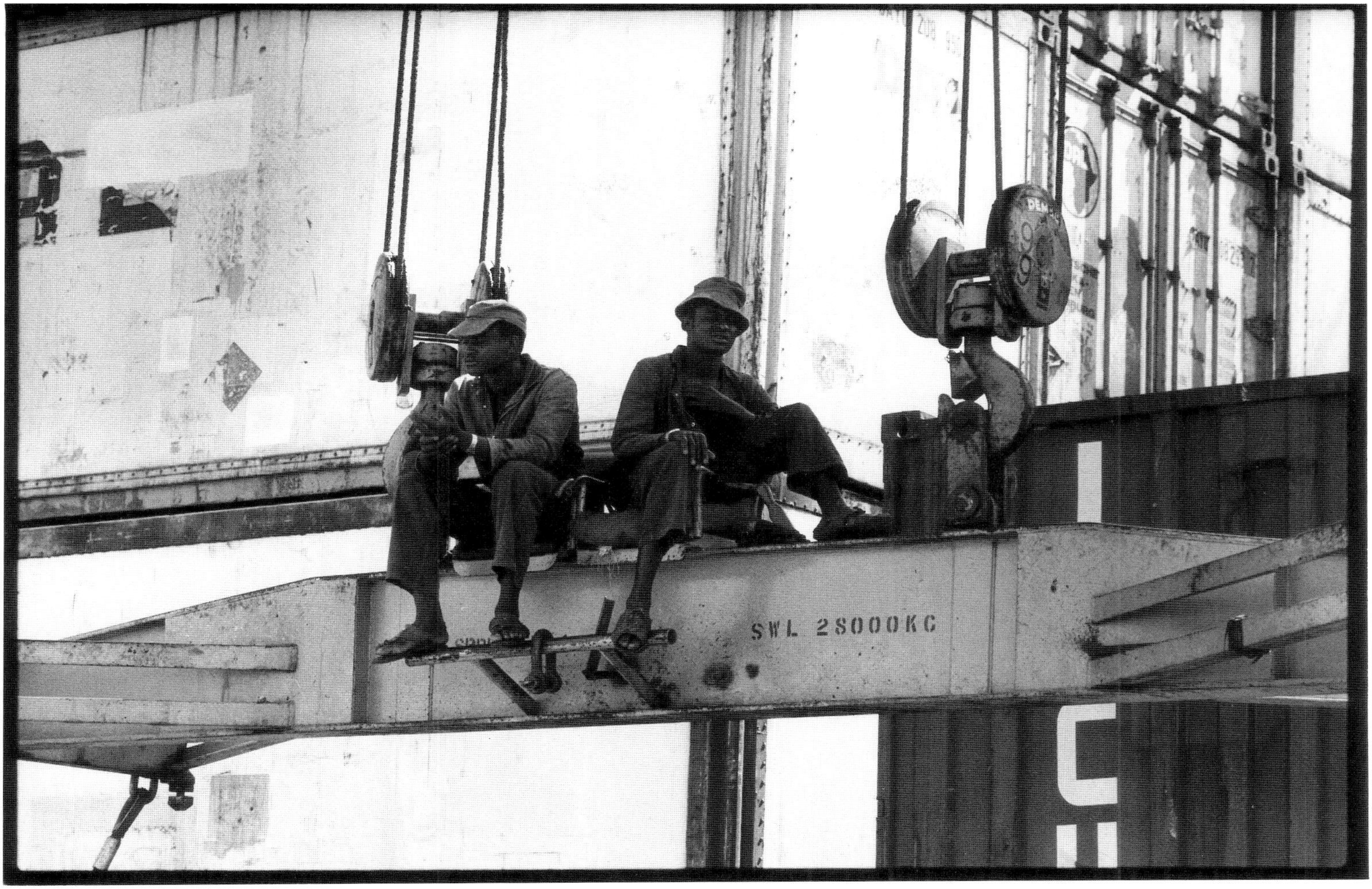

Zimbabwe bears all the outward signs of a highly industrialised nation. However, as a landlocked country it is entirely dependent on others for import and export routes to the sea. South Africa successfully controls this via Beit Bridge (see picture on page 70) through Zimbabwe's south.

Zambia

'So we have an obligation, a political obligation, a moral obligation, to assist those who want to establish their own elementary human rights in their own country.'

Kenneth Kaunda, President of Zambia

'The South African regime knows that it's fighting a losing battle. What it is now trying to achieve by destabilising Frontline States is to delay the day when apartheid is no more.

Now, just now, we've got a number of South Africans under custody, recently arrested for programmes which would lead to the destruction of our property and possibly would result in deaths of human beings. They have been training 120 Zambian dissidents with the help of the rebels in Angola, the UNITA rebels. We know they are training about 2,000 Zambians in Namibia. All this obviously is meant to destabilise us even more and the only crime we have committed is to look after the refugees here and the ANC. So we have an obligation, a political obligation, a moral obligation, to assist those who want to establish their own elementary human rights in their own countries. This is what we're doing for South Africans, and what is more the ANC have done Zambia a tremendous service. It was on our soil that they passed another resolution deciding they were going to continue to be non-racial, and to us in Zambia this is an important element in their policies which we support fully.'

Kenneth Kaunda, President, Zambia

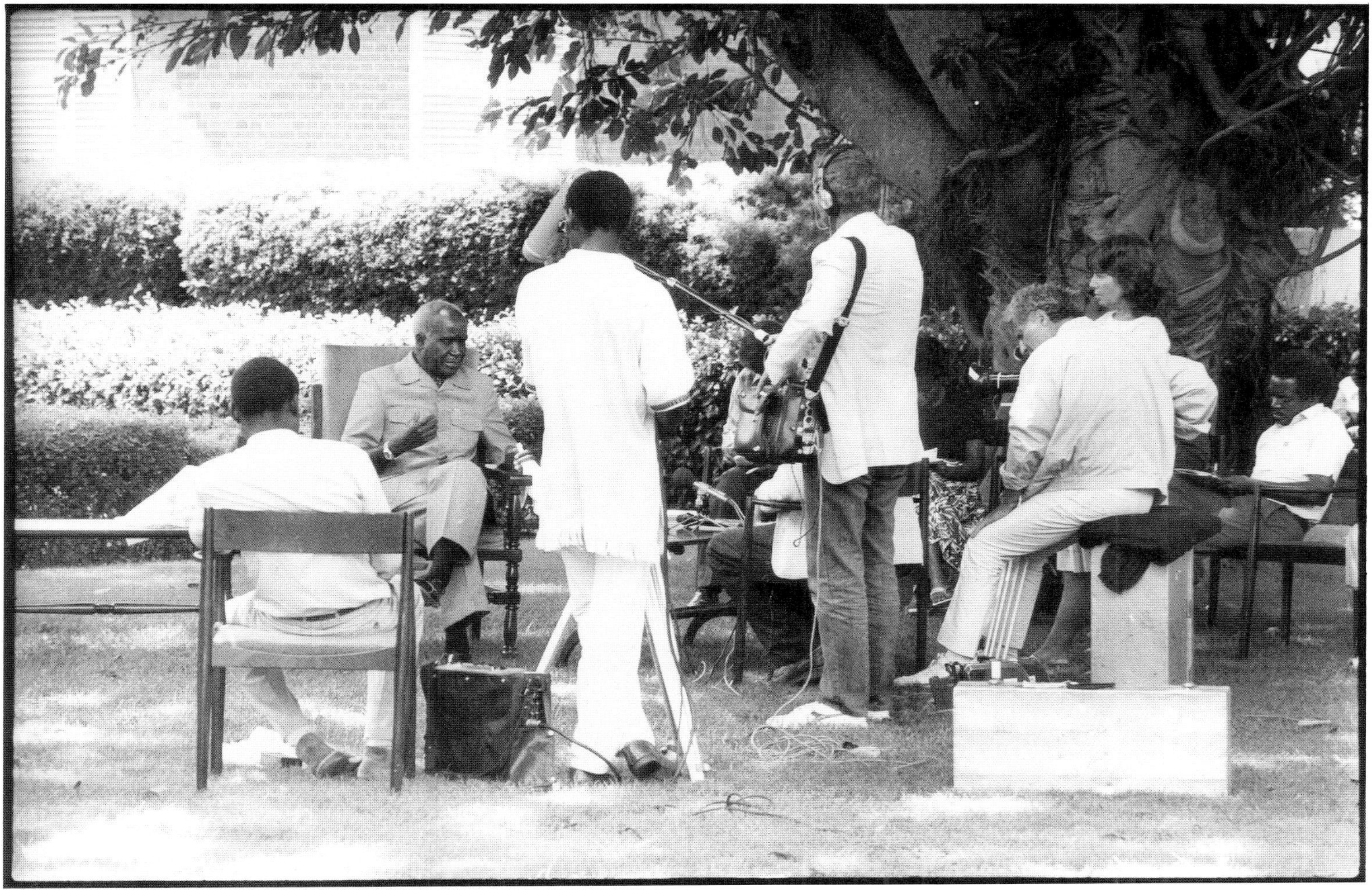

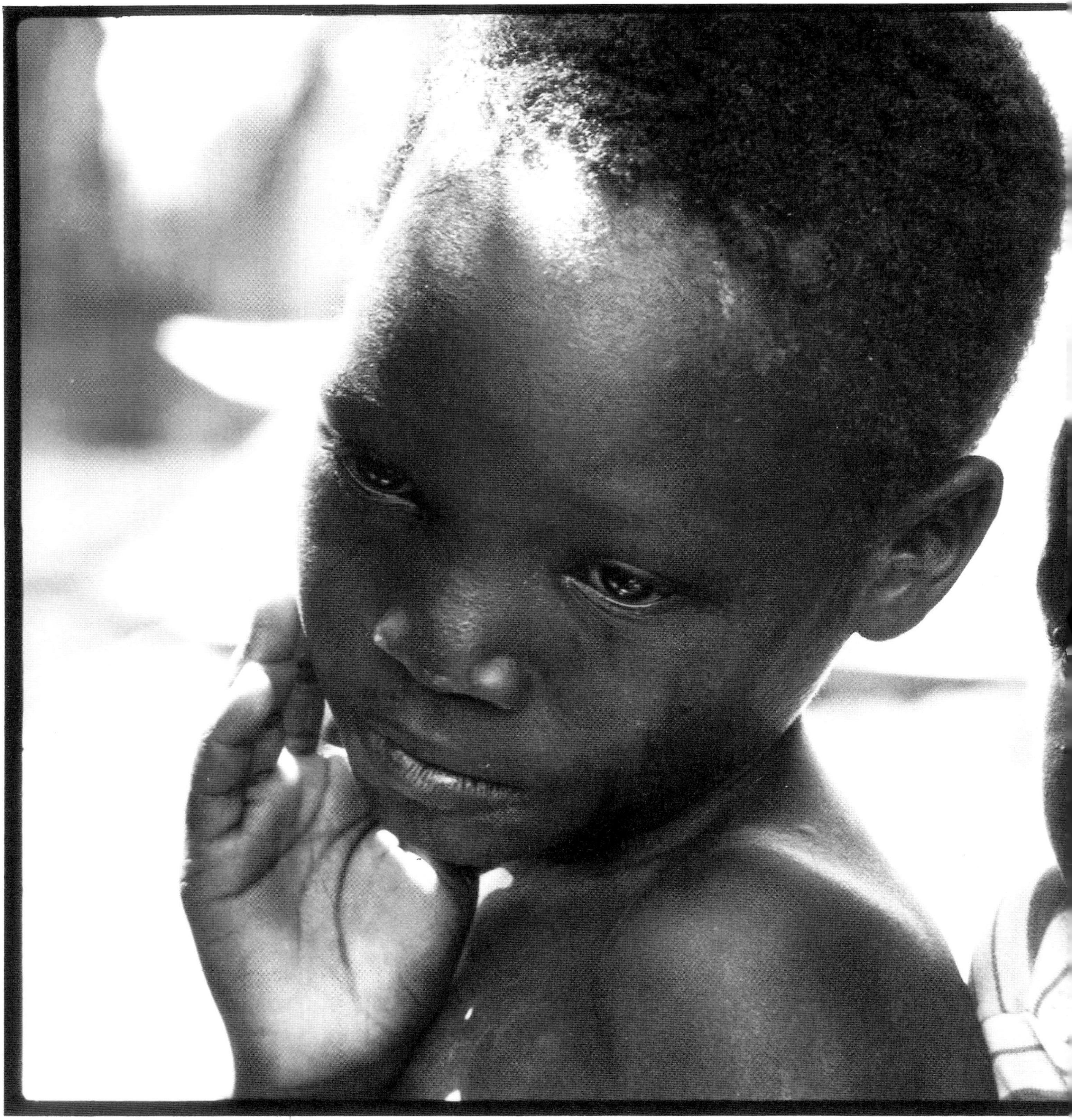

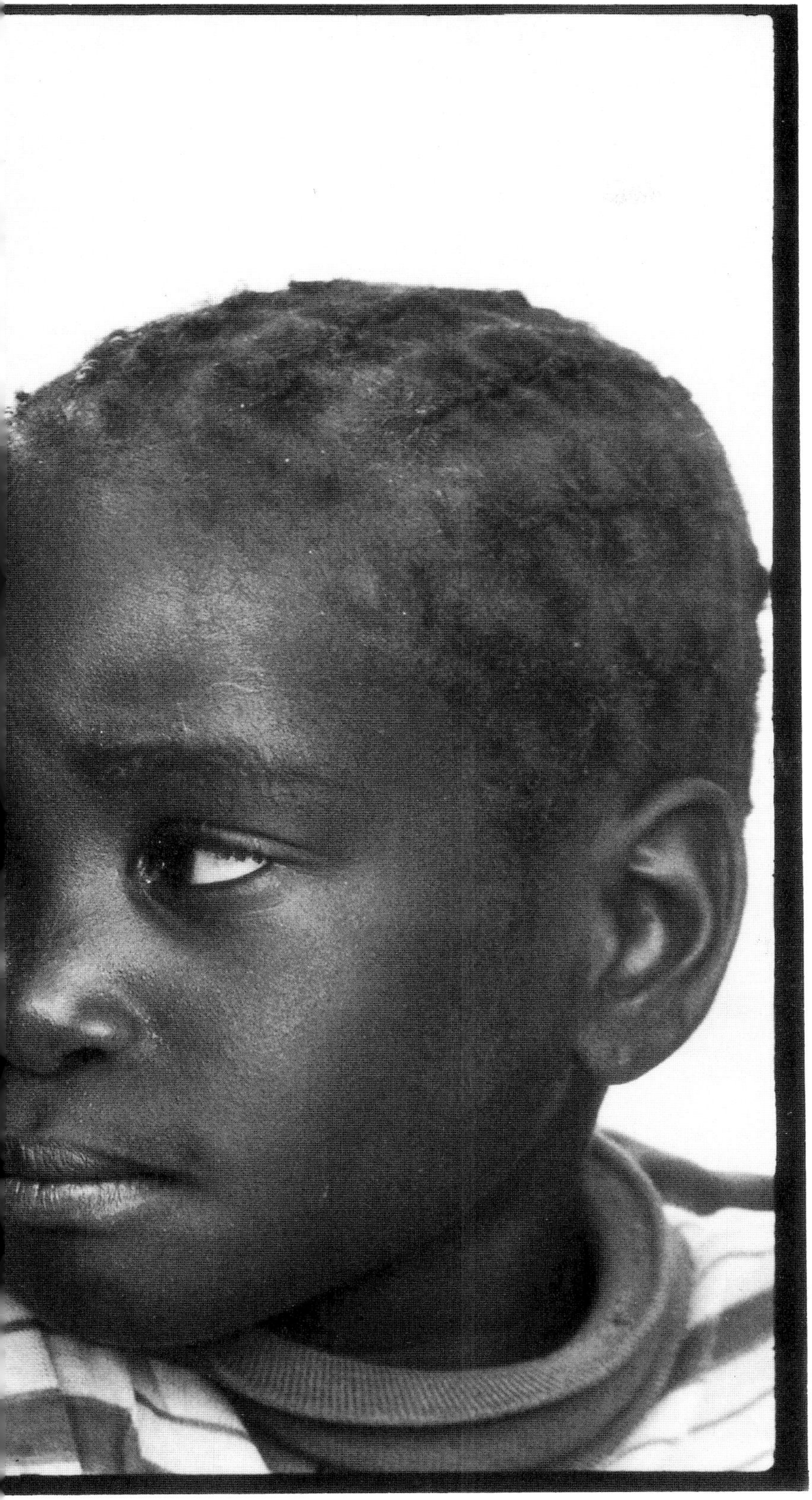

Zambia is having to cope with more than 130,000 refugees who have poured into the country from the war zones in neighbouring Mozambique. More refugees arrive every day, many at this camp at Luangwa. They are arriving in Zambia from all points — in the east from fighting and famine in Mozambique; in the south from Namibia and South Africa; in the west from the devastation in Angola; and in the north from Zaire. Conditions at this camp are typical; malaria is endemic, fuelled by poor water and lack of medicines. Many refugees arrive with nothing, many without clothes, and makeshift 'tailoring' is all that they can expect.

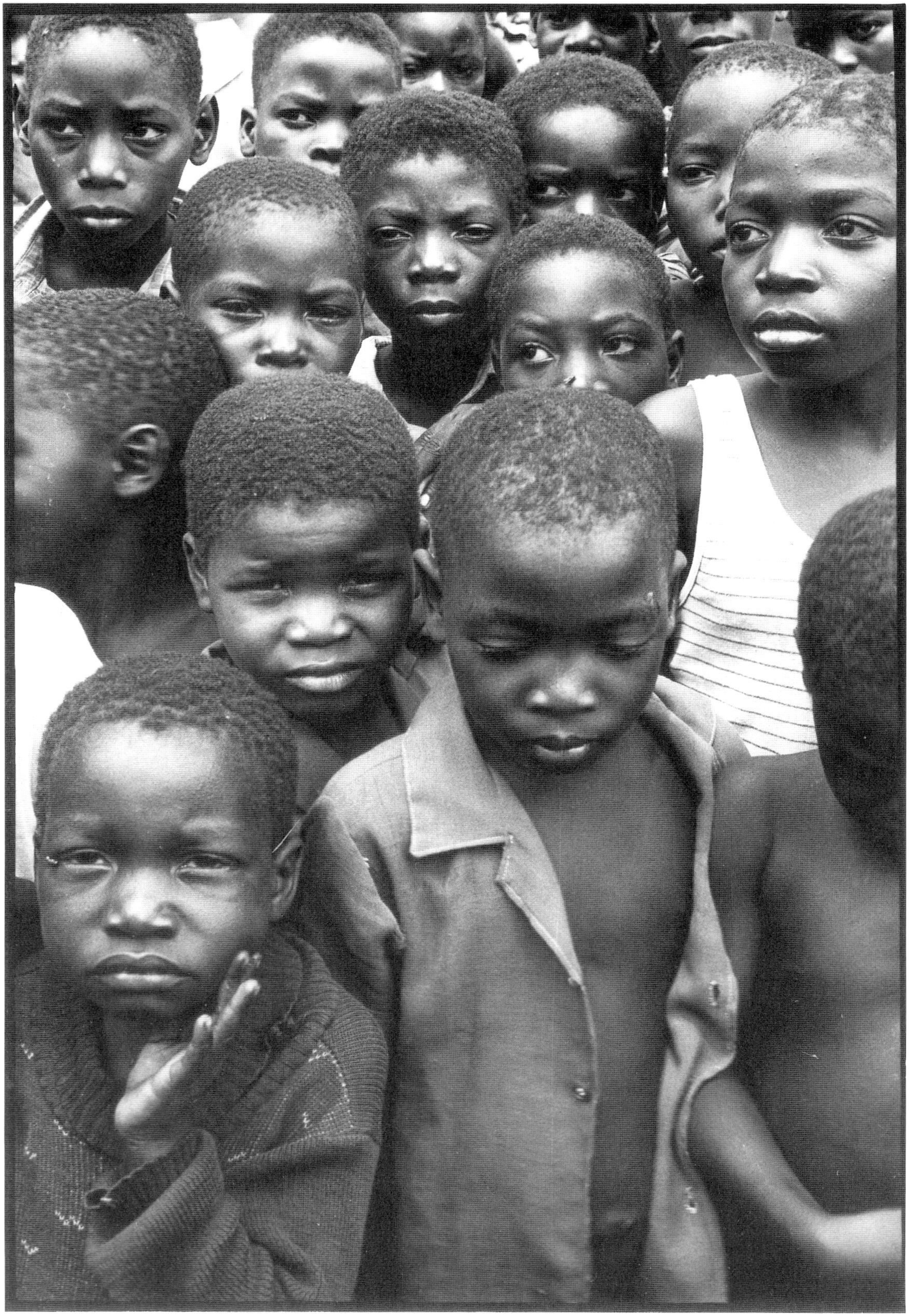

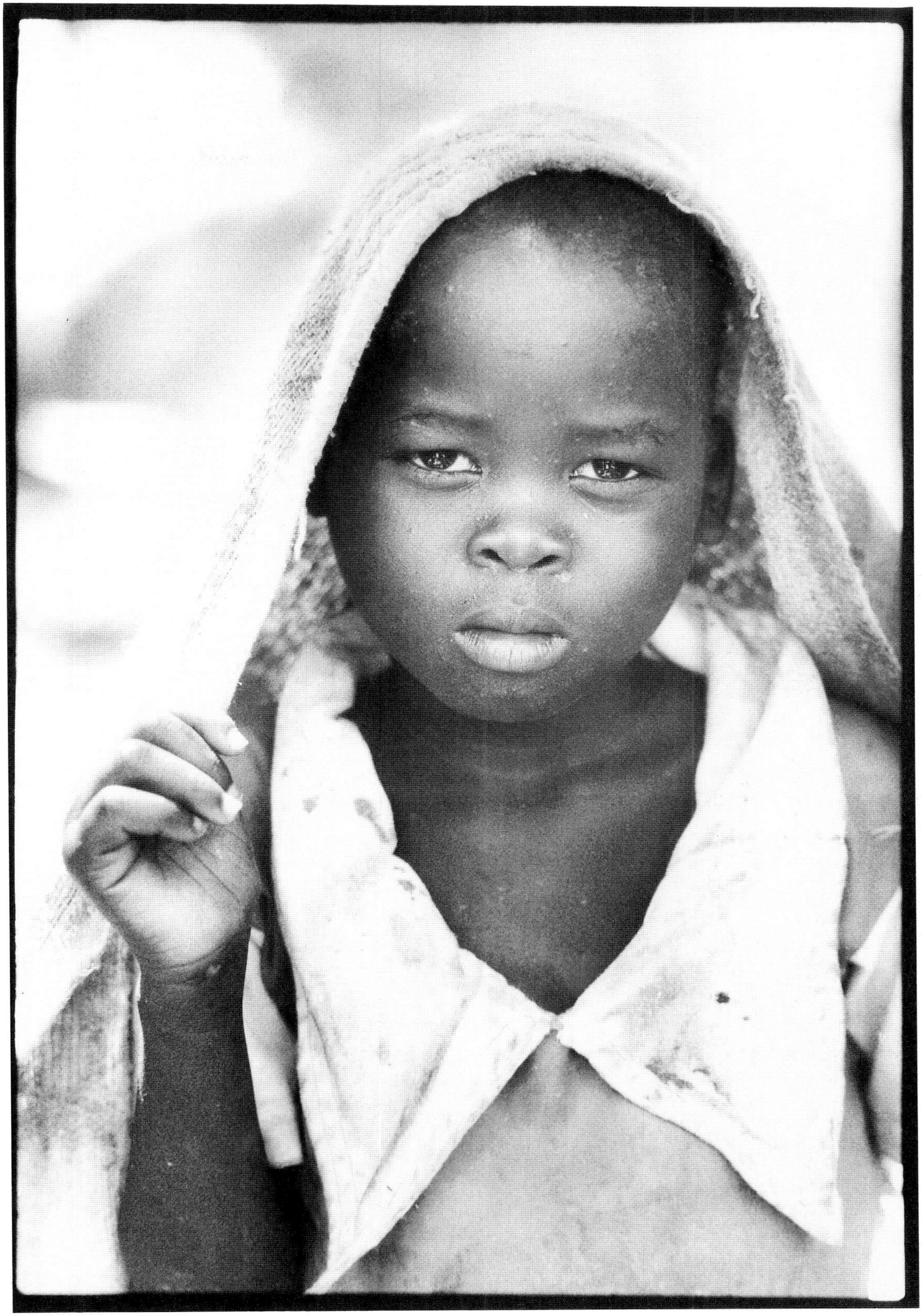

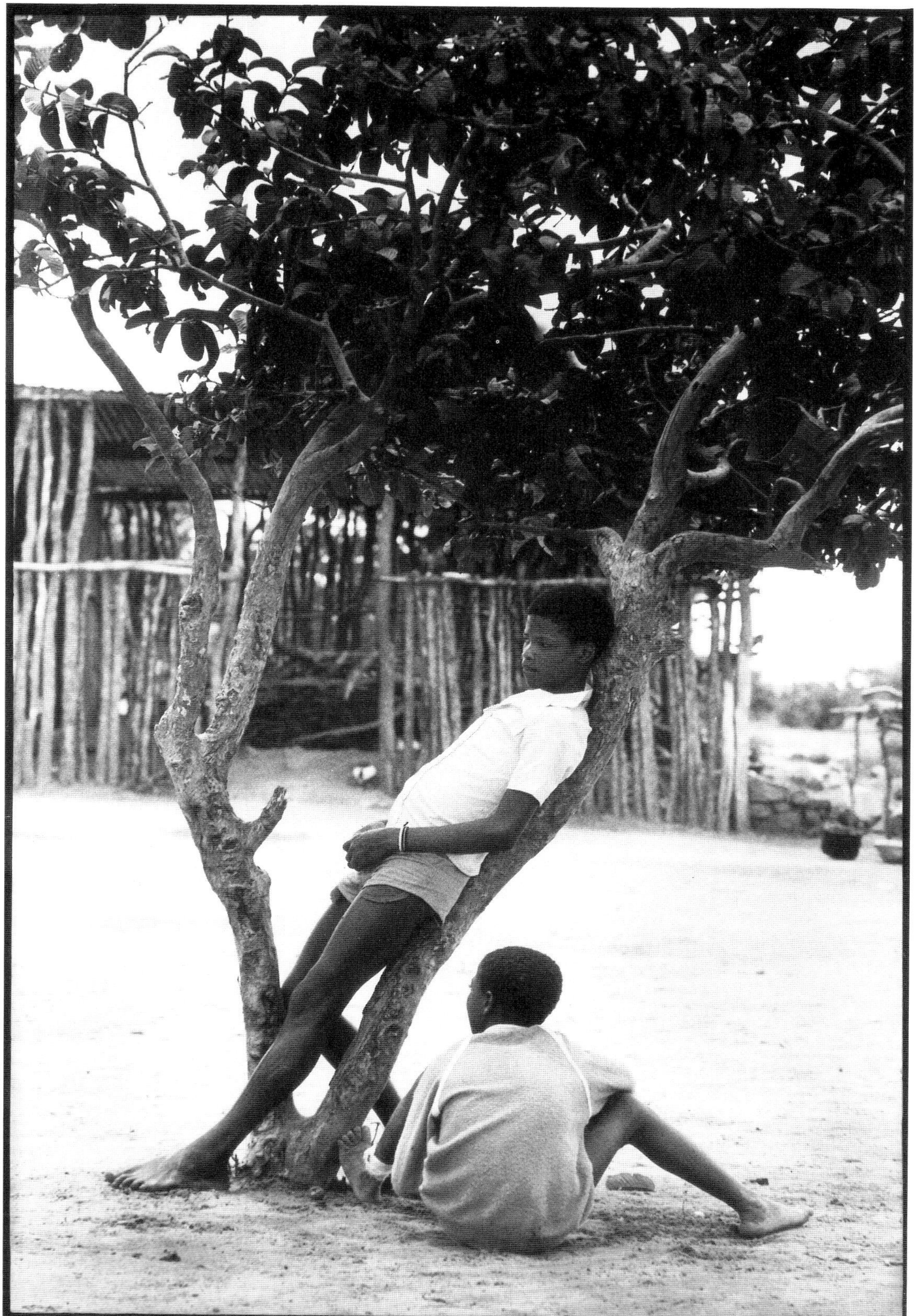

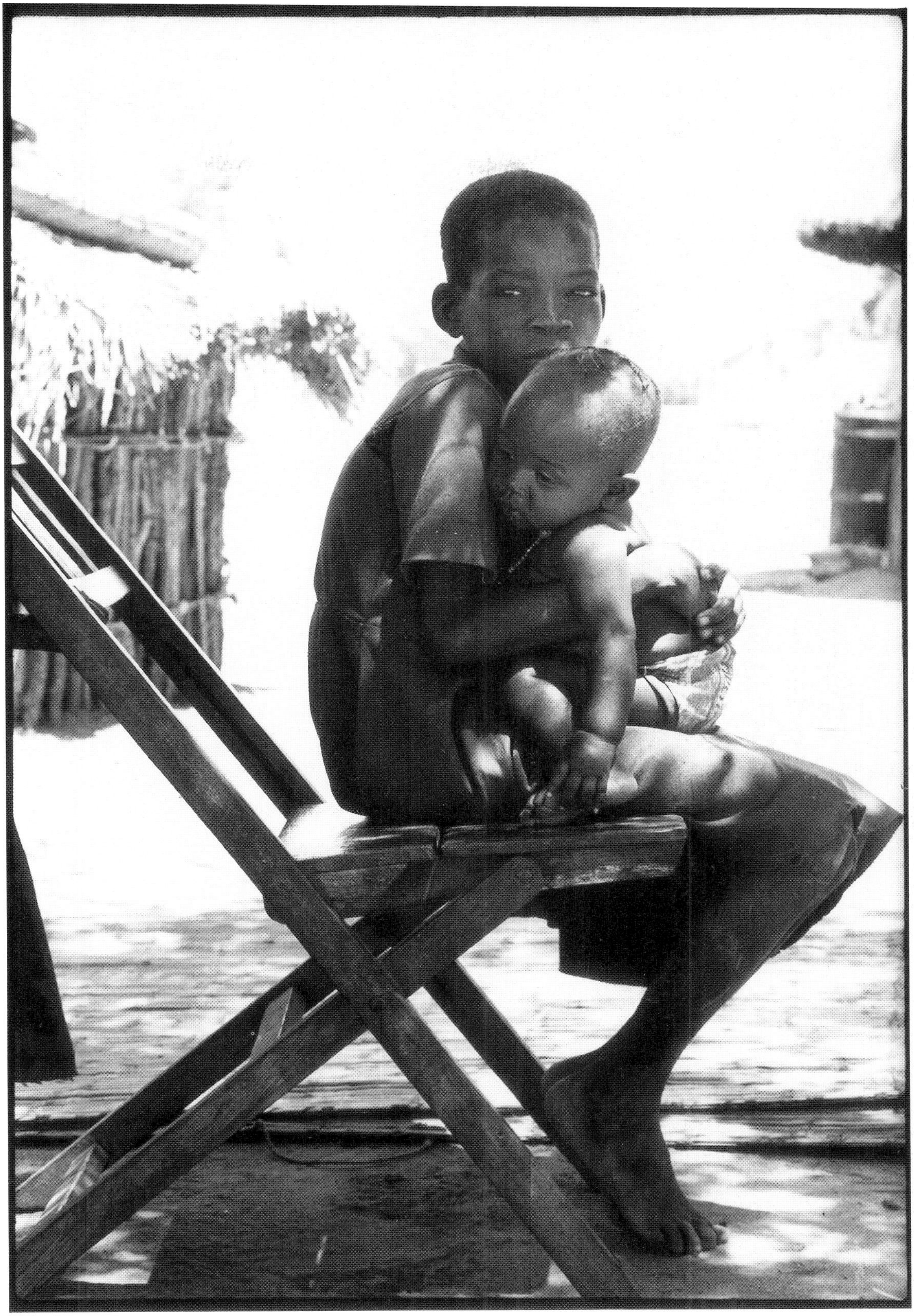

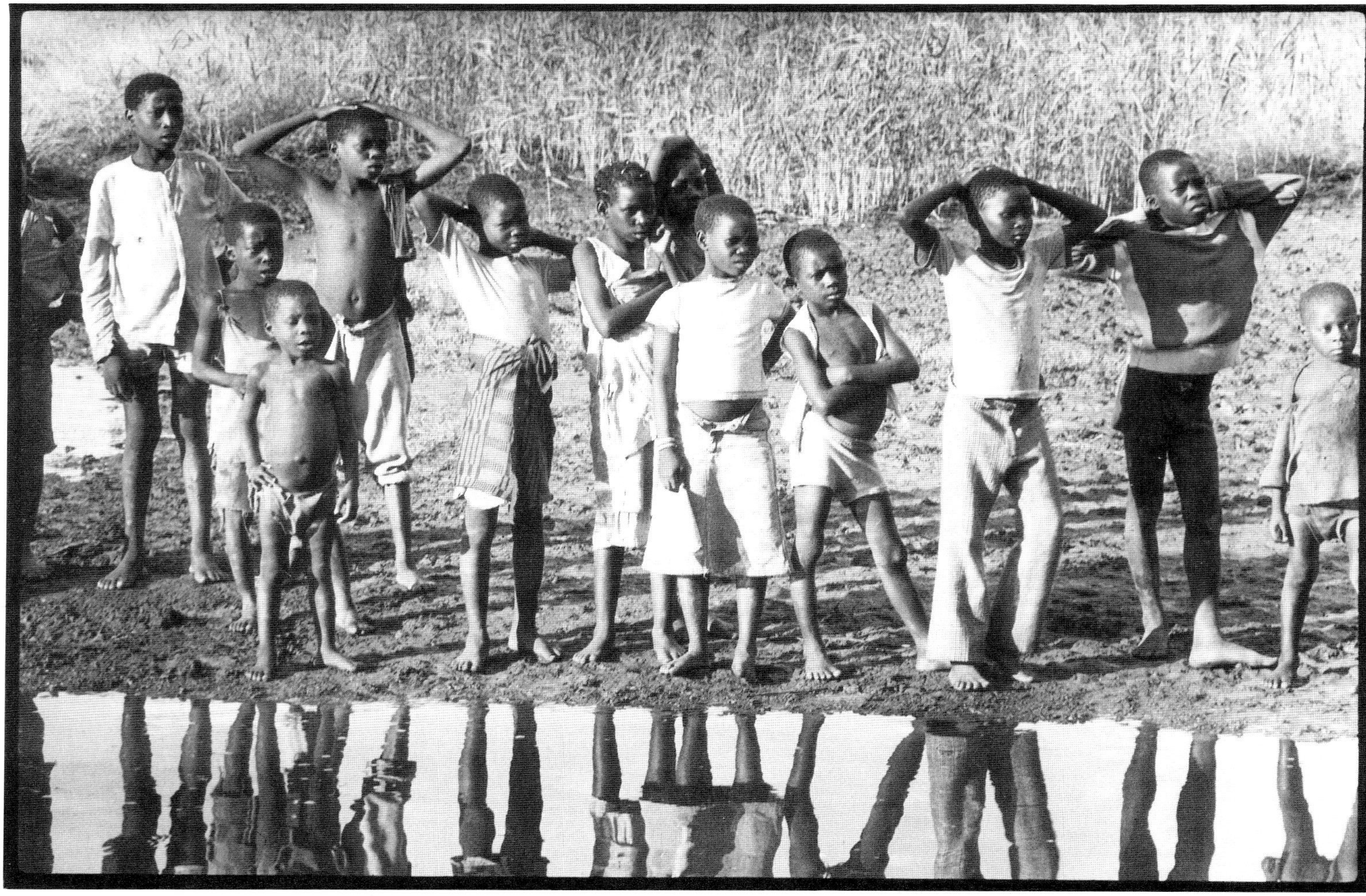

'We are here in Zambia because Renamo (MNR) is attacking our villages. When Renamo approach the villages they don't do good things. They burn houses, they steal clothes, almost everything is taken from the houses. They burn the entire village. Once they kidnapped the children. They took them into the bush. When it happens, we all run away, yes, that is why I'm here in Zambia. It is to flee from the war isn't it? In Mozambique there is a war and that war, let us say, is of the armed bandits who are massacring innocent people — people without guilt. If they came across me, even worse because I am young. I would be kidnapped and taken into the bush and I would find a group of these men and would start to fight against my brothers or my sisters. So in order for this not to happen, I had to flee to this place, where there is nothing, but where I am free. I am doing what I can; when later Mozambique will be peaceful, I will go back to my area. I want to go back to my home.'

Mozambican refugee, Luangwa camp, Zambia

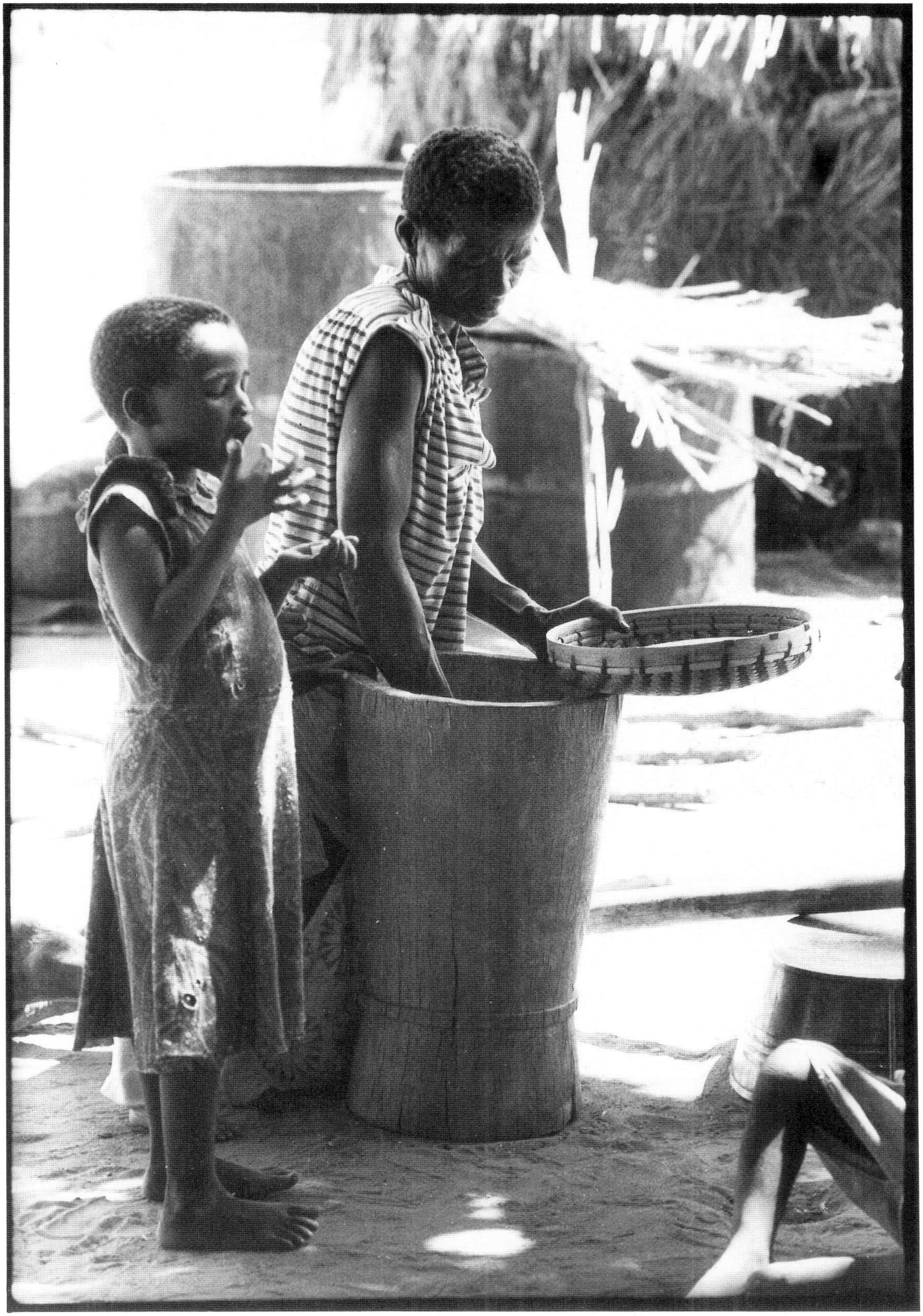

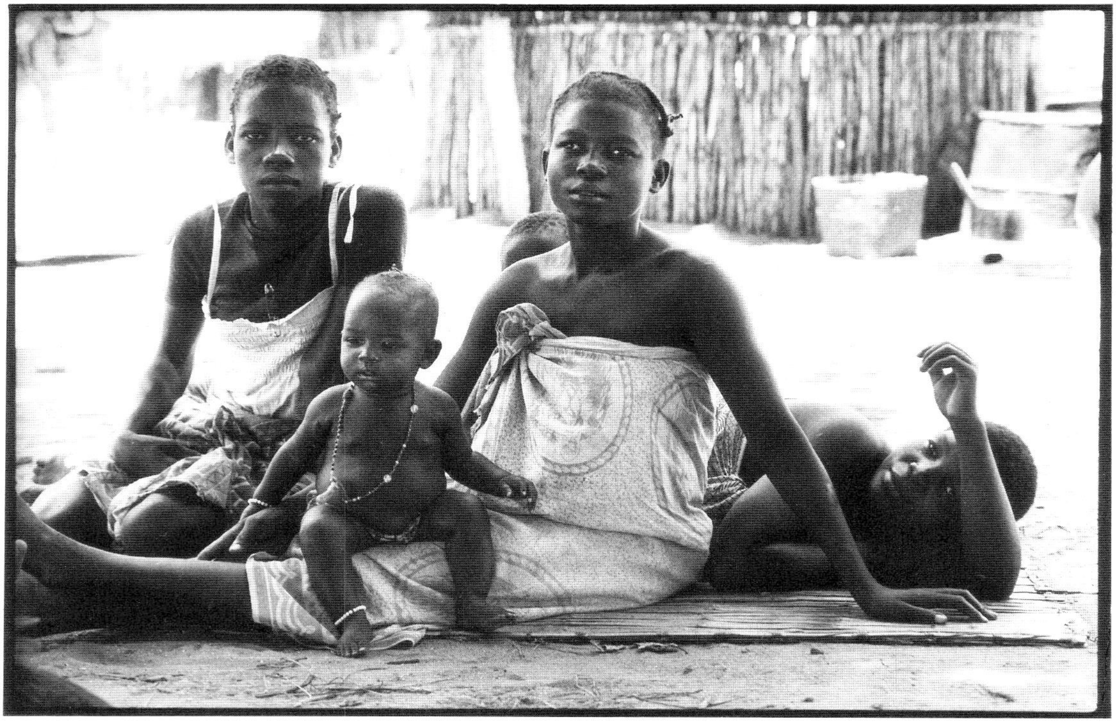

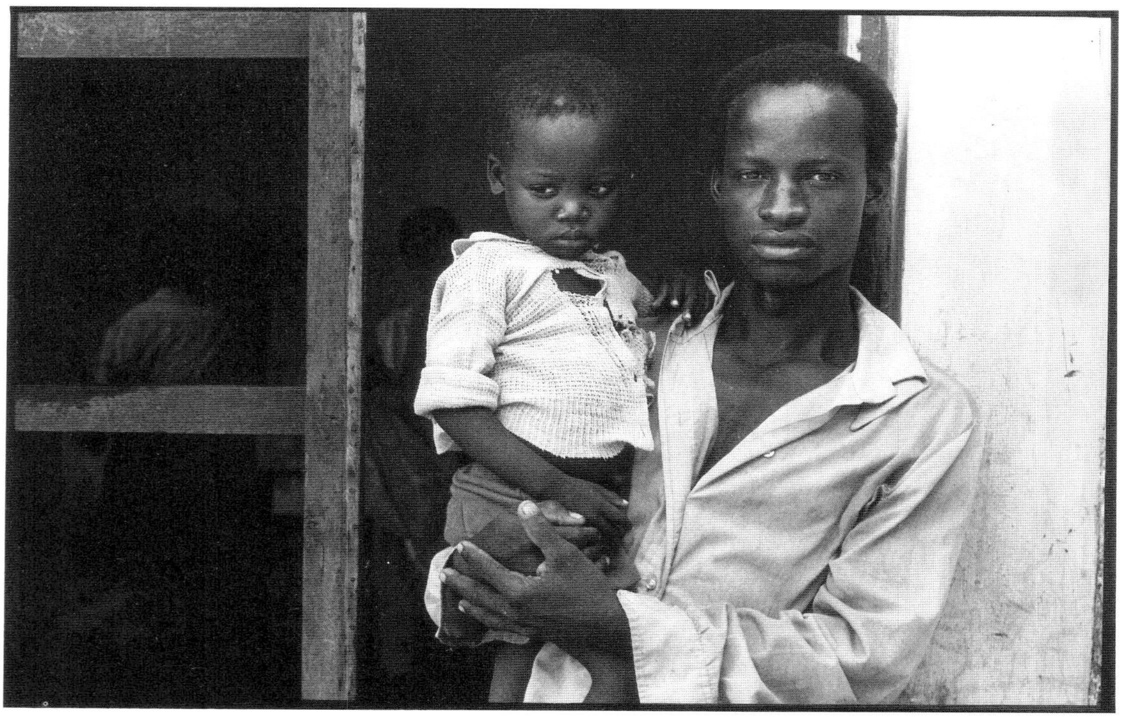

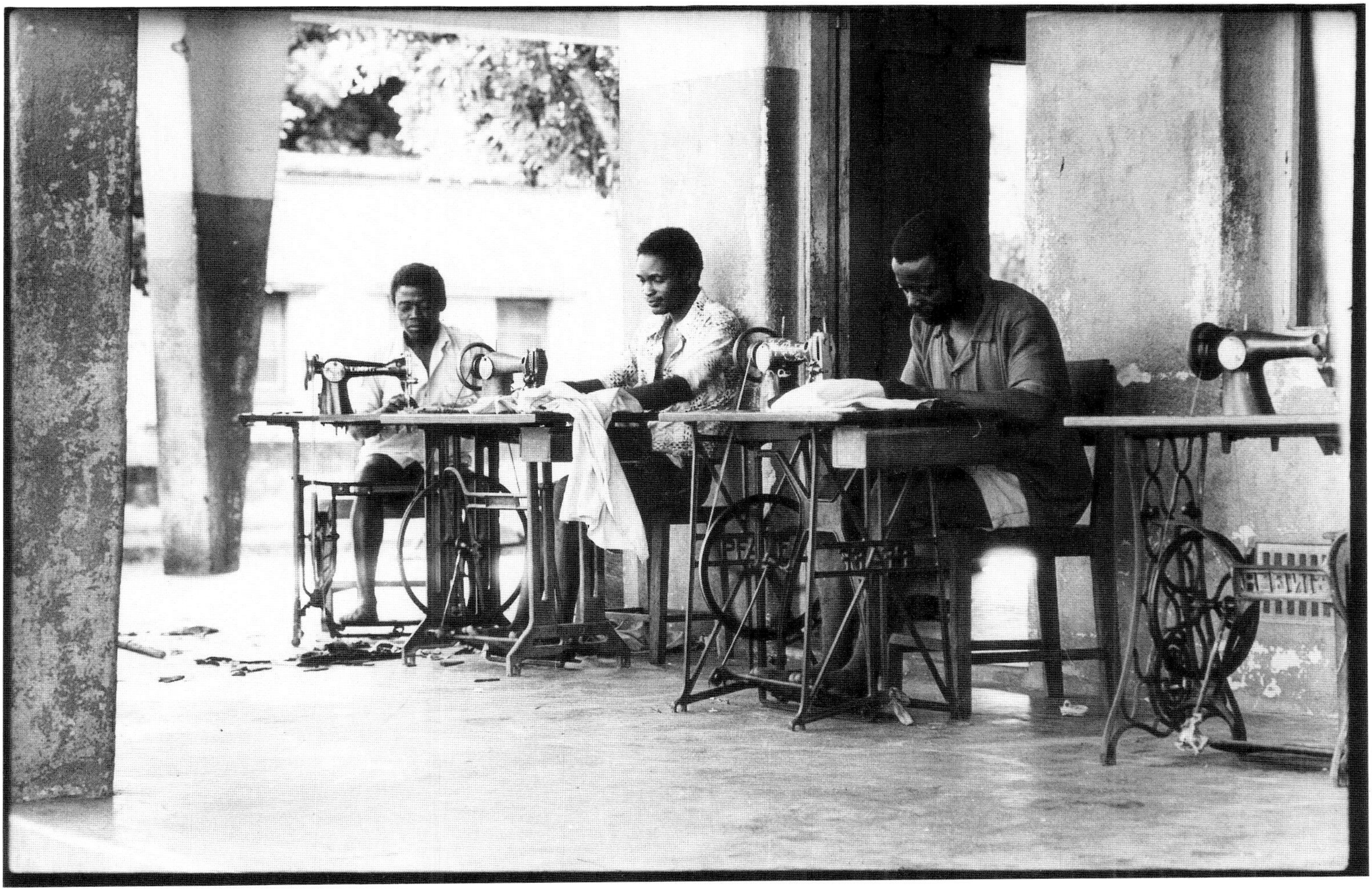

Angola

'It is the question of the war. This war which is imposed on us by the South Africans. If there were no killings, I would not be afraid to be there. But the principle thing is that they kill — and I'm afraid of being killed.'

Angolan refugee

War in Angola has been on a wider scale than anywhere else among the Frontline States. South Africa has invaded several times and maintains a continuous presence in parts of the south. The first South African invasion took place in 1975 to try to prevent the new MPLA government taking power at the time of independence. In 1975 both Angola and Mozambique won independence from Portugal. The new governments took over nations with largely illiterate populations and economies which had been systematically sabotaged by the departing Portuguese. Since then both nations have been ravaged by war — in Mozambique one of terror and destruction, in Angola a more conventional war conducted by the South African Defence Force and UNITA, the rebels backed by South Africa and the USA. Neither UNITA nor the MNR could have survived without this backing. Angola is the only oil producer in the region and its extensive deposits make it relatively wealthy. With peace, Angola could become a major fuel supplier to the region. Oil income also means that Angola cannot be squeezed economically, in the same way that South Africa can squeeze Mozambique and the land-locked countries.

Oil installations have been among South Africa's direct targets in Angola. At an oil refinery and storage depot at Namibe, South African commandos launched a relatively successful attack. They destroyed three storage tanks, but the main explosive charges were placed on a tank that had been emptied for cleaning. Had a

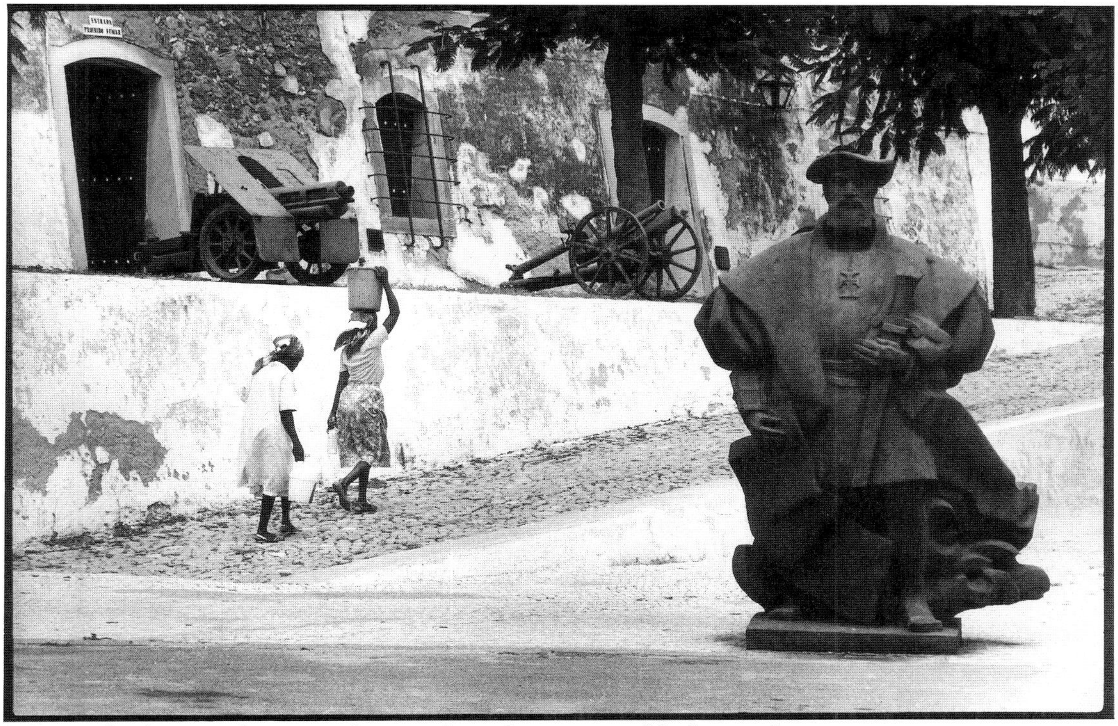

The military museum, above Luanda, was originally established to house weapons from previous conflicts. It now also has an increasingly large display of South African weapons, including planes, tanks and a range of small arms and land-mines.

full tank been chosen, the entire depot would have been destroyed.

Since 1975 there have been many South African incursions into Angola. On 4 May 1978, the South African Defence Force attacked a Namibian refugee camp in Kassinga, killing 612 refugees, 12 Angolan soldiers and three Angolan camp workers. There have also been major attacks at Boma, Moxico province in which 98 died, and aerial bombings of the Huila Timber factory and Leba mountain road. At the time of writing (March 1988) a major battle was taking place, with 9,000 South African troops deep inside Angola.

In 1984, Captain Wynand Petrus Johannes du Toit of the South African Defence Force, launched an operation to destroy the oil storage tanks at Cabinda Gulf. 'We were transported to near Cabinda by the South African destroyer *Jan Fouchier*. We landed by inflatable boat at the bay of Malimbu and the nine man team including myself went ashore. There were six oil storage tanks and we would divide into three teams, each team carrying three mines. Unfortunately everything did not go according to plan, due to a lack of information. We did not know of several FAPLA bases in the area. We lay in the bush but FAPLA patrols were all around and came across some of our group. Our group was nearly through the FAPLA lines when a FAPLA soldier saw us and opened fire. The two men with me were killed and I myself was injured.'

Capt du Toit was released in a 'prisoner swap' in 1987 — he was greeted in South Africa by President Botha.

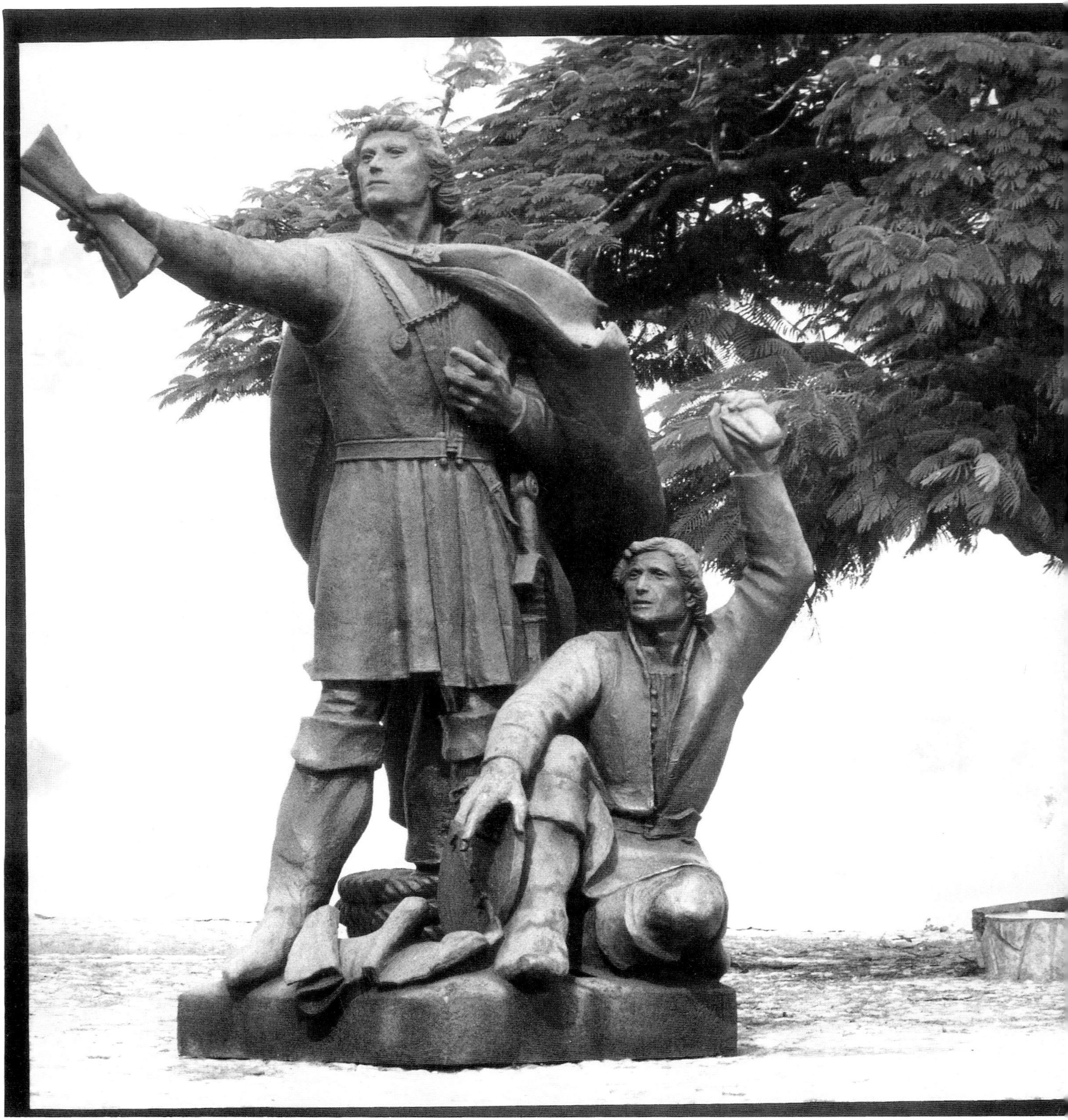

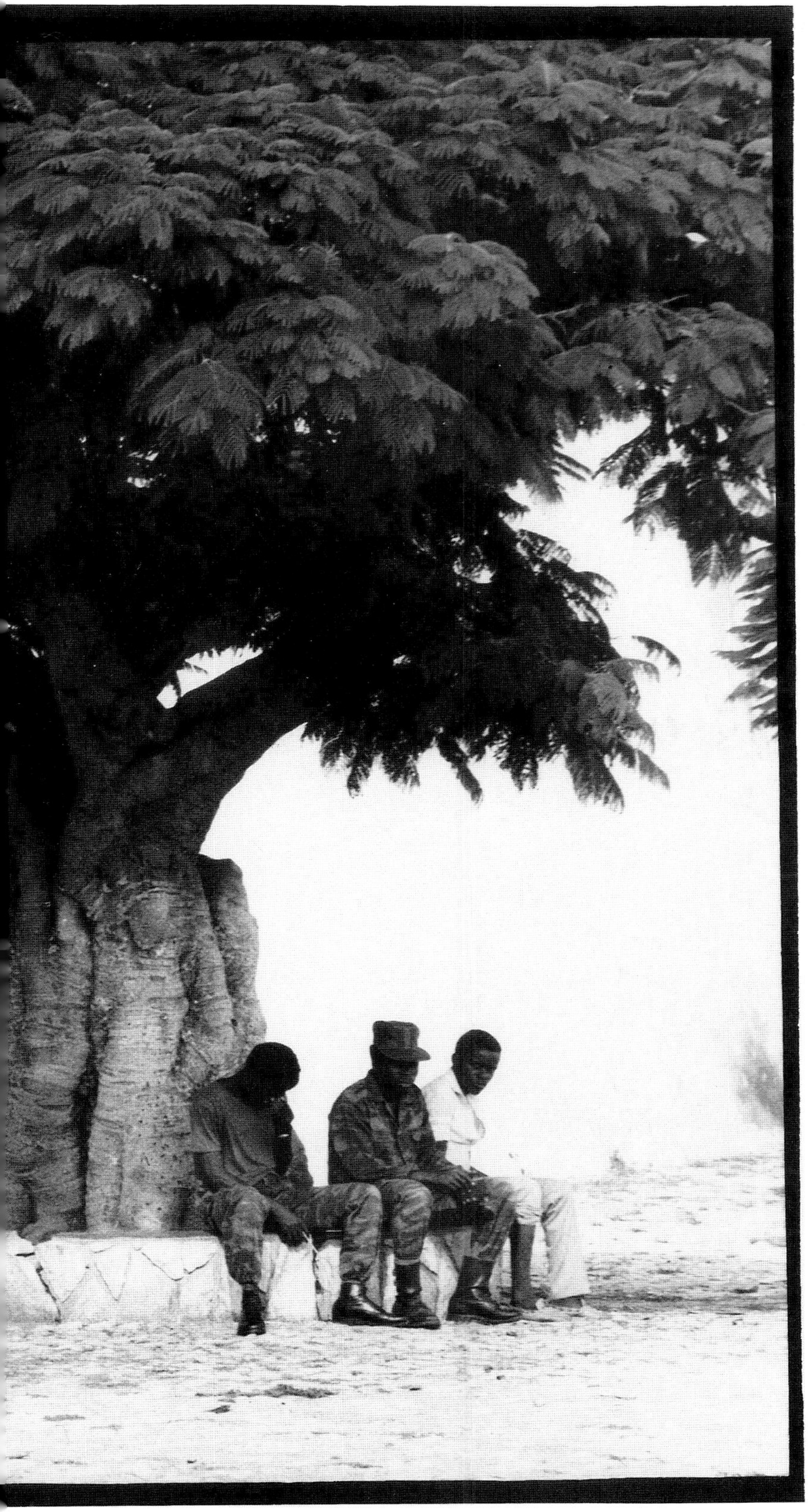

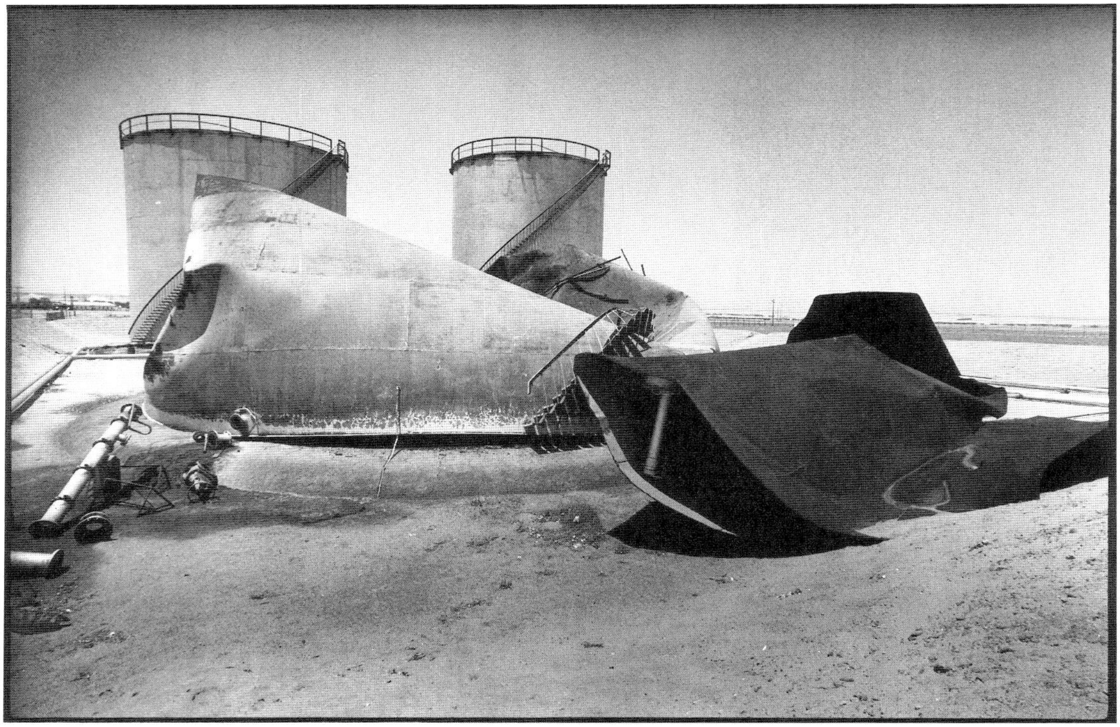

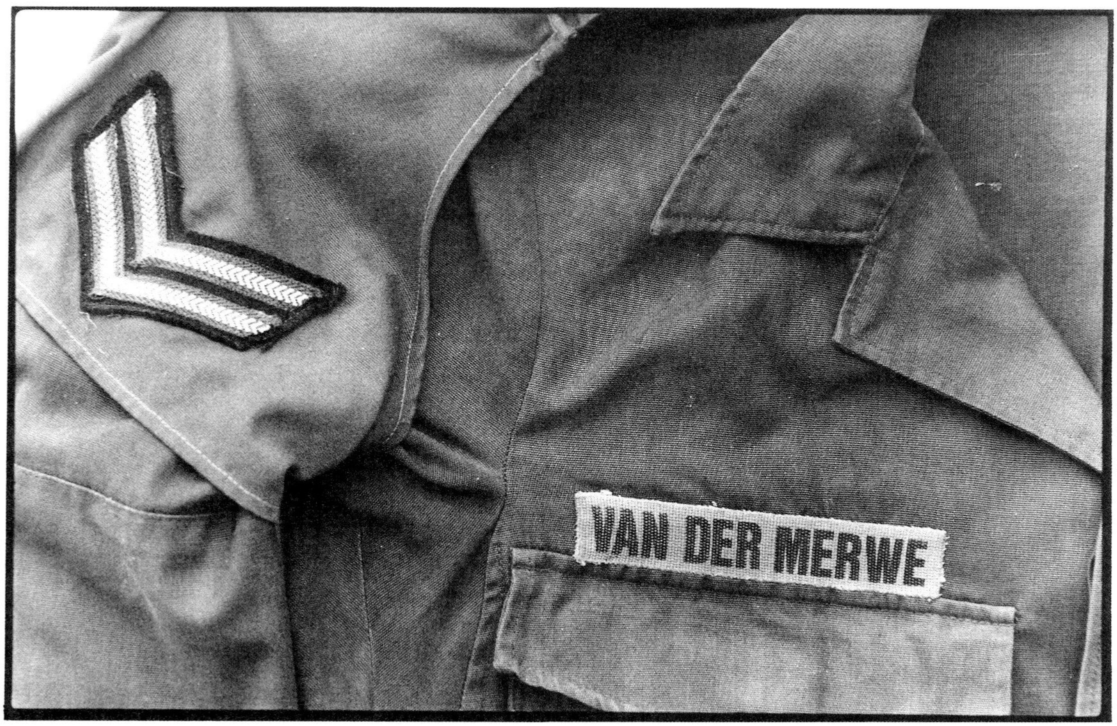
VAN DER MERWE

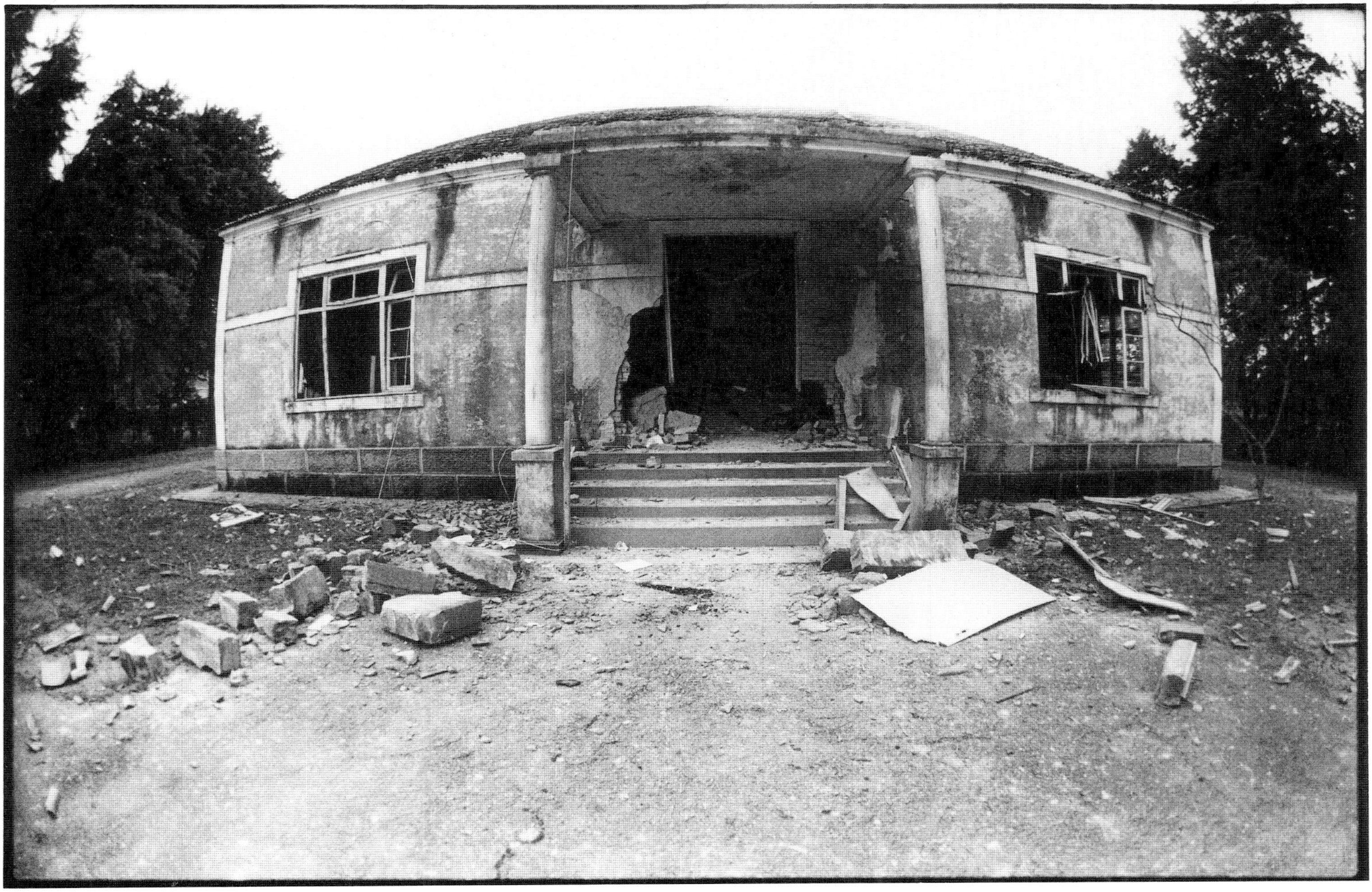

'Well, it was a sabotage action of UNITA obviously. It is a building belonging to the Faculty of Agricultural Sciences. This faculty runs courses on veterinary medicine and agronomy. The action took place at night, at daybreak, and you can see the state of the buildings. You can see the equipment not destroyed has already been taken out.

When in fact the confrontation is not possible, when there is nothing more to do, there is only pure and simple destruction which is left over, which does not have anything to do with military objectives. In fact, that is the only possible explanation. An attitude which shows there is no other objective for UNITA than pure and simple destruction of institutions and structures of economic and social interest for the People's Republic of Angola.

The importance? You may imagine. A laboratory which gives support to a veterinary medicine course. This is a Faculty for Agrarian Sciences, a higher education institute. So we are here to train higher agrarian technicians which are extremely necessary for the country. The number of qualified people in the country is very low and we are the only institution in the country providing this type of activity.'

Dean of College

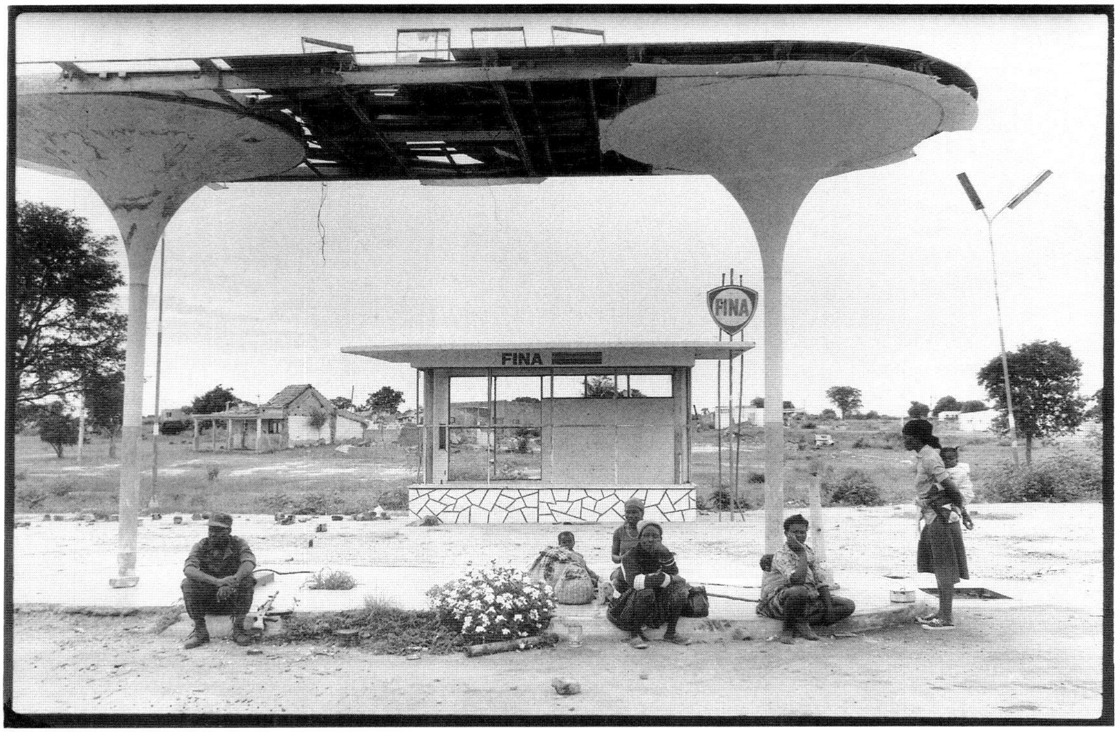

Disabling people, disabling chances of material progress and peace: those are the aims of the rebels. By the destruction of places which could help revitalise the economy, and the constant threat of bombs and mines, the Angolans are prevented from rebuilding their society. Together, South Africa and the rebels have destroyed vast areas of southern Angola with the displacement of hundreds of thousands of people.

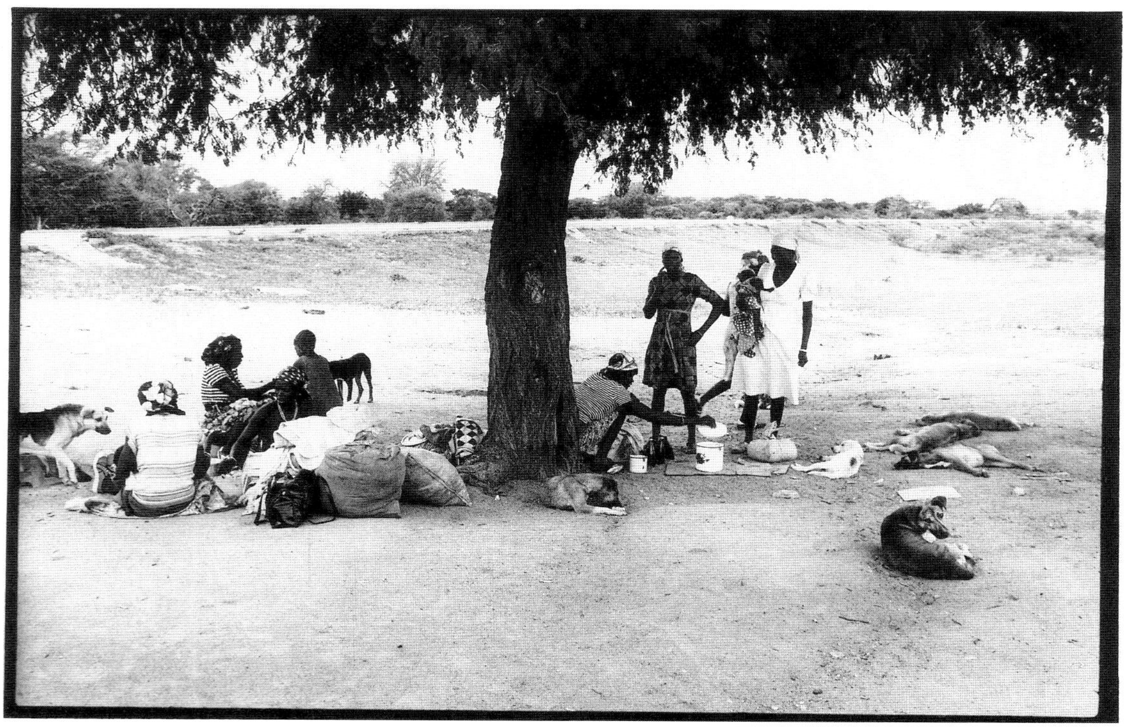

'It is the question of the war. This war which is imposed on us by the South Africans, who are killing and violating, stealing the cattle, all the belongings of the Angolan people. That is the main reason why we came here. There we had everything. In our homes we had not only food, but we were also privileged — our land, belongings, animals, we had everything. But here we don't — it's a great difference. I would really like to go back. If there were no killings I would not be afraid to be there.

But the principal thing is they kill and I'm afraid of being killed.'

Angolan refugee

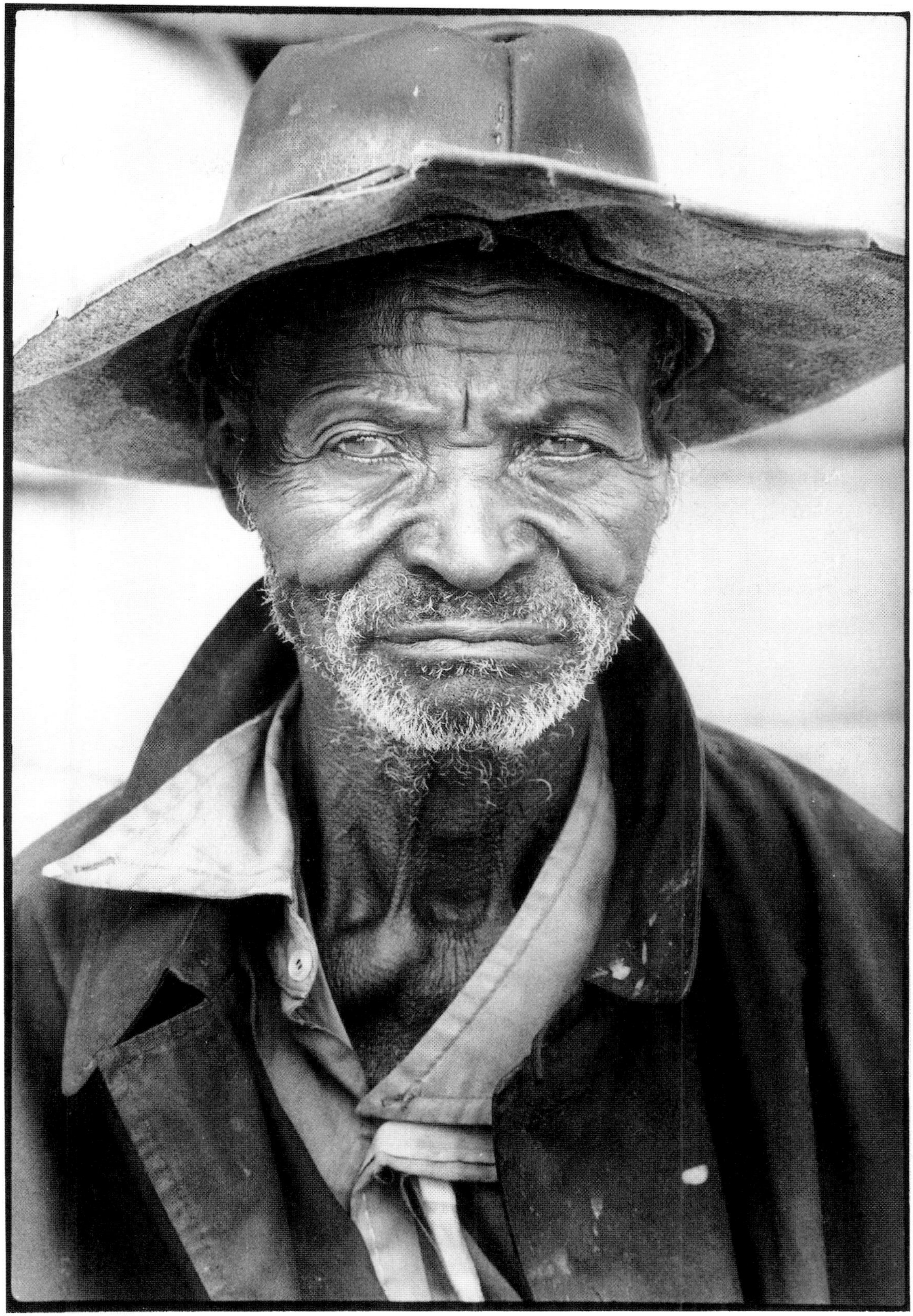

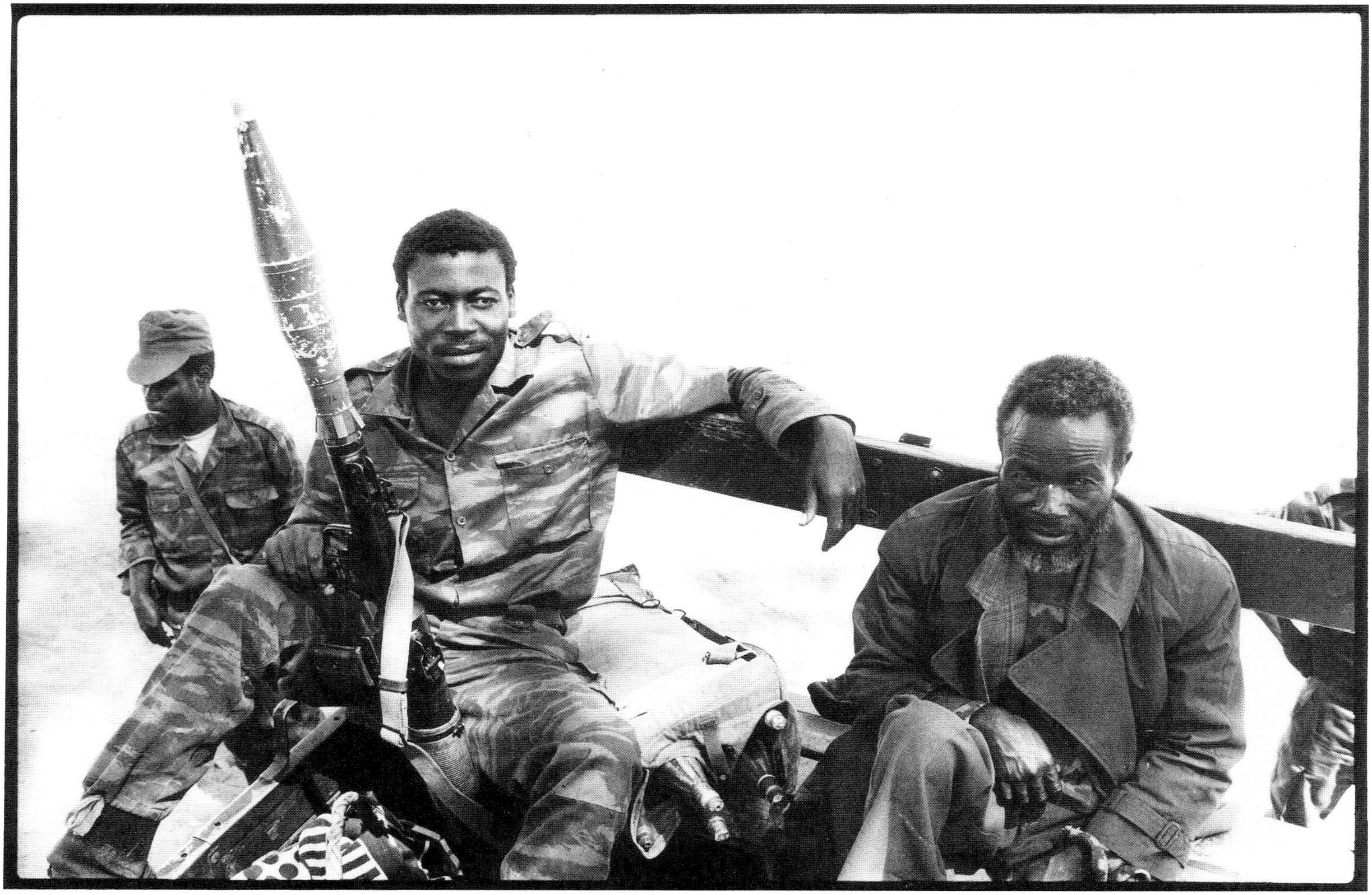

'Previously many people were living here, about 80,000 inhabitants, and we had many things — proper housing, shops, good farming areas. There was a hotel here, people would come to stay. But now there is nothing, there are very few people left here because of the incursions from the South Africans who always attack us. The buildings are destroyed, there is nothing here now, nothing. The only people left are us, the soldiers, and the sick and elderly who cannot leave on their own.'

Angolan commandant, Masvinga, southern Angola

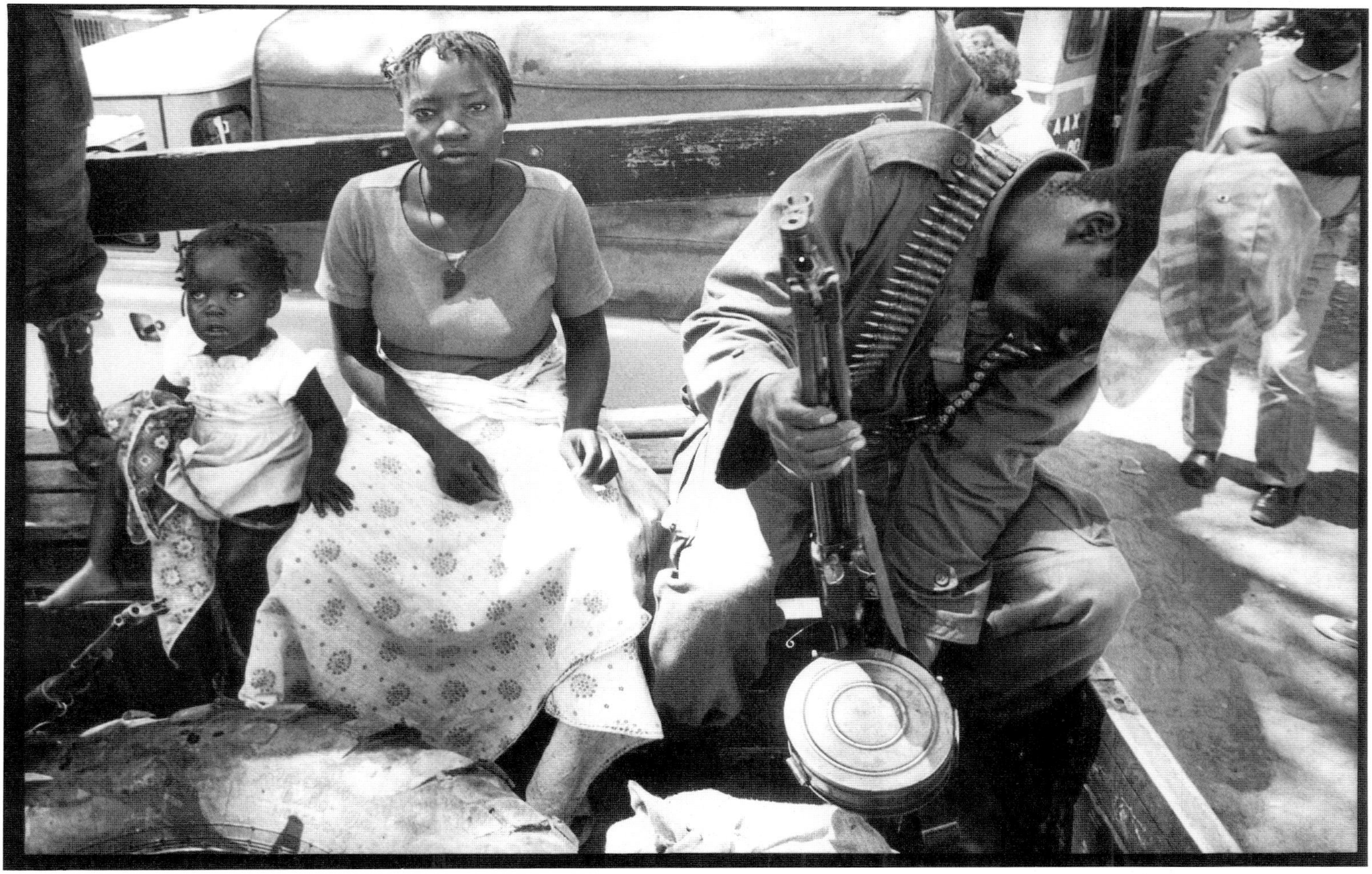

'The people who live here? Everybody knows beforehand the policy of UNITA against the people. Because the people know when UNITA comes they kill defenceless civilians. Because they don't fight against our units, they come to rob. Even yesterday evening, a civilian came here: a group of UNITA, on the road to Changongo, came and plundered the things of the population; they stole clothes, food, blankets — that is what UNITA does against the population. And the people really know who is defending them.'

Woman refugee

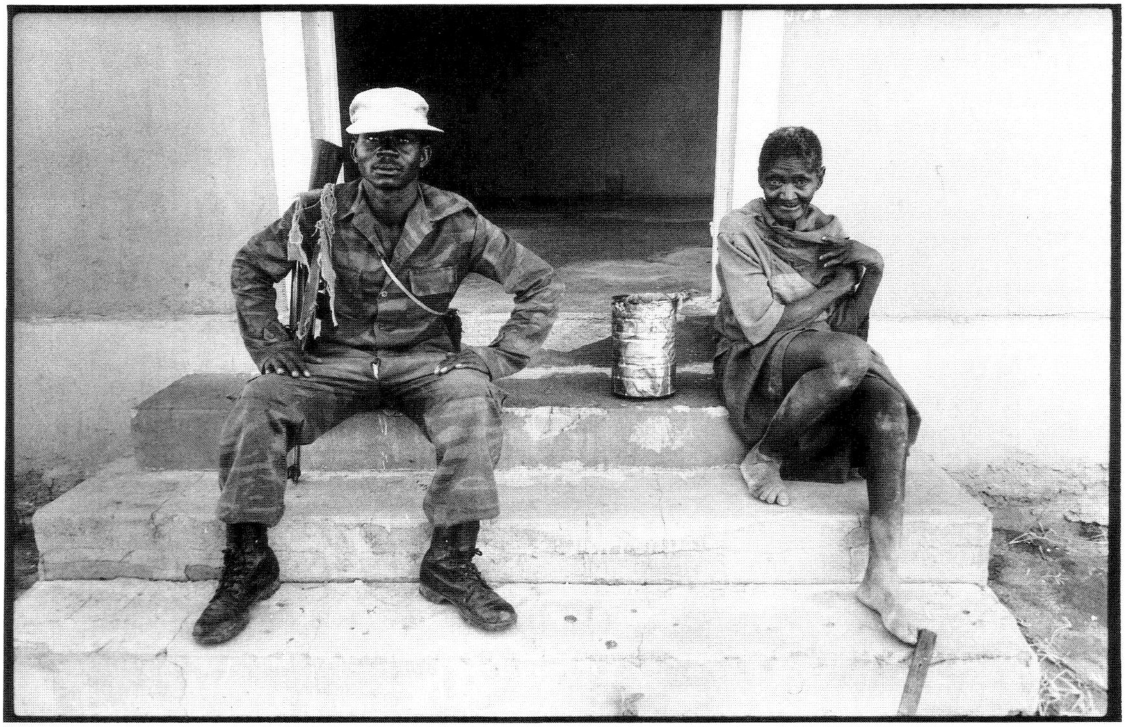

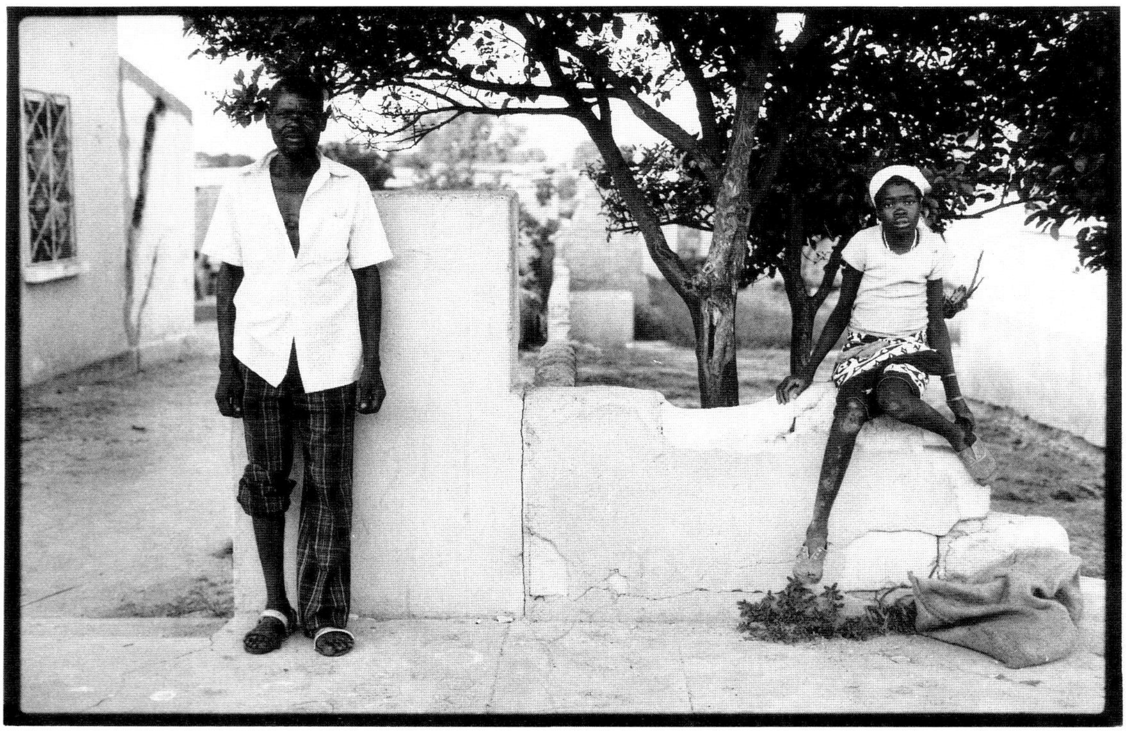

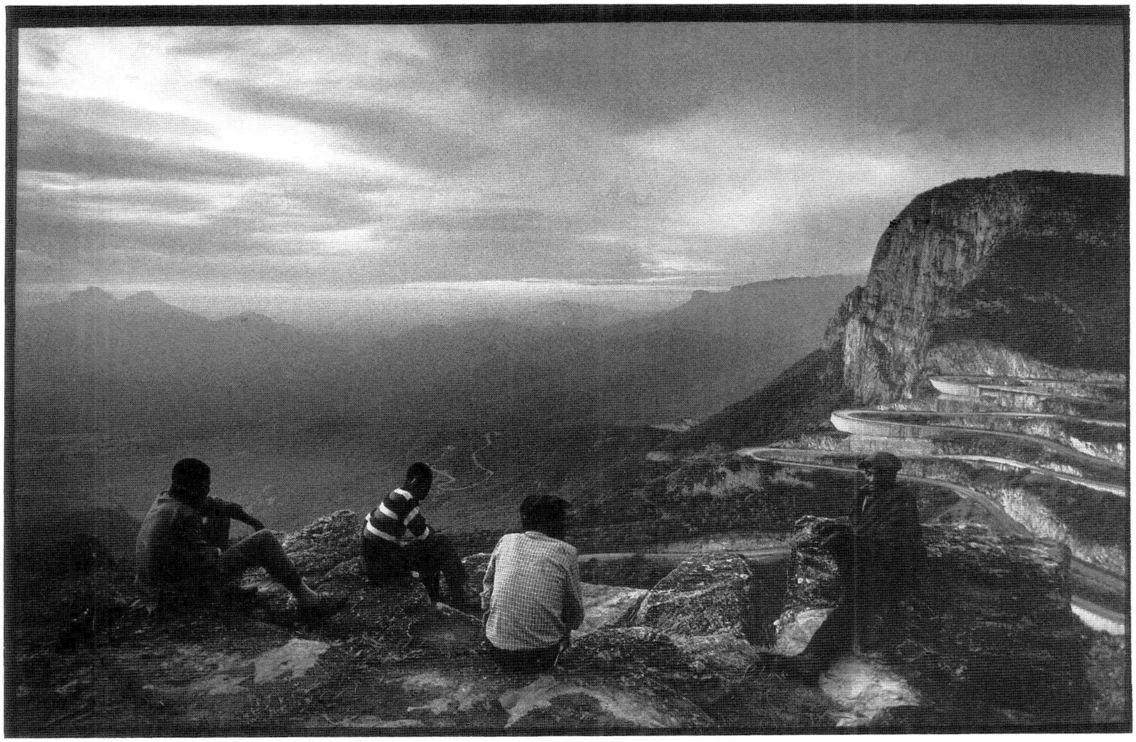

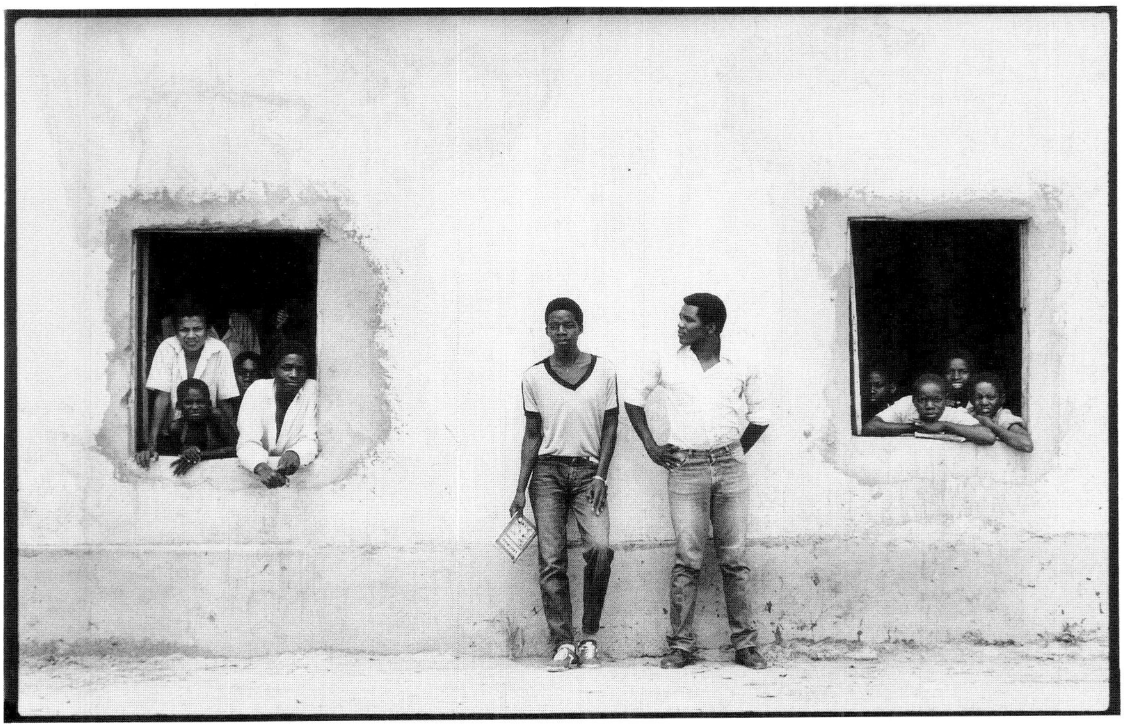

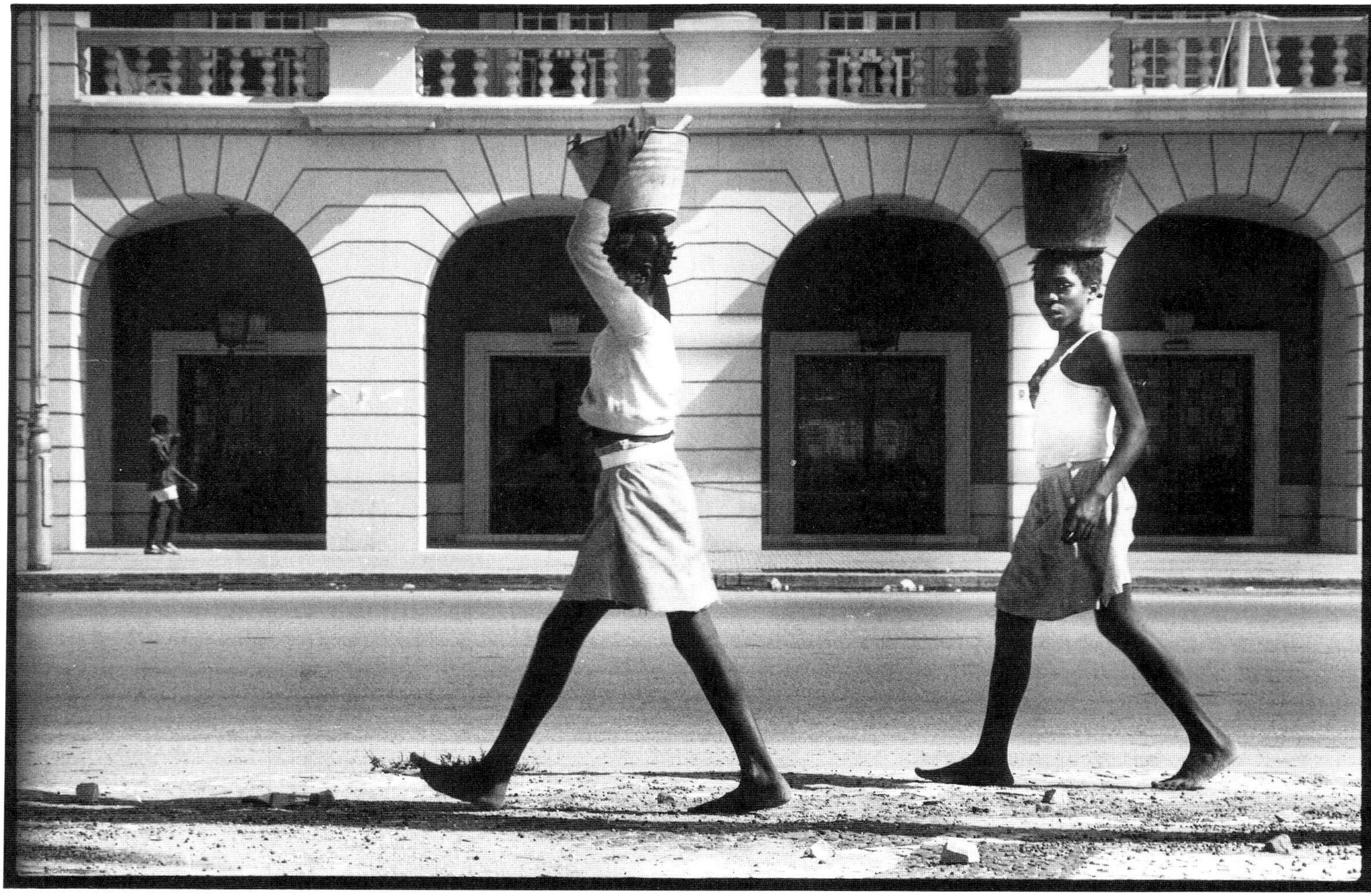

One of the first casualties of war is the water supply. Luanda has been without mains water for seven years, and the grand façades of the Portuguese waterfront buildings are a backdrop for the city's inhabitants who must carry water from standpipes to their homes.

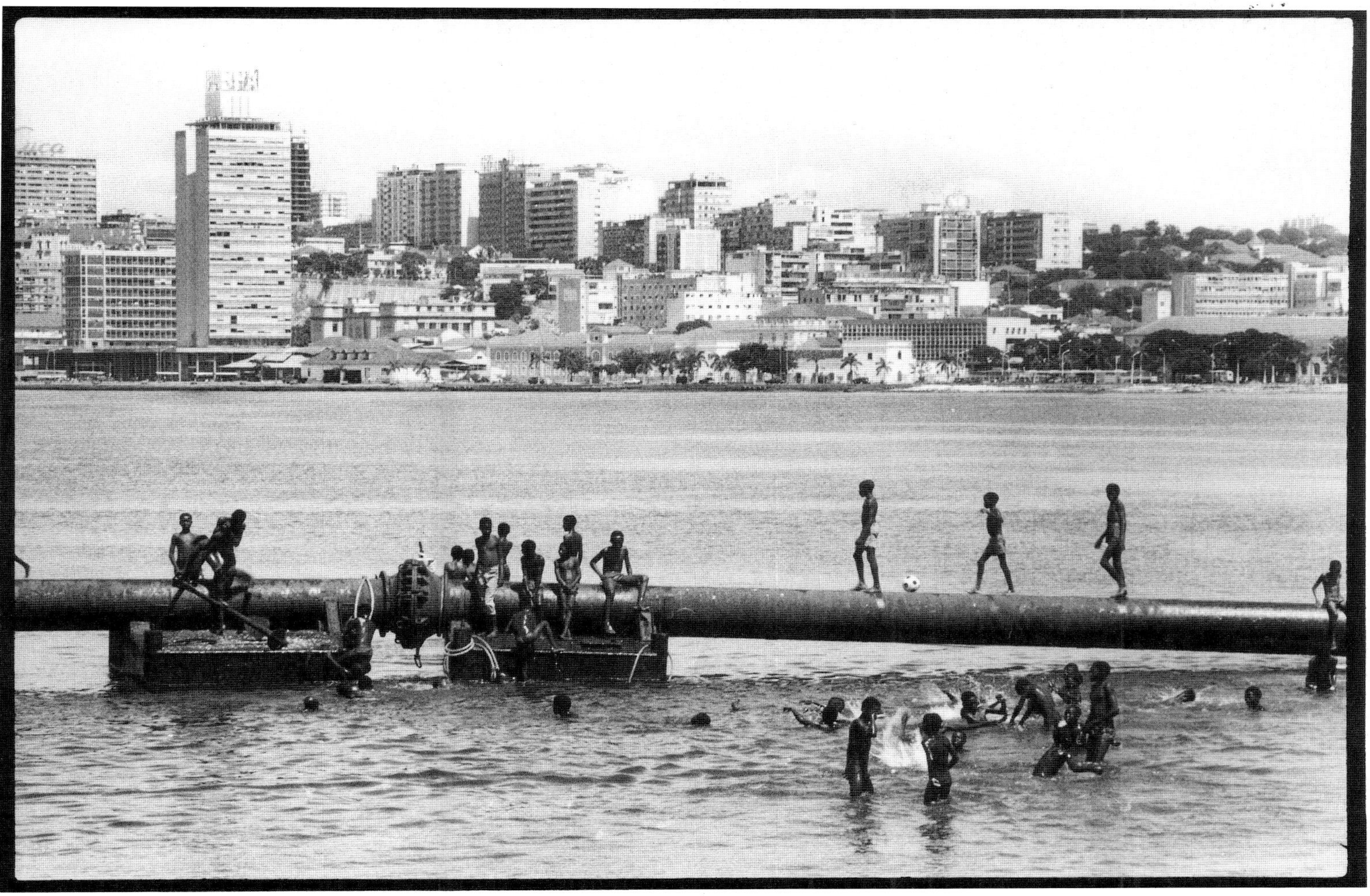

The waterfront façade of Luanda looks just like the waterfront of any major town. But up close the buildings are crumbling, starved of mains water for seven years, and with an intermittent electricity supply. Food and general supplies are erratic.

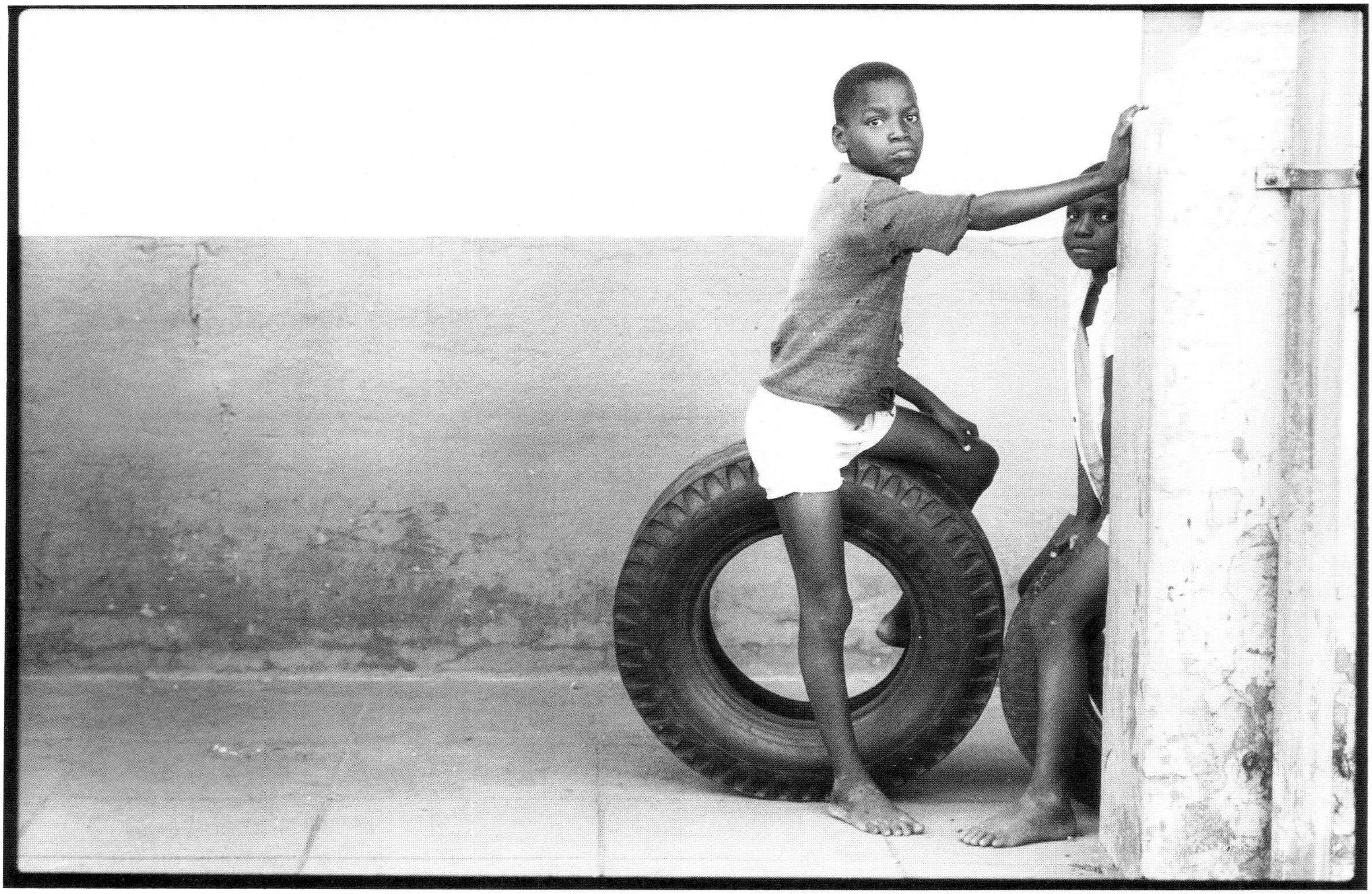

Mines are sown in the fields where people go to work. Few are killed but many are seriously maimed. The clear intention is to tie up as many resources as possible in caring for the wounded.

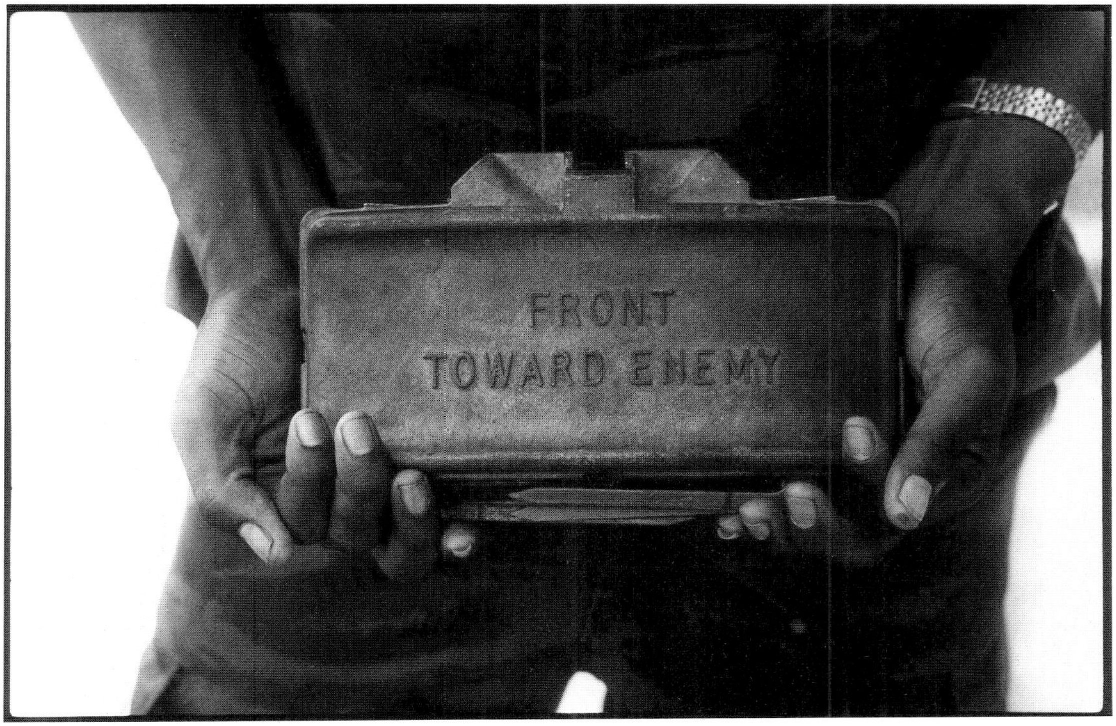

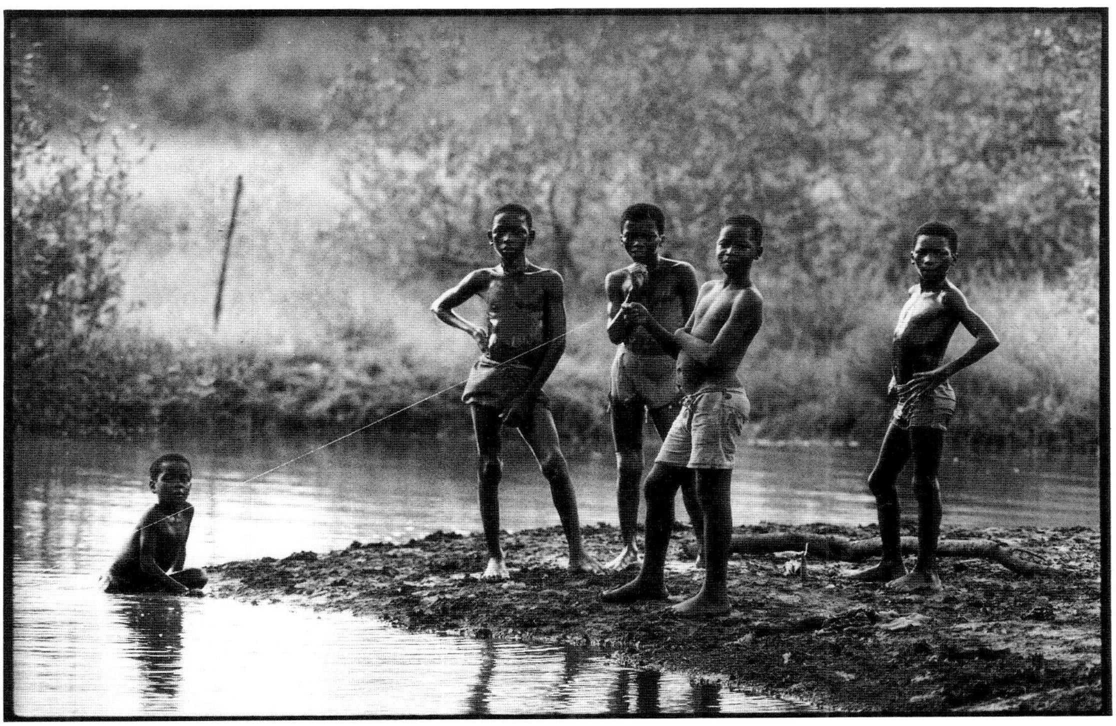

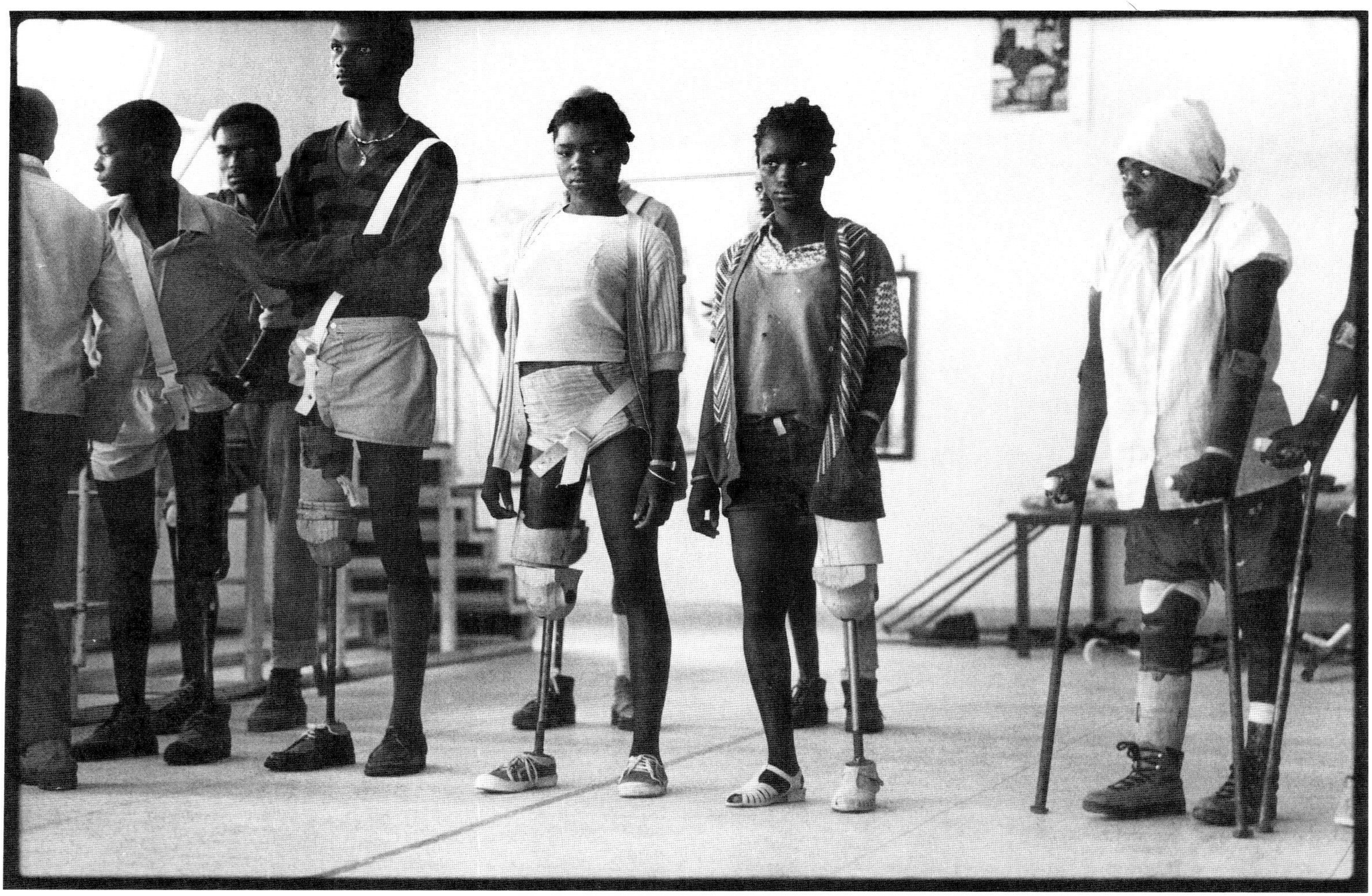

There are perhaps 20,000 limbless people in Angola. The lucky few have access to the Red Cross hospital in Huambo, where they can be fitted with artificial limbs and taught to walk again.

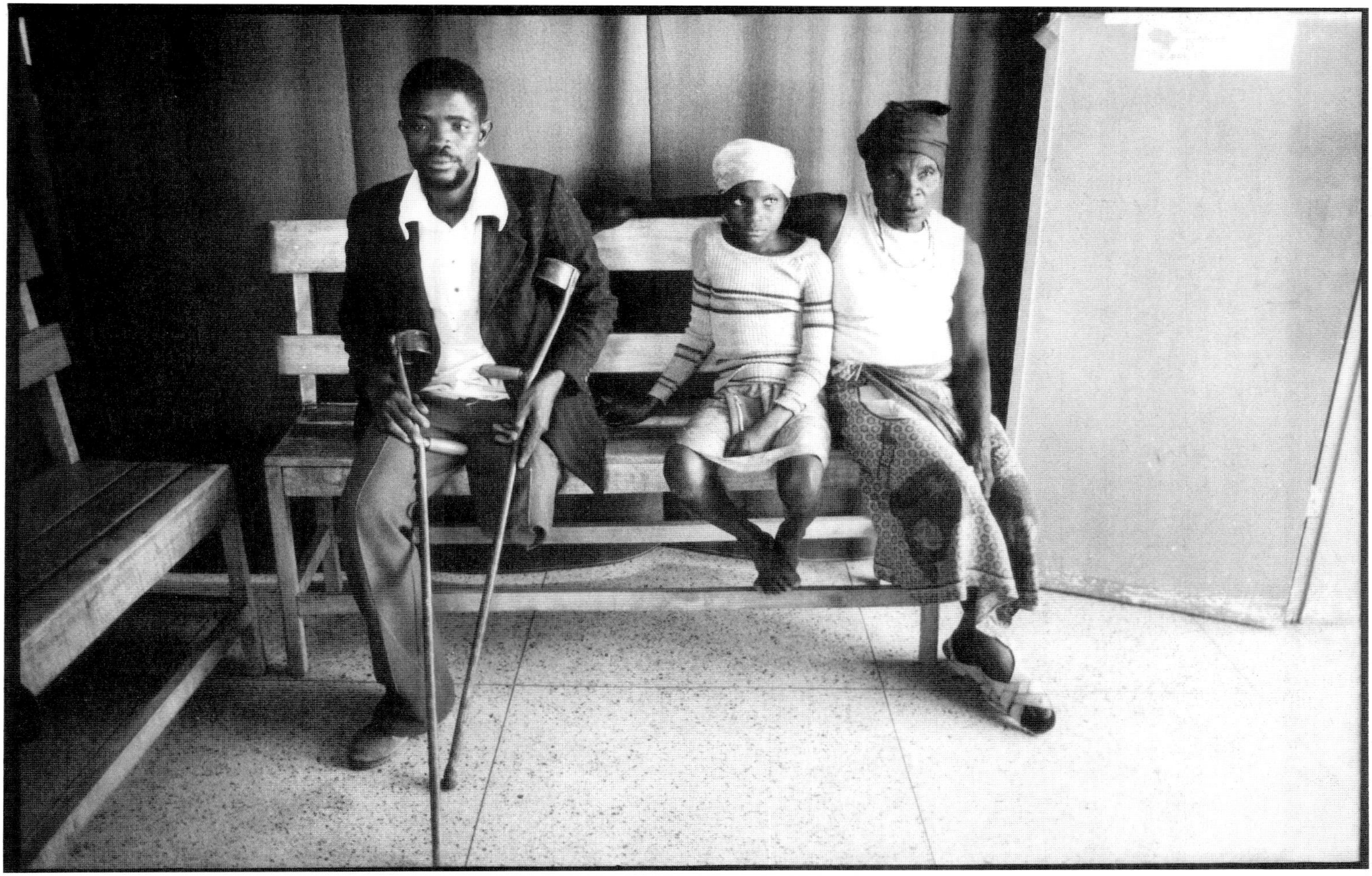

'Mainly they are victims of war. Very rarely you have an accident victim, but we fit them too, but I think that 95 to 98 per cent of them are victims of war. So they lose their legs because of an explosion from an anti-personnel mine.'

Swiss doctor, Red Cross hospital, Huambo

'I lost my leg because of a mine. We were going to work on the land. On the way to the land there was an electricity post, and they had mines down next to it, and I wanted to pass there because there was a path, and I wanted to pass and then I stepped on this mine.'

Little boy, patient at Red Cross hospital, Huambo

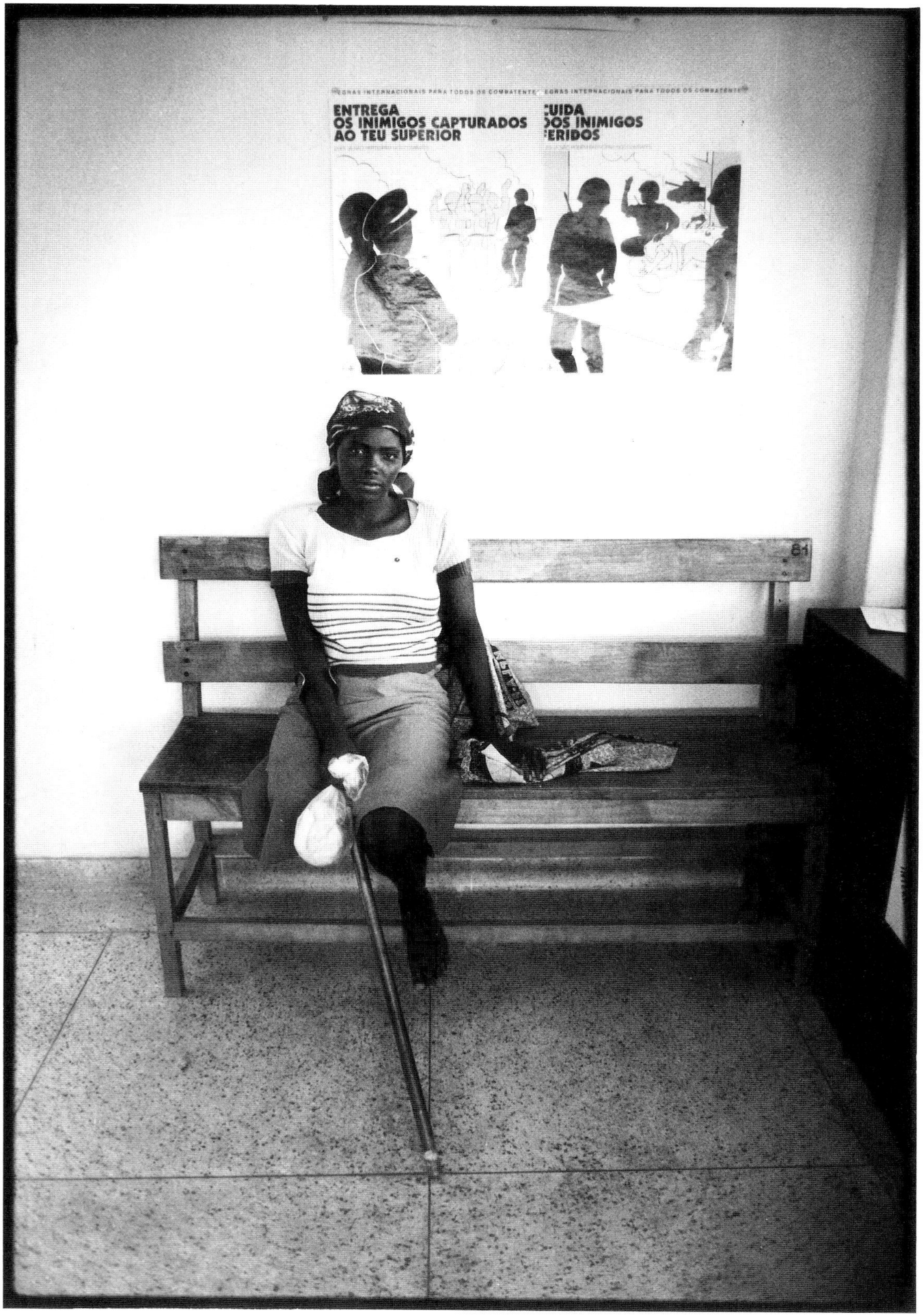

Doctor: 'How many children do you have?'
Patient: 'I have seven.'
Doctor: 'Seven children. Husband, do you have?'
Patient: 'Yes, a husband and seven children.'
Doctor: 'Who do you think put the mines which did this to you?'
Patient: 'I don't know, I don't know who did it. I was working in the fields and it started to rain. I said, I will stay here because it is raining, and because I have the baby. I will stay here under a tree. And then I stepped on the mine and the baby was on my back.'

Red Cross hospital, Huambo

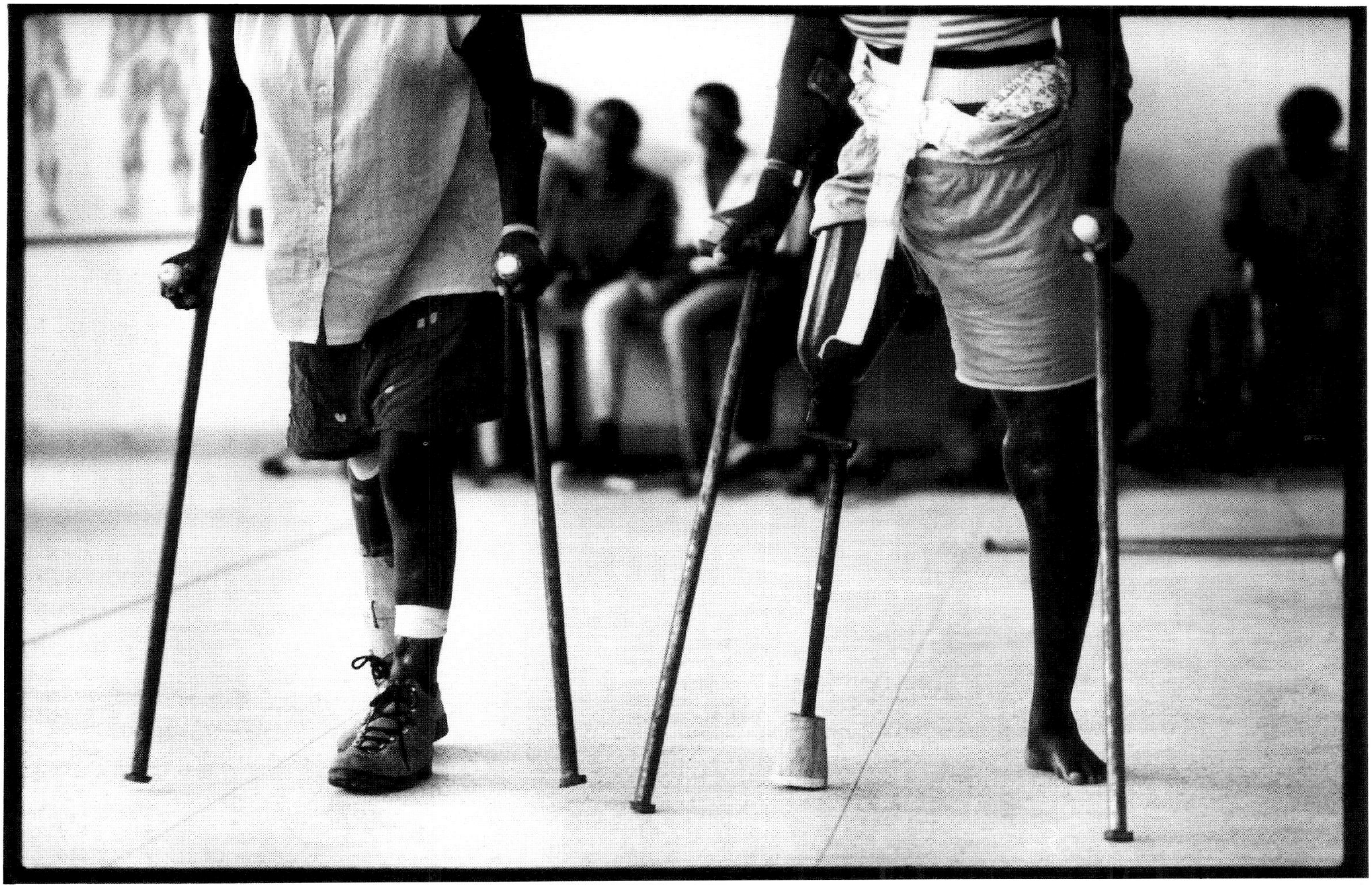

'I will explain this problem: it seems that these people who are armed and shoot at children, women and old people, these people do not have any education. They don't know anything. Because how can a normal person shoot at children? I have never seen that! Is that good sense, I am asking? Before I thought, this cannot be true. Before I saw it with my own eyes, I did not think this could exist. Never! How can they shoot at children, small and big children? It is very difficult to look at these children. How are they going to live? How are they going to take care of their food?'

Russian doctor, Huambo hospital

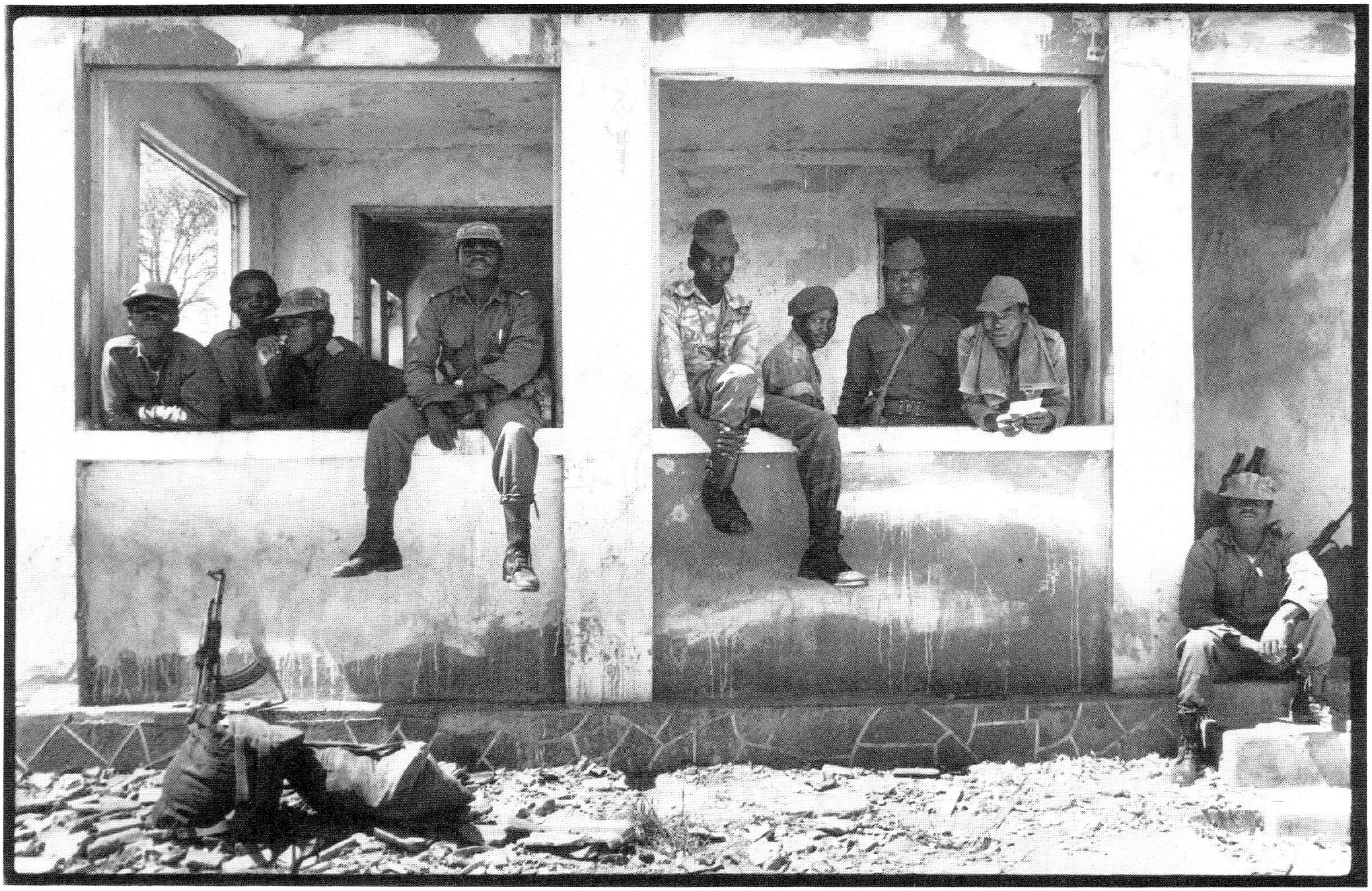

'Many of these soldiers have been based along the southern front for up to 11 years. Supplies of all kinds — food, medicine, weapons and spares — are erratic and never sufficient. Many of the soldiers have not been home to their families for years.'

Angolan commander, Xangongo

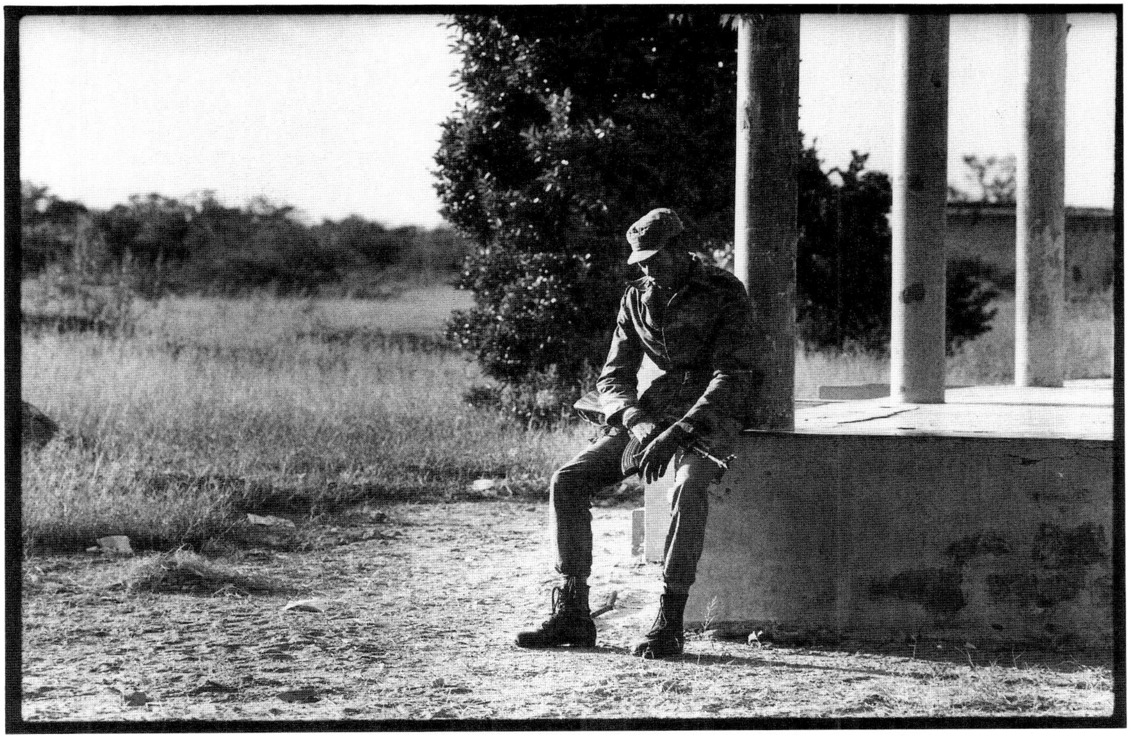

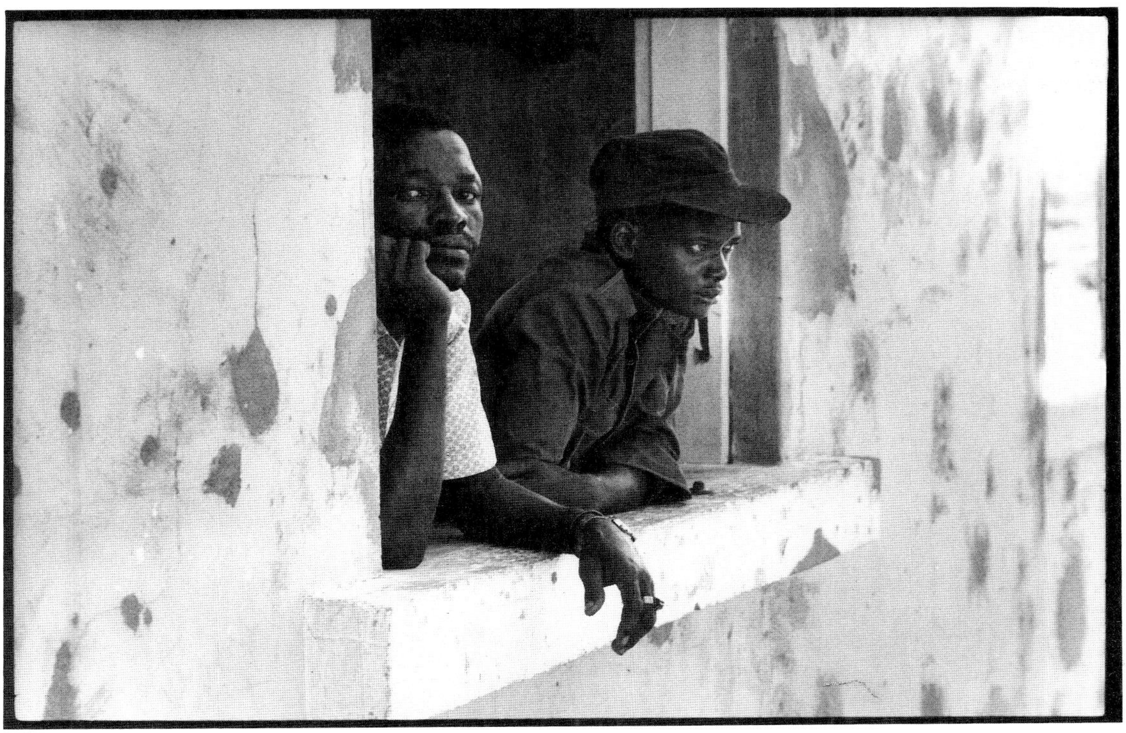

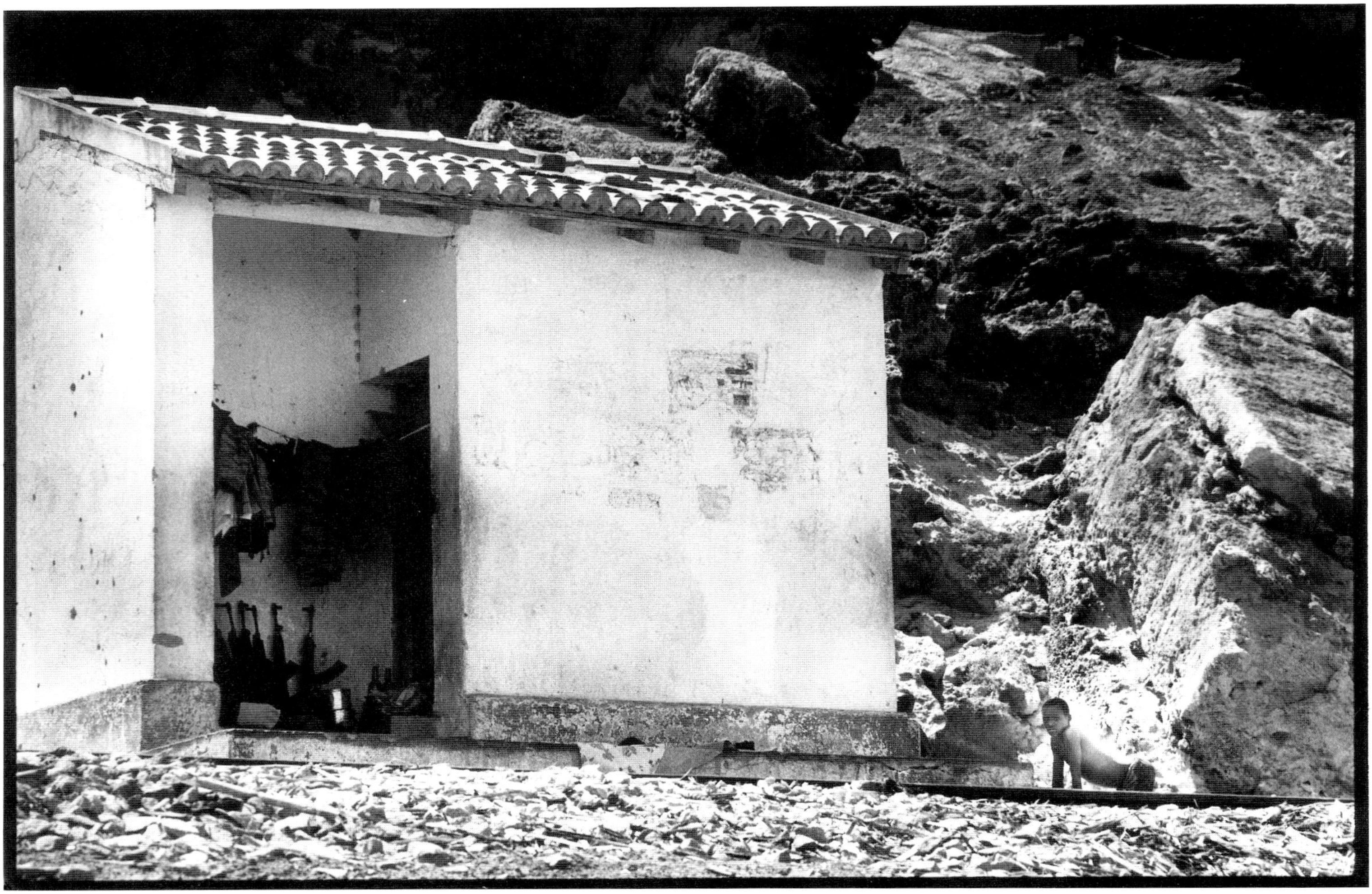

Near Namibe, in southern Angola, a soldier protects a small bridge that has been the subject of frequent attacks.

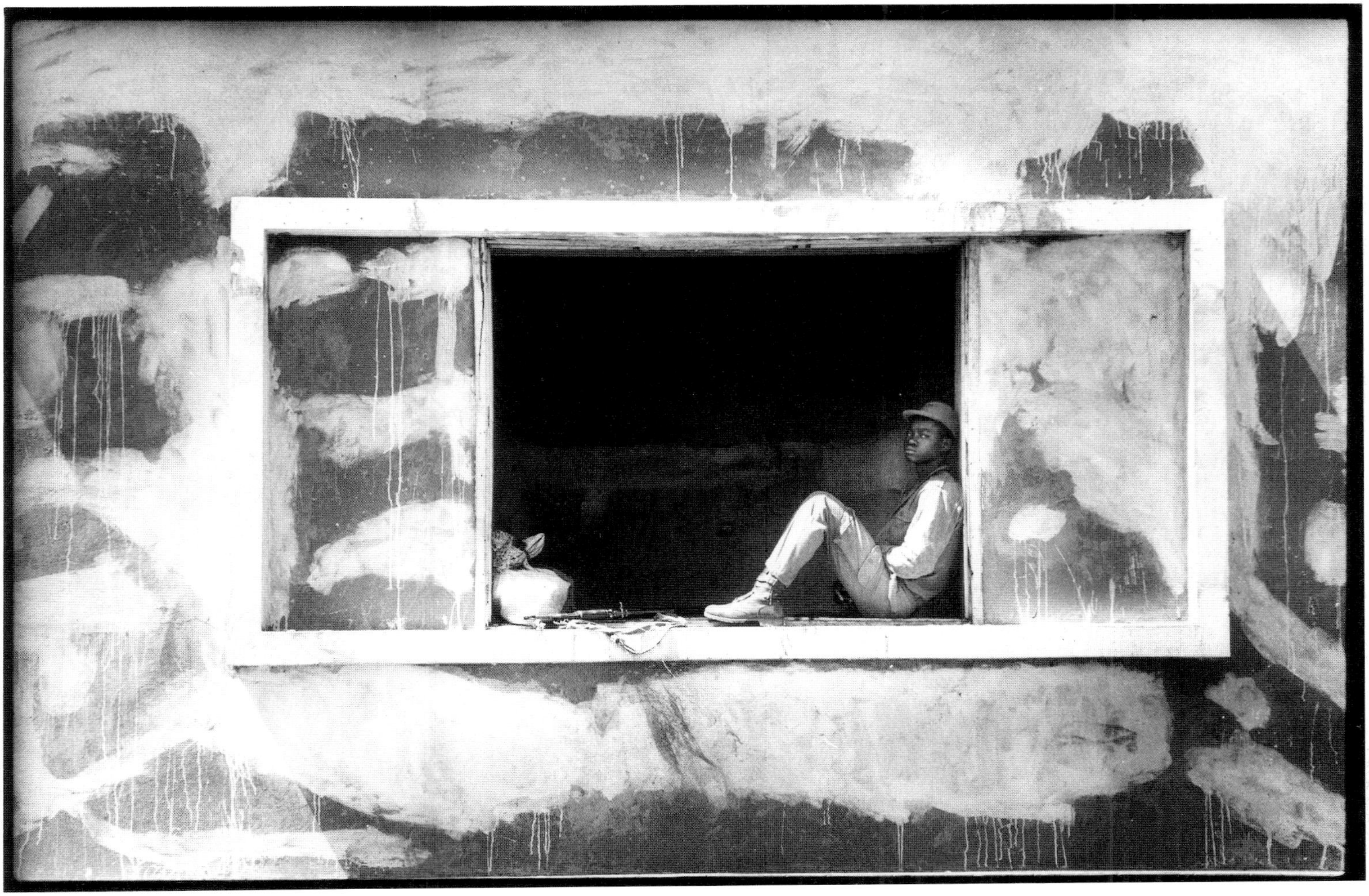

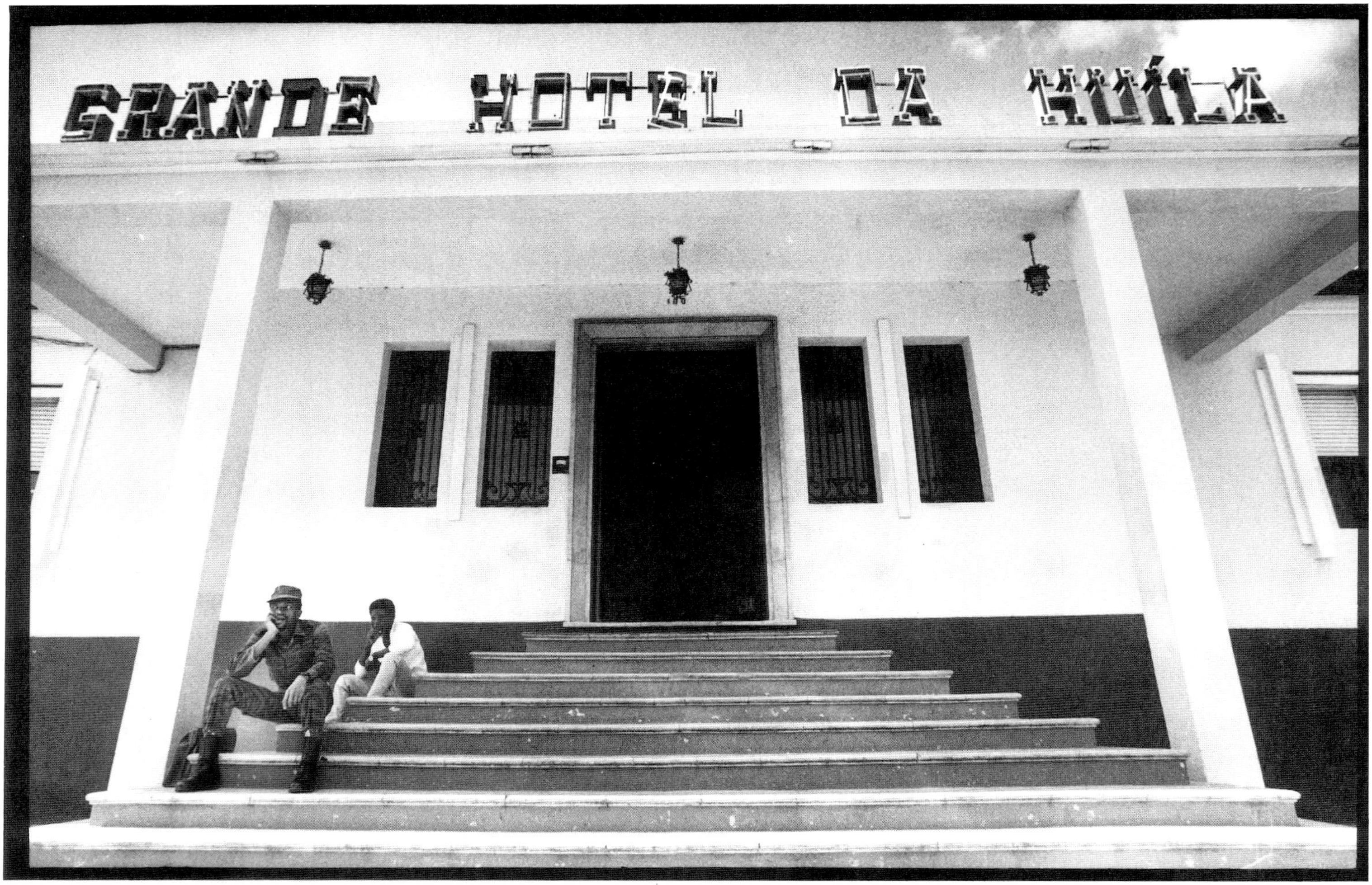

Angola's hotels have found new occupants. Formerly popular holiday areas, such as Huila in the south, are in decay. The Grande Hotel da Huila was a favourite rest for visitors from Luanda; it now plays host to senior military personnel and the occasional journalist.

'Well, at the moment our enemy, our principal enemy, as the spearhead of the South Africans, is UNITA. But UNITA does not undertake direct actions. It is the South Africans who come, and after defeating our units, they leave UNITA. And when UNITA notices our forces, they withdraw again. Ah! If UNITA would not have the South African support, they would not have the means to carry out these actions.'

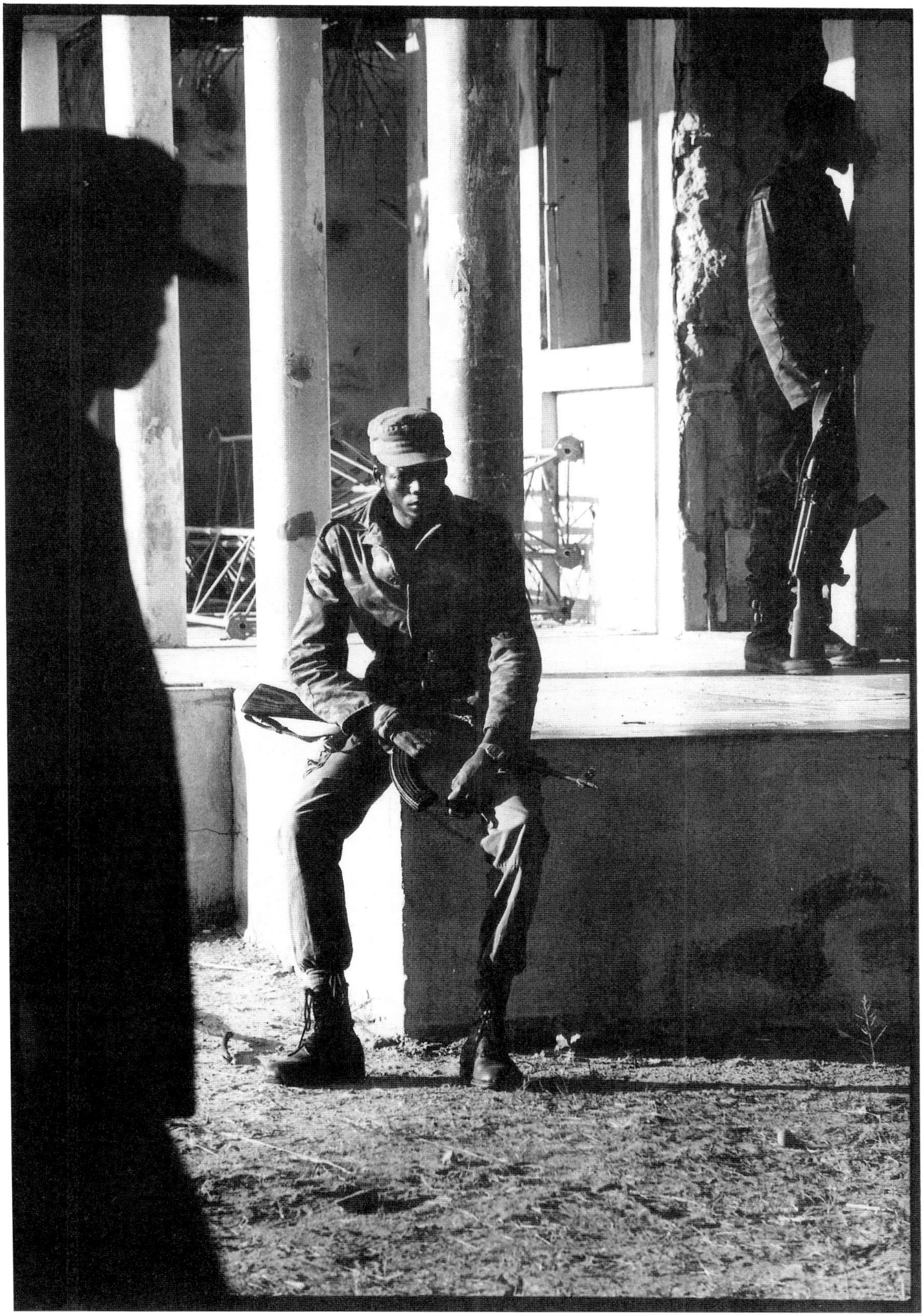

'They do not need to defend themselves against the neighbouring countries. The neighbouring countries don't want to attack South Africa. They don't have the capacity to attack South Africa. The neighbouring countries are merely saying what the rest of the world is saying — that they're opposed to the apartheid system. It can't really succeed ultimately because the end of apartheid depends on two things — the struggle of the people inside South Africa and secondly international pressures which do not have to come from the neighbouring countries. It's the international community and no amount of aggression against neighbouring countries is going to save apartheid . . .

They have less reason now in terms of the ANC to want to attack the Frontline States because the struggle is developed to such a high level within the country, and that is really not as a result of anything the neighbouring countries are doing. But of course the regime is desperate and in desperation they are hitting out at everything and at everybody.'
Oliver Tambo, President, ANC

'The human cost is very high but we must say we, in Zimbabwe, and the same applies to governments within the Frontline States, we regard this human cost as part of the price that we must pay in order to eliminate apartheid from the international system. It's a crime against humanity. It's the most diabolical racist system that has been known by mankind and just as it took the deaths of many people to eliminate Nazism in Europe, it will take the deaths of many people to eliminate apartheid in Southern Africa. It's the price that we must pay and we are determined to pay it.'
Minister Nathan Shamuyarira, Zimbabwe

'The result of all this is that we are not able to stand up to them in economic terms, in military terms, but we have one superior weapon — moral right, political morality is with us. They have a rotten system to defend and nothing like that is defendable in the long term. So, we are ready to sacrifice as we have done before, and that sacrifice, that spirit of sacrifice, is more than enough to destroy the apartheid regime, strong as it is in economic terms, strong as it is in military terms. Victory is certain in the end.'
Kenneth Kaunda, President, Zambia

LIST OF PHOTOGRAPHS